The Circle
of Discrimination

The Circle
of Discrimination

An Economic and Social Study of
the Black Man in New York

Herman D. Bloch

New York: New York University Press
London: University of London Press
1969

For: *Joyce, Leslie, and Kate*

Contents

Introduction   ix

1   Afro-Americans in Colonial New York: An Institutional Setting for a Vicious Circle   1

2   The New York Afro-American and Employment, 1777–1920   19

3   Discrimination in Employment Against the New York Afro-American, 1920–1965   47

4   Job Entry, Occupational Mobility, Income, and Economic Security   69

5   Afro-Americans and the Trade Unions, 1866–1910   79

6   Afro-Americans and the Trade Unions, 1910–1965   97

7   The New York Afro-American's Battle for Political Rights, 1777–1865   153

8   The New York Afro-American's Battle for Political Rights and the Emergence of Political Recognition, 1865–1900   169

9   Afro-Americans in New York: A Circle of Discrimination, 1625–1965   197

10   Some Afro-American Reactions to the Circle of Discrimination   221

Epilog   235

Notes   239

Introduction

Usually, in an open class society such as is generally ascribed to the United States, vertical mobility is possible, and has taken place, as is exemplified by the successive waves of immigrants and their offspring who have attained varying degrees of such mobility. Each new wave of immigrants has replaced the longer established immigrants on the lower rungs of the social ladder. However, the historical progress of the immigrant has not applied to the Afro-American. The latter's failure to achieve upward mobility can be linked, chiefly, to a continuing pattern of social and economic discrimination. The effects of such discrimination on the New York Afro-American is the special concern of this study.

Similarly, colored American reaction to this discrimination is of primary importance, since it elicited the white man's retaliation and led to increased black subordination. Thus, a circle of discrimination and Afro-American counteraction has followed a continuing pattern of thrust and counterthrust in the relation of the white man to the Afro-American and vice versa through the years 1625 to 1965.

The early basis for the white man's attitude toward the Afro-American stems from "historical accident." Because of the American colonies' lack of an indigenous labor supply, the colored American was forcibly transplanted to Colonial America, where he was placed in a peculiar property relationship, giving rise to the attitude that the

Afro-American, as transplanted slave labor, had to be kept in check through subordination. In time this subordination created a proscribed way of life for the Afro-American. Later, it was reflected in the white man's image of the colored American, enforcing a continued belief in the black man's racial inferiority. The historical development of Afro-American subordination and how it affected the colored American's status in New York City society will be detailed in our study.

Once the Afro-American was assigned a low social and economic status, his life activities had to conform to this ascribed status. In a class-oriented society this meant the lowest stratum in society. In turn, this assigned low socioeconomic status bred continued racial subordination, even in instances where a favorable change in the colored American's economic position has been followed by an imperceptible alteration in his social status. For example, in the early 1960's the son of the American United Nations official Ralph Bunche was denied membership in the Forest Hills Tennis Club, despite his father's eminence, because of his color. Moreover, the colored American has been excluded from many occupations, displaced from occupations he has held by incoming immigrants, or in stringent times even displaced by native labor. This noncompetitive social and economic position has had multiple manifestations at different times and different places.

A theoretical framework for the circle of discrimination has emerged from our investigations, yielding the following salient features: (1) the Afro-American's subordination to the white man; (2) his social subordination, limiting his economic or employment opportunities; (3) his restricted social mobility, even when he has been able to elevate his economic status; and (4) his noncompetitive employment status because of social discrimination.

While it may be noted that the above is subject to *inverse causation*, the end results would be the same. Thus, you may start with the supposition that the lack of an indigenous labor force— economic need in William Graham Sumner's sense—allowed for the ascription of heathenism, which was synonymous with inferiority. This ascribed social subordination led to limited economic or employment opportunities, which in turn led to restricted social mobility. Regardless of economic elevation, restricted social mobility had to conform to fixed social status, which often meant that the white man had to be given priority in employment. In any case, the black man was limited to the lowest strata in our class society, and it is fairly manifest that his visibility made it possible to enforce this type of social subordination.

It matters little whether we start from a sociological or economic base. Each factor derived from the data should permit some formalization, since each represents specific interaction between economic and social processes wherein the complexities of the problem appear in their full manifestations. Viewed in combination, the four features form a nucleus for the evaluation of the Afro-American problem in the North.

Before proceeding with an examination of each of these features, it should be emphasized that all are inextricably interwoven, and that the abstraction of a single factor for analytical purposes has been done only for the sake of clarity. The constant interaction of the various factors form an integrated whole.

In a class-oriented society, artificial subordination of a particular ethnic, or minority, stock may have a multiplicity of bases. They may stem, individually or severally, from such diverse sources as biology, economics, sociology, culture, or politics. Therefore, in any given situation one aspect may be singled out as primary, and the others made to appear dependent. For example, it has been contended that the colored American is by nature mentally and physically inferior because of his evolutionary level. It has also been alleged that this belief is substantially grounded in various Afro-American physical characteristics, such as prognathism and greater susceptibility to certain diseases (tuberculosis, nephritis, and so on). Utilizing such an argument as a base, it has been relatively simple to extend such allegations to include the concept of *noblesse oblige*, or the white man's burden. Ultimately, this type of reasoning has led to the Afro-American's being made an outsider in white society.

Likewise, subjugation of the Afro-American may be imputed to the white man's belief in his social and economic superiority, as evidenced by the Dutch patroon system in New York or by the Dutch West India Company's manumission of "bonded servants," the latter an act that had explicit social and economic implications. Then again, it may arise from economic imperialism, as revealed in the desire of the English to exploit the transplanted Afro-American. This subjugation was attempted by the enactment of various laws restricting manumission; in accord with the economic tenets of mercantilism.

Racial subjugation, which is a form of class subordination, may also arise from cultural differences based on divergences in religion, language, and customs. Historically, for many American minority stocks, the original cultural barriers have been mitigated. This has not been the case with the colored American. Other bases for subjugation have arisen from changes in the relative proportion of a minority's population ratio to that of the "dominant group," as illustrated in the instance of the Eurasian in India. Eventually, the original basis for race prejudice may be forgotten. Once it is rationalized and institutionalized, it acquires a modus vivendi of its own.

In focusing our attention on the New York Afro-American, we found that racial subordination was apparent when most Afro-Americans were put into a preconceived composite image, or "collective representation." Once placed in this stereotype, they were rarely judged as individuals, but rather as a group with assigned "outsider status" in our class society.

We shall deal first with the institutional setting of the *Circle of Discrimination,* stressing the combination of a partial feudal system comingled with the emergence of a class system. Then, we shall develop some of the employment practices used to maintain the Afro-American's "outsider status" in society. Later we shall deal with craft unions, beginning with the year 1866—the year marking the formation of the first nationwide confederations of labor—and such practices as restricted entry into a trade. Subsequent chapters will deal with the Afro-American's battle for political rights during the period 1777–1900.

All of the material developed to this point will be utilized to show the *Circle of Discrimination,* as it affected the Afro-American in New York between 1625 and 1965. During this period, the Afro-American tried to break out of this vicious circle by employing various measures—measures that had been helpful to other minority stocks in their upward striving for social and economic status. These measures failed, however, to achieve the degree of success for Afro-Americans in New York or in any other part of the United States that it did for the Greeks, Italians, Hebrews, and most other nationalities that came to seek a new opportunity in a new land.

Among many Afro-Americans there is an acceptable nomenclature as to how they wish to be designated. In descending order, the preference is: Afro-American, Black Man, Colored American, and least of all Negro. To many, the last designation, Negro is linked with slavery and is viewed as derogatory. With this qualification in mind, the names Afro-American, Colored American, Negro American, and so on, have been used interchangeably.

There are a few persons who deserve special mention, since they urged me on when the task appeared overwhelming. They are: Professor Herbert Blumer and the late Professor Maurice R. Davie. For permission to use the author's previously published material, I do thank the editors of *Phylon, The Journal of Negro History,* and *The International Review of Social History.*

Afro-Americans in Colonial New York: An Institutional Setting for a Vicious Circle

Although the current controversy as to whether Afro-Americans were or were not treated equally with white indentured servants before the 1660's was opened by Mary and Oscar Handlin in their article, "Origins of the Southern Labor System," [1] there is a literature on the controversy dating back to the 1890's. [2] In their *Race and Nationality in American Life*, [3] the Handlins reiterated their thesis: "Slavery had no meaning in law; at most it was a popular description of a low form of service." [4] Thus Afro-American status was that of "servants in the laws and [they were] identified and treated as such down to the 1660's." [5] Although the Handlins stressed the law as the line of demarcation between equal and unequal treatment, they did not perceive the change as being abrupt between the period prior to, and that after, 1660. Rather, they contended that "social attitudes transformed in the 1660's [could not have been] immediately reflected in every legislative action of the decade." [6]

On the other hand, Carl N. Degler [7] developed the thesis that a "pattern of discrimination against the colored American antedated legal slavery"; [8] since discrimination preceded slavery, it had to condition it. In other words, "long before slavery came into legal existence," after the 1660's, American race prejudice had its origins in the "social atmosphere of the early 17th century." [9] Hence, legalized slavery was a reflection of the institutionalized bias that paved the way for the laws legalizing Afro-American inferiority. [10] Thus with the aid of some historical evidence, Degler concluded that the Afro-American was "accorded lower status than any white man," [11] even before the 1660's.

Professor W. D. Jordan attempted to mediate the Degler-Handlin dispute in his article, "Modern Tensions and the Origins of American Slavery." [12] Before Jordan suggested a common denominator,
"mutual causation," to bridge the gap between Degler and Handlin,
he offered some historical material favorable to both parties. Then
he proceeded on the premise that both contestants

> predicate two factors, prejudice and slavery, and [each de-
> mands] a distinct order of casuality. [Viewed in terms of]
> mutual causation, slavery and prejudice [were the] species of
> general debasement of the Negro . . . [and] both may have
> been equally cause and effect . . . dynamically joining hands
> to hustle the Negro down the road to complete degradation.
> [Hence], the urgent need for labor in a virgin country guided
> the direction which debasement took, molded it . . . into an
> institutional framework. [But] the economic practicalities [that]
> shaped the external form of debasement should not tempt one
> to forget . . . that slavery was at bottom a social arrangement,
> a way of society's ordering its members' [statuses] in its own
> mind.[13]

Like most trucelike solutions, Professor Jordan's failed to satisfy
either of the disputants. Other scholars joined the controversy, and
each new contestant suggested a possible approach to the problem;
each offered some new historical evidence; and each sought to settle
the question with a degree of finality.[14] The question still remains
controversial.

The role played by the Dutch in New York with respect to
de facto or *de jure* discrimination was never mentioned in the
Degler-Handlin discussion. Since the Dutch did hold the colony for
some 40 years before the 1660's, their attitudes toward the New
York Afro-American should be of some interest, even though it does
not permit for wide generalization. English attitudes toward the
Afro-American from 1664 until the American Revolution are less
relevant to the Degler-Handlin discussion, because both parties
agree that after 1660 both *de jure* and *de facto* discrimination were
prevalent throughout the Colonial period.

The material that follows stems directly from our main hypothesis, that the social and economic conditions that underlay the
principles of mercantilism were directly responsible for "modern
colonialism." It is also relevant to the Degler–Handlin discussion.[15]
In turn, these principles formed the basis for the formation of the

New York Afro-American's circle of discrimination. Thus it was the mercantile philosophy practiced by the Dutch West India Company that was responsible for the company's subjugation of the Afro-American.[16] In part this premise is based on the fact that, originally, Afro-American slavery "came to be accepted as morally right and economically necessary," [17] even though it was without warrant in legislative law, unknown in natural law, and not recognized by common law.[18] Thus when the Dutch introduced slavery into New Netherland, "it was introduced by custom in accord with the spirit of the age and the common practice of nations; [later], it was regulated by municipal law." [19]

Without being aware of the differences between Degler and Handlin, William Graham Sumner in his classic book *Folkways* offered an explanation for the apparent differences between the two. He noted that socioeconomic discrimination could start as a more, become a folkway, or be institutionalized and later formalized into law. Sumner defined folkways as

> the habits of the individual and customs of the society which arise from efforts to satisfy needs [in the case of the American colonies, the lack of an indigenous population to develop the territory, plus the white man's need to emulate the estate system prevalent in Europe]. In time [these individual habits and customs of society, arising from needs, won] authority, [became] regulative for succeeding generations and [took] on the character of a social force.[20]

In such manner, status can be created by mores and folkways even before laws are enacted; laws formalize what already has been institutionalized. Thus,

> status [is] a direct product of the mores, distinguishable from institutions and contract. . . .[21]
>
> . . . Folkways change their character when they become laws. Acts under the laws and institutions are conscious and voluntary; under folkways they are always unconscious and involuntary, so that [the latter] have the character of natural necessity.[22]

Unless legislative acts come out of the mores, they usually fail, "because they do not affect ritual, and because they always aim at greater results than [are] possible in a short time." [23] Hence, stemming from existing mores, with prior accepted ritual black codes could be more readily incorporated into the existing institutions and contracts. These codes were merely an extension of consciously accepted conditions and would not disturb the social equilibrium.

AFRO-AMERICANS UNDER DUTCH RULE, 1625–1664

Although both the Dutch and the English subscribed to some tenets of mercantilism in their attitudes and practices toward Afro-Americans, there were important differences between the two countries. The Dutch did offer possible manumission, a change in social status, and some economic fulfillment in terms of land grants; the policy of the English circumscribed both the manumitted Negro American and the slave. Thus under Dutch rule

> most of the slaves in the province of New Amsterdam, from the time they were first introduced [circa, 1625] down to 1664, had been the property of the Dutch West India Company. Each male slave had a small plot of land to work for his own benefit, and he was not without hope of [partial] emancipation. However, under English rule, the slave's condition was clearly defined by law and was one of great hardship.[24]

The fur trade and its exploitation, taxation, regulation, and control must be visualized as the chief line and color of any picture of early New Netherland. The Dutch West India Company's main objective was conquest and commerce, not colonization.[25] This economic philosophy was incorporated in the preamble of the Dutch West India Company's 1621 Charter, which declared that the States General of the Netherlands regarded the prosperity of the country as consisting "principally in navigation and trade." [26] In the New World one such source of economic opportunity was to be found in ". . . cod fishing . . . [and] traffic in good skins and furs, which were to be got at a very low price." [27] Another source of exploitation was suggested by the Dutch West India Company when it stated that

> direct trade between New Netherland and Brazil would cause the former, by slave labor [to] be more extensively cultivated

than it has hitherto been, . . . Slaves, . . . being brought and maintained [in New Netherland] at a cheap rate, various other descriptions of produce would be raised, and by their abundance be reduced in price, so as to allow, when occasion would offer, of their advantageous exportation hither and to other parts of Europe.[28]

The log of the slaver St. John attested to the advantage set forth by the directors of the company as to the lucrativeness of the slave trade, since slaves averaged between $100 and $150 per person.[29] It also revealed the status of the Afro-American when it referred to bills of lading signed by a Mr. Blaes, which were little different from inanimate cargo.

> We weighted anchor by the order of the Honorable Director Johan Valkenborch . . . to proceed on our voyage to Rio Reael [Rio del Rey], to trade for slaves for the honorable Company. . . . Nothing was done [on this trip], except to trade for slaves. . . . We turned over to Adriaen Blaes, the ship's 195 slaves . . . for which bills of lading were signed . . . [plus] receipts for remaining merchandise.[30]

The Dutch West India Company's zone of settlement, which encompassed Long Island and the Hudson River Valley with its two principal river towns, New York and Albany, reinforced the thesis that the company was not interested in colonization. Thus, by 1664 all but two of the patroonships had been repurchased by the company. The patroons alleged that the company was primarily interested in trade and not in establishing a colony of farms.[31]

It was the lack of a large, dependable, exploitable, and indigenous population,[32] plus a failure to obtain sufficient recruits from the Old World, that brought the Afro-American into sharp focus as a source of cheap and dependable labor. (The importation of the colored American fits Sumner's need theory.)

The introduction of slave labor, although it consisted of involuntary servitude, furnished the numbers and dependability necessary to exploit the natural resources of the colony and offered a social structure—master-servant—similar to the status structure then current in Holland. Thus, "under Dutch rule the slave trade was a property right of the Dutch West India Company," [33] a monopoly that permitted the company to earn huge profits in accord with the tenets of mercantilism.[34] It was the combination of slaves working the company's land—land allotted to Afro-Americans—and slaves employed by the patroons that enabled the company to exploit the New World's natural resources.[35] The company profited further by transporting the New World's resources in its own bottomry.

It was either in 1625 or in 1626 that the first Afro-Americans, eleven males, were brought to New Amsterdam as bonded slaves. A group of female slaves was added in 1626.[36] No additional slaves were brought to New Amsterdam until after the establishment of patroonships in 1629.[37]

Under the Charter of Freedoms and Exemptions, which established the patroon system on June 7, 1629, any stockholder of the company could acquire the title of "Lord" by establishing a colony of 50 or more persons, each above fifteen years of age.[38] These patroonships were to take the form of feudal estates—each a "perpetual fief" and a "perpetual inheritance with its promoter in full possession of feudal rights." [39] Although absentee peerage may have acted as a strong inducement to recruit workers from Holland, these promotional campaigns failed to alleviate the labor shortage.[40] One reason given was that in Holland, "all who [are] inclined to do any sort of work . . . procure enough to eat without any trouble." [41] Most of the workers brought over from Europe at great expense found work other than agriculture more lucrative.

> The temptation held out by the fur trade was so irresistible, that the servants, or "boere-knechts," who were brought over from Holland, were soon seduced from the pursuits of agriculture.[42]

Failure to induce enough European workers to migrate to the New World and develop agriculture caused the company to plead with the States General of Holland that

> colonizing such wild and uncultivated countries, demand more inhabitants than we can supply . . .[43]

> [Therefore], it is deemed proper to permit, at the request of the Patroons, colonists and other farmers, the conveyance thither of as many negroes as they are willing to purchase at a fair price.[44]

Thus, farmers, patroons, and company became dependent upon Afro-Americans for their labor supply, which in time became "one of the staples of the country." [45] This "staple," arising from the economic and social needs of New Amsterdam, in time became legitimized. It became part of the mores for succeeding generations and finally took on the character of a social force.[46]

Since slavery had declined in Europe, "yet was being revived in a deadly form in America," [47] support is given to the thesis that the Afro-American's inferior status was an outgrowth of the mores created by need (labor shortage). In time these mores were to give way to conscious and voluntary institutions, or laws. Even though a decree was issued declaring that the original "Negroes taken from the Spaniards being all slaves, were on account of their long service manumitted" [48] by an act of the director and council of Netherland on Feb. 24, 1644, the Afro-American's newly acquired "freedom" did not erase his social inferiority.

> Having considered the petition of the Negroes named: Paul D'Angola, Senion Congo, [*et al.*], who have served the Company 18 to 19 years, to be liberated, especially as they have been many years in the service of the Honorable West India Company here and have long since been promised their freedom; also that they are burdened with many children so that it is impossible for them to support their wives and children as they have been accustomed to do, if they must continue in the Company's service. Therefore, we, the Director and Council do release them and their wives from slavery, . . . where they shall be able to earn their livelihood by Agriculture, in the land shown and granted to them.[49]

If these had been the only conditions connected with manumission, it could be stated that these new freedmen were on their own. However, their previous involuntary servitude was to be manifested in socioeconomic subordination, because manumission was dependent

> on condition that they, the above named Negroes, shall be bound to pay for the freedom they receive, each man for himself annually, as long as he lives, to the West India Company, or its Deputy here, 30 skepels of Maize, or Wheat, Peas, or Beans and one Fat Hog, valued at 20 Guilders, which 30 skepels and the hog they, the Negroes, each for himself, promises to pay annually, beginning from the date hereof [1644], on pain if any one shall fail to pay the yearly tribute, *he shall forfeit his freedom and return to the Company's slavery.*[50]

His lifelong indebtedness to the company distinguished the Afro-American from any other type of bonded or indentured servant in the colony and expressly revealed his subordinate socioeconomic status in Dutch society. A further condition reinforced his subordinate status: the children of the "new freedmen," or those yet to be born to them "shall be bound and obligated to serve the Honorable West India Company as Slaves." [51]

The critical labor shortage was not alleviated by the "freedmen" and their offspring, since the Dutch West India Company, on May 27, 1647, again pleaded with the States General of Holland to permit the import of additional slaves to New Amsterdam. An affirmative response did not come from Holland until 1652. The new order permitted the importation of slaves directly from Angola,[52] but curtailed the monopoly power of the company by extending the privilege to the colonists together with permission to use their own vessels in the importation of slaves.[53] Subsequently, in 1664, before the Dutch relinquished their authority to the English, the Dutch administrator Peter Stuyvesant gave eight half-slaves their complete freedom, plus land grants near his bowery.[54]

AFRO-AMERICAN EMPLOYMENT IN COLONIAL AMSTERDAM

Since the Dutch West India Company was primarily interested in exploiting the natural resources of its colony, it offered its slaves many opportunities to develop manual skills in accord with their innate and acquired abilities. This attitude was entirely consistent with the company's charter—export for profit. The original eleven bonded slaves and their women were employed as agricultural laborers on the company's plantations.[55] Later, both slaves and "freedmen" were employed as stevedores and deckhands on the company's vessels. On land, these slaves became builders of roads and repairers of public installations and were frequently used to maintain Fort Amsterdam.[56] They built the original wagon road between New Amsterdam and Harlem in a further example of their occupational mobility.[57]

Attitudinally, the Dutch New Amsterdam burgher was not swayed too much by color; rather he was greatly influenced by the nature of his religious faith. Those "freedmen" who accepted the religious teaching of the Dutch Reformed Church and did not compete seriously with the Dutchman, had on the whole many opportunities. E. L. Raesly contended that the free Afro-American lived with "the colonists on terms of perfect equality. . . . Of course to enjoy such sweet fruits, . . . a New Netherland African had to be a free man." [58] As late as 1670–1671, such fortunate individuals numbered no more than about a dozen. A brief examination of the records reveals that five patents were issued to former slaves; two in 1643 and three in 1647.[59] Thus under Dutch rule the Afro-American could hope for possible manumission and even some equality of social and economic status with the white burgher.

AFRO-AMERICANS UNDER ENGLISH RULE, 1664–1777

Although English conquest of New Amsterdam brought with it a new political, social, and economic life for many of the colonists, the Afro-American's socioeconomic status regressed. The English assured the Afro-American a helot status by instituting a complete set of legal controls that extended to most forms of activity and included restriction of manumission and social and economic mobility. There were occasional exceptions, as in the manumission of a personal slave following the owner's death, but even these manumissions became difficult to fulfill because of the special restrictions placed upon all future manumitors. Two such manumissions were those by Alice Crabb, whose will provided in 1685 for her "negro man's . . . freedom and liberty" after her death; and by the Smith family, whose will left "a slave to their son Job for 12 years," to be freed after the slave had completed his term of servitude with Job.[60]

In spite of such occasional manumissions ("tokenism"), most Afro-Americans refused to accommodate to the conditions imposed by the English, and their refusal took the form of riots and insurrections. Such refusal to accept an artificially imposed inferior status was revealed by the passage of the act of 1702, entitled "An Act for Regulating Slaves." [61] It stated that Negro Americans "have been found often times guilty of Confederating together in running away, or other ill practices." [62] Since the Afro-American frequently refused to obey the law, a new law was passed to strengthen the previous laws. Thus in 1706 Lord Cornbury issued a proclamation.

I am informed that several negroes in Kings County have assembled themselves in a riotous manner, which if not prevented may prove ill consequence; you [Justices of the Peace] . . . are

required and commanded to take all proper methods for seizing
and apprehending all such negroes. . . . *If they refuse to submit themselves, then fire on them, kill, or destroy them . . .
and for so doing this shall be your sufficient warrant.*[63]

The frequency with which new laws were promulgated to in-
hibit the Afro-American and the extreme penalty for disobeying
these proclamations indicated that the Negro American's hostility
toward white society remained unabated. Thus again in 1708 a
group of slaves in Newton, Long Island, rebelled and killed seven
white persons. The town's legislators refused to remedy the causes
for rebellion and instead enacted another regulation aimed at "pre-
venting the Conspiracy of Slaves." This time the justices were given
carte blanche to avoid any further outbreaks and to secure the
public tranquility.[64]

Apparently the 1708 law proved ineffective, since some Negro
Americans resorted to the Insurrection of 1712.[65] Governor Hunter
told the Lords of Trade in London:

> The bloody conspiracy was put into execution . . . when they
> [Afro-Americans] resolved to revenge themselves for some hard
> usage . . . from their masters. . . . One cuffee, a negro slave
> of one Vantilburgh, set fire to an outhouse of his master. Both
> the noise of the fire and the glare of burning timber attracted
> some of the town's people and upon their approach several
> armed slaves killed a few whites. [Immediately, thereafter, the
> governor sent a detachment of soldiers to put down the rebel-
> lion. In Court were some 27 condemned], and it took the testi-
> mony of a slave witness to convict the suspects, [since] without
> [his] testimony very few of them could have been punished.[66]

Again English recrimination took the usual form. Another law
was passed in December, 1712 to prevent, suppress, and punish "the
Conspiracy and Insurrection of negroes and other slaves." [67] The
intent of this new law was to "reduce the practice of existing manumission." The terror of slave uprising that obsessed the colonials de-
manded strict regulation of all Negroes.[68] The 1712 law also was
intended to restrict the existing economic mobility of freed Afro-
Americans. Thus the new law incorporated a provision forbidding
any Afro-American or mulatto slave granted manumission to enjoy,
"hold, or possess any Houses, Lands, Tenements, or Hereditaments
within the Colony." [69]

Having placed special restrictions upon previously manumitted Afro-Americans, the question was what to do about future manumission. The legislators therefore incorporated a provision in the law discouraging the release of personal slaves in anyone's last will and testament. In part, this provision stated that in order to prevent a freed slave from becoming a public charge, the future manumitor had to place in escrow "a security of not less than £200. This security was to be distributed to the freed slave at the rate of £20 per annum over a ten year period." The rationale behind this provision was based on the supposition that Afro-Americans were like culturally deprived children, "idle and slothful people," and when emancipated would become public charges.[70] Thus, future manumission carried with it a double cost: the loss incurred by not selling the slave at the market price, and the subsidization of the new "freedman" by having to dole out his escrow over a period of years.

If the new law had been enforced it would have erased even the semblance of any possible manumission. Although the statute was moderated in 1717, the revised law still required the placing of £200 in escrow, this money to be used on a contingency basis. Should the freed Afro-American become a public charge, the money would be used to reimburse the public authorities. This created a dual problem for an owner of slaves: (1) the Afro-American's blocked economic mobility made him especially prone to becoming a public charge, thus increasing the likelihood of the escrow money's being used to maintain him; and (2) the tying up of a sizable sum of capital would make even a "benevolent" slave owner hesitate to part with his personal property. How effective English law was in restraining possible manumission [71] was illustrated by census data covering the last decade of the 17th century and the third quarter of the 18th century—the latter, shortly before the American Revolution. In 1698 it was estimated that slaves in New York constituted at least 10 per cent of the total population. Thus, out of an estimated total population of 18,067, some 2,170 were slaves; again in 1771, New York's slave population was estimated at 19,883; over 17 per cent of an estimated total population of 168,007.[72]

> There were so few [Afro-Americans] who were free [in 1771] as to render negligible [their] effect upon the population.[73]

There are other estimates of the slave population for New York City and the province of New York that tend to reinforce the above percentages. According to U. B. Phillips, at least one tenth of the householders in New York owned slaves by 1750; [74] the institutionalization of slavery was also manifested in the fact that "Yankees who moved to Westchester and Long Island were quick to purchase slaves." [75] This institutionalization was reflected in the colonial Englishman's attitudes toward manumission and continued at least until the first decade of the 19th century. Thus,

> in most of the British colonies [on this side of the Atlantic Ocean], heavy taxes were imposed on manumission, and as late as 1802, a law was passed on Northern Leeward Island requiring the owner of slaves to register his slaves for manumission and to pay £500 into the public treasury. [76]

To develop a consistently complex system of legal controls and to maintain the institutionalized status of the Afro-American, English colonials supplemented their restrictive manumission laws to make them all-inclusive. Thus, in addition to their repeatedly emphasizing the slave's chattel status, the English denied the Afro-American the possibility of acquiring middle-class family values and limited the educational opportunities of both freed Negro Americans and slaves. The English did not stop here. They restricted the potential development of the colored American's economic horizon by artificially restricting his economic mobility.

The mark of Ham pursued most manumitted slaves, making it easy to distinguish them from the rest of the population. For example, Alice Crabb's personal slave was easily recognizable, since his "earmark [was] registered in the book of earmarks." [77] There were other indications of the slave's chattel position as evidenced by the common council's passage of laws to protect real and personal property. In March, 1681 the council's law "prohibited the entertainment of slaves in houses, the selling of liquor [to slaves]." Like other enactments protecting personal and real property, this law sought to curtail potential rebellion and runaway slaves and inflicted economic loss on the slaveowner. [78] Annotation of the 1681 law by the 1683 act implied that the establishment was further fearful of financial loss to its citizens. The common council's 1683 act limited assemblage to no more than four slaves, at any time or at any place within the city, except on their master's service. [79]

Again in 1692 the common council of New York showed its concern with keeping the Afro-American in "his place" when it ordered that any slave "found making noise, or playing on the street on Sunday was to receive 20 lashes at the whipping post, unless the owner paid 6 shillings to excuse the same." [80] If comparison can be made, it revealed a socioeconomic status of slaves similar to that of animals by making the master responsible for any and all acts of his moving personal property.

All of these attempts to "cow" the Afro-American were not fully realized, since there were some slaves who showed an overt hostility to these artificial restrictions. One occasion arose on Aug. 19, 1696, when Mayor Merritt ordered a group of noisy slaves to disperse. They refused to obey the mayor's order. The latter threatened them with corporal punishment, and a slave named Prince showed his defiance by striking His Honor "on the face." [81]

The English, ever optimistic that the law would ultimately resolve their difficulties with the slaves, passed another law in 1702, reducing the number of slaves permitted to assemble anywhere in the town from four to three. Slaves were denied their day in court except to testify in "cases of Plotting or Confederacy among themselves." [82] One authority, who supported the idea that Afro-American slaves were no different from other types of property, stated that "entries of purchases and sale of negroes appeared mixed with those of cattle; combined entries of births, or babies with asses and oxen appeared on numerous occasions." [83] S. McKee, Jr., another authority on the Colonial period, reinforced this contention when he stated that slaveowners in New York intentionally "brought them [slaves] together for laboring purposes, sanctioned their reproduction and then separated them as casually as they did live stock." [84]

The elite's social needs—need for servants—required that Afro-Americans conform to the white man's stereotype. Thus the latter organized to prevent passage of a bill presented to the Colonial Assembly on April 27, 1699.

A Bill for facilitating the conversion of Indians and Negroes (which the King's instructions require should be endeavored to be passed), would not go down with the Assembly; they [the assembly, consisting of landed gentry, merchants, *et al.*], had a notion that the Negroes being converted to Christianity [would alter the heathen's status in the eyes of God], would [then] emancipate them from their service, for they have no other servants in this country, but Negroes.[85]

Fear of the Negro's conversion to Christianity dated from the 15th century, when increased prejudice against "the enslavement of men from Christian countries" was reinforced by the church's denouncement of the practice and her threat to punish her subjects who did not adhere to this doctrine. However, "these scruples, did not extend to unbelievers, who were usually thought to be undeserving of freedom." [86]

To dull the Afro-American's mental state and to maintain his "outsider status," the establishment sought to restrain "the education of negro slaves . . . , [and] as a general rule, [education was] forbidden, or at least not promoted, or encouraged in the English Colonies." [87]

EMPLOYMENT OF NEW YORK AFRO-AMERICANS UNDER ENGLISH RULE

The changeover, politically, from Dutch "absentee-ownership" to English resident proprietorship witnessed a decided increase in the total number of white inhabitants in New York.[88] This population change was partly attributable to the fact that the English "fostered agriculture and the welfare of their colonies, unlike the Dutch who lacked interest in the welfare of their province," other than to milk it for possible profit.[89] The change also increased the number of white freemen, bringing a conflict between the free white laboring classes and the landed gentry. White workers sought a monopoly of economic chances and, like the landed gentry, resorted to the law to gain their ends.[90] Thus admission to freemanship (a local license to practice a trade) was denied to "free and slave Afro-Americans," thereby blocking their entry into the skilled trades.

Although the conflict was most pronounced in those towns where a considerable slave population existed, "evidence of conflict [was] found in virtually every sizable town on the Atlantic Coast." [91] New York City was no exception, because when regular carmen were discharged as a body, everyone within the city was given the liberty and license to serve for hire or for wages as carmen *with the exception of slaves*.[92] The continued blocking of economic opportunity for Afro-Americans was manifested again in 1686 when the city's handicraftsmen prevailed upon the council to issue an order stating that "noe Negro or Slave be suffered on the bridge as Porter about any goods either imported or exported from or into this city." [93]

One indication of the white craftsmen's success in monopolizing the trades and blocking the economic mobility of Afro-Americans was attested to by the Earl of Bellmont in 1699. He contended that there were fewer than 100 common laborers to be had in the entire New York province despite the high wage of 3 shillings per day. Such common labor as was performed was restricted mainly to Negro Americans. White workmen had trades, or kept sloops, which afforded them better incomes.[94] Not content with their monopoly of the trades, porters filed a sworn complaint in 1691 attesting that the practice of employing colored Americans "soe impoverished them, that they cannot by their labors get a competency for the maintenance of themselves and families." [95]

The quest for power to restrict the economic chances of the black man was heard across the Atlantic when, in response to the white man's plea, the English Parliament passed the Act of 1732, specifically excluding Afro-Americans in the colonies from being employed in the manufacture of hats, an industry then flourishing in New York.[96] The white outcry against the colored American continued unabated, as is illustrated by Governor Clarke's response to a petition presented to him in 1737. The governor informed the legislature that

> artificers complain and with too much reason of the pernicious custom of breeding slaves to trades whereby the honest and industrious tradesmen were [being] reduced to poverty for want of employ.[97]

In spite of the pleas made to the governors of the New York province of the "intolerable competition" between the whites and the Afro-Americans, there actually existed a critical labor shortage, which was evidenced by the liberal admission policy of white non-residents to freemanship (another manifestation of the Negro American's inferior status in society). Since freemanship was a prerequisite to entrance into the crafts, it held a dual importance: (1) Economic mobility and opportunity were dependent upon admission to free-manship—a step in the direction of economic security and elevation of economic status. It could also be a way in which the slave could purchase his freedom. (2) The freemanship fee was made extremely low only because there was a critical labor shortage. Thus, economic security and opportunity bore a definite relationship to freemanship because of the relatively high wage scale enjoyed by New York City craftsmen when compared with that of laborers.[98] Furthermore, if there had been an oversupply of craftsmen, the city's common council would not have lowered the admission fee for freemanship. Politically, it would have been inexpedient to lower the fee if there had been an abundant supply of labor.

Despite the pleas of Colonial workmen to various governors that many Afro-Americans were depriving them of employment, these same governors decried the existence of high wages (usually an indication of a labor shortage). In 1701 one colonial governor wrote to King George III:

> To make a soldier work, . . . is to alter the nature of man. Idleness is the great motive to many of them, which makes them leave their trades and to enter the King's service, and though they are willing to work when they please and can have liberty, yet, do not like to be compelled thereunto, *especially for one third part of the wages a Negro slave receives in New York for splitting fire wood, carrying the hod.*[99]

Again we note that government officials resorted to the employment of Afro-Americans, either because of the shortage of labor and/or the high wage structure, which forced the utilization of Negro Americans to keep the cost of maintenance down. In writing to the English king, the governor of New York said:

> I could in no way perceive that it was possible for such sums of money to be expended for Fort James [formerly Fort Amsterdam], except by pulling down and building up again the Kitchen and shed which hath been repeated several times by taking the Dutch tiles from off the great house and covering it with shingles, altering the stairs and such other practices by which soldiers, his own servants, and negroes [were] employed.[100]

The labor role of Afro-Americans between 1664 and 1776 was summarized by one authority:

> The slaves were largely unskilled laborers and the wording of protests against the training of slaves to crafts would indicate the exceptional nature of [Afro-American] skilled labor. [In other words, the white man maintained a closed shop.] [101]

On the eve of the American Revolution the relative position of the Afro-American relative to the white freeman was described as follows:

> In general, . . . slaves were forbidden to assemble without permission and presence of responsible whites, were not to own, or to carry guns of any kind, were not to trade, buy, sell, or engage in any other economic activity without permission of their masters, were not to be off the plantation grounds at any time, or on the streets after 9 or 10 in the evening without written permission, were not to practice, or administer medicine, were not to lift their hands against any white person, were not to be taught to read or write.[102]

By the time the colonies had succeeded in overthrowing English control, slavery had become a *national institution*, fully implanted in all 13 colonies, and the newly formed political confederation did not change the Afro-American's second-class social, economic, and political status.[103]

CHAPTER 2

The New York Afro-American and Employment, 1777–1920

The society that emerged from the Dutch effort to translate a declining European "estate society" and English efforts to install their aristocracy differed markedly from either concept. It was, instead, a class society; still in embryo, but definitely class-oriented. CLASS SOCIETY

A class society is a stratified one, even as are caste or estate societies, but the criteria for stratification are different. Unlike the caste society, where one is born into a particular status, or the estate society, where the eldest son inherits his father's domain, class society criteria allow for vertical mobility regardless of ancestors. Thus, theoretically, in a class society each person can make a niche for himself based on the innate and acquired abilities prescribed by the surrounding environment. For some, however, the circle of discrimination, based primarily on visibility, circumscribes opportunity.

For Afro-Americans, the relative "freedom of entry" into most occupations reached its zenith after the close of the Colonial period. Although slaves pursued occupations chosen by their masters, "freedom of occupational entry" was basically determined by the profit motive, which was in turn governed by the principles of supply and demand. Since the Northern economy was based primarily on commerce, manufacturing, and small-scale agriculture, the scarcity and uncertainty of obtaining free white labor made it economically feasible to use Afro-American bondsmen. They performed a multiplicity of tasks: as barbers, carpenters, cabinetmakers, sawyers, blacksmiths, printers, and maritime workers. On the farm, the slave was put to work on the production of foodstuffs and dairy products and

in sheep raising.[1] The savings effected by the use of slave labor
was best exemplified by John Adams' comment, that the release of
his slaves cost him "thousands of dollars for the labor and subsistence of free men, which I might have saved by the purchase of
Negroes at times when they were cheap." [2]

To maintain the balance of trade, an import tariff was proposed
on slaves. Many merchants opposed it, citing as their reasons: (1)
The scarcity of laborers and artisans, which could be alleviated only
by the import of additional slaves. (2) The need for the import of
slaves to reduce the "exorbitant price of labor and . . . bring our
Staple Commodities to their usual price." [3]

During the Revolution, available slaves and the few black
freedmen continued to have some access to many trades because the
labor shortage was aggravated by the urgent need for manpower
to fight the war. Too, since many slaves were owned by the "Tories,"
it was feasible for the anti-British to offer freedom to all slaves
who joined the Revolutionary cause.

However, such "relative freedom of entry" as colored Americans
had in the specialized trades was curtailed at the end of the Anglo-
French War. After the downfall of Napoleon, the influx of foreigners to the United States reversed the situation and intensified
economic discrimination in the North. Afro-Americans were restricted to menial tasks; they were barred from most unskilled jobs
when in competition with whites, and they were excluded from
professional activity because of their lack of education. If the Afro-
American was fortunate enough to acquire "some modest wealth
and wished to invest it in land, he was constantly in danger from
land sharpers and speculators who, in one way or another, found
him the fairest game of all to cheat and rob of the little he had
acquired." [4]

When slavery was legally abolished in New York State in 1827,
employment opportunities for the Afro-American became even more
restricted.

> Freedom offered legal protection but not political, social and
> economic equality. Until the post-Civil War era, in fact, many
> Northern whites maintained a careful distinction between
> granting Negroes legal protection—a theoretical right to life,
> liberty, and property—and political and social equality.[5]

The Afro-American's second-class status had become institutionalized.[6] This branded status was manifested in the intensified efforts

of whites to restrict further the free Afro-American's social, economic, and political status; with special restrictions on most job opportunities (which reached a high point about 1860, when a plateau was established). The displacement of Afro-Americans by white immigrants in employment merely accentuated the subordination of the Afro-American to all whites, including whites illiterate in both their native tongue and the English language and lacking a knowledge of American customs. These employment restrictions continued until World War I, when mass immigration to the United States virtually ceased. Again, production needs for the supply of our own and our allies' armed forces created an acute labor shortage, and Afro-Americans found new employment opportunities. However, the signing of the 1918 Armistice, again brought an abundance of white labor and economic regression for the colored American.

EMPLOYMENT IN NEW YORK, POST-REVOLUTIONARY TO 1820

The American Revolution, with its accompanying changes in the economic, political, and social life of the thirteen colonies, failed to alter the Afro-American's "outsider status." In some instances the post-Revolutionary period found certain tradesmen antithetical toward further colored American manumission: a fear based on potential economic competition with the freedman. Also, having the black man as a competitor meant occupational and social debasement.[7] Abigail Adams wrote to her husband, John Adams:

> I have been much diverted with a little occurrence . . . which serves to show how little founded in nature the so much boasted principle of liberty is. (Specifically, she was referring to the exclusion of Afro-Americans from the skilled trades.) [8]

Actually, she should not have been so "diverted" by the continued practice of overt and covert discrimination against the colored American, because Americans as colonials had practiced discrimination for over one hundred years under English domination. Even before she wrote to her husband, discrimination against the Afro-American had become institutionalized.

Shortly after the Revolutionary War, manufacturing expanded

rapidly, offering wider economic opportunities. Illustrative of this economic growth was the record of exports from the Port of New York. By 1791, exports had grown from almost nothing to $2,505,465. Later, they expanded at an even faster rate. Thus by 1800 they had grown to $14,045,079 or six times as large as in 1791.[9] But, continued economic expansion failed to integrate the freedman or slave into factory life.[10] This trend continued despite the increase of slaves in New York from 2,103 in 1786 to 2,369 by 1790.[11] In 1790, Afro-Americans accounted for 9.9 per cent of the total population.[12]

It is interesting to note at this point that the first retail outlet for manufacturing appeared in New York City around 1790. It was known as the "slop-shop." This type of outlet sold loose, unfinished garments; the customer was expected to turn up his own cuffs or hems, to make buttonholes, and to sew on buttons.[13] Tailors hired garment cutters to cut the material to pattern and then contracted the work out to seamstresses. Many of these garments were distributed to women to work on at home, or sent to farmers' wives who would sew the cut pieces during the winter months when chores were at a low ebb. Thus, to some degree, piece work, or "bundles," were already in practice in the needle trades in the 18th century.

One of the first attempts to list occupations open to New York Afro-Americans appeared in the *Minutes of the Proceedings of the 4th American Convention of Delegates from the Abolition Societies in 1787*. It stated that

> [Although the precise] number of people of color in the State of New York is not known, [the 1800 census listed 20,613 [14]], it exceeds 2,000 in the city. [It was 2,868 in 1800.[15]] Names of one thousand [in the city] were collected and of these more than half were free, employed as servants, laborers, sailors, mechanics, etc., a few were small traders . . . [their] condition was tolerable.[16]

One occupation omitted was that of restaurateur, which offered a good income to at least a few Afro-Americans, notably Samuel Fraunces, who owned the historic Fraunces Tavern in New York City, where George Washington bade farewell to his troops.

The order of occupations probably resulted from tallies taken of the 1,000 names collected, with the highest number in a given occupation listed first. Coincidentally, Charles S. Johnson offered a similar occupational listing, with emphasis on the personal service trades.

> Time was when the small cluster of descendants of the benevolent old Dutch masters and of the free Negroes moved with freedom and complacent importance about the *intimate fringe of the city's active life.* These Negroes were barbers, caterers, bakers, restaurateurs, coachmen, all highly elaborate personal service positions.[17]

The "intimate fringe of the city's active life," or the institutional boundaries set by white society, forced the Afro-American into personal-service, rather than the skilled, trades. President Adams' wife Abigail offered an example when she wrote to her husband abroad in February, 1797.

> Master Heath has opened an evening school to instruct a number of apprentices [in] ciphering, at a shilling a week. . . . James desired that he might go. I told him to go with my compliments to Master Heath. . . . After about a week, Neighbor Faxon came . . . to inform me that if James went to school it would break up the school, for the other lads refused to go. "Pray, Mr. Faxon, has the boy misbehaved? If he has, let the master turn him out of school." "Oh! no! There was no complaint of that kind, but they did not choose to go to school with a black boy." "Is there not room enough to go to school with a black boy?" "Yes!" "Did these lads object to James' playing for them when at a dance?" "Oh, it is not that I object, or my boys, it is some others." [18]

It was arguments such as those employed by Faxon that cast aspersions on "the principle of liberty, and equality," the only grounds upon which the equality of rights ought to be supported, and so loudly enunciated during the Revolution.[19]

During the first decade of the 1800's there were some societies that felt that the Afro-American's lot was improving. Thus, in 1803 the Abolition Societies held a convention at which some New York delegates discussed the Afro-American freeholders.

> [The] increase in the number of freeholders among the free blacks is an evidence of the progress of industry and sobriety

and economy, and strengthens them to hope that they will gradually emerge from their degraded condition to usefulness and
respectability.[20]

The same optimistic note that the Afro-American would find "usefulness and respectability in the near future" was pronounced time
and again at subsequent society meetings, but the phrase "Negro's
degraded condition" was never omitted in describing his situation.

The Abolition Societies met again in 1805, and the New York
delegation again suggested that the "degraded condition" would
disappear in the future. Meanwhile, the emphasis was shifted to
educating the freed Negro American's offspring in order to raise his
economic status. In other words, if there was hope, it would be
realized by the new generation of Afro-Americans. Thus,

> the education of your offspring is a subject of lasting importance
> and has obtained a large portion of your attention and care.
> In this, too, we call upon you for your aid; many of you have
> been favored to acquire considerable portions of property and
> consequently enabled to contribute in some measure to the
> means of educating your offspring.[21]

However, the educational salvation achieved by the white immigrants' offspring proved negligible in the Afro-Americans' case.
When the colored man's aspirations on the craft level or on the
level of higher education were achieved, more often than not he
found it difficult to compete with the white man for available jobs.

The termination of the Napoleonic Wars saw a revival of white
immigration to America. Since New York was one of the main
ports of debarkation, many immigrants remained in the city because
of insufficient funds to move elsewhere. These white foreigners were
granted preferential treatment in employment, and gradually were
able to displace the Afro-American.[22]

Of all the city's diverse groups, the only ones that had difficulty
in obtaining employment were unskilled laborers,

> and among them in particular the Negro. The free colored
> people had grown steadily more numerous following the pas-
> sage of the 1799 Act; [the number of free Afro-Americans rose
> from 6,382 in 1800 to 9,823 in 1810, . . .[23]

Likewise the number of slaves had decreased from 2,868 in 1800 to 1,686 by 1810]. . . .[24]

Still the masses of Negro workers remained unskilled, turbulent and somewhat of a problem. Shortly before the 1820 decade was ushered in the increased number of unskilled foreign born laborers began to meet difficulty in settlement.[25]

In 1818, shortly after the Napoleonic era, the economic difficulties plaguing the unskilled Afro-American began to encompass even their educated brethren. The Abolition Societies were informed by the New York Mission Society that the former's plan (Afro-American salvation through education) was a dismal failure. The Mission Society pointed to the fact that many Afro-American children had completed acceptable courses at the New African Free School but had found it extremely difficult to enter "some useful trade or employment." [26] Afro-American parents discovered that the children "educated at their schools had been suffered after leaving it to waste their time in idleness, thereby incurring those vicious habits which were calculated to render their previous education worse than useless." [27] To alleviate this difficulty an indenturing committee was formed to assist the educated youngsters in finding placement.

Although there was a discernible segregated black community in New York as early as 1800,[28] many Afro-Americans could still be found throughout the city. In integrated areas, the whites lived in the dwellings above ground and the Afro-American in the cellar apartments. (Segregation, as the term is used today, took effect in New York City around 1840.) Since situs mobility was possible, and housing accommodations depended upon income, Dr. John H. Griscom's description of a given health district revealed the low economic status of many Afro-Americans. Doctor Griscom, who was connected with the city's Department of Health, depicted the condition of many Afro-Americans in 1820 as follows:

There were some 562 blacks [who] inhabited the infected district [fever ridden] of whom 119 lived in cellars; of these 119, 54 were sick of the prevailing fever, and 24 died. . . . Out of 48 blacks in 10 cellars, 33 were sick, of whom 14 died, while out of 120 whites, living immediately over their heads, in the same houses, not one even had the fever.[29]

THE ESTABLISHMENT OF AN AFRO-AMERICAN JOB CEILING: 1820–1860

There is some evidence that an Afro-American job ceiling originated in New York shortly after the Anglo-French Wars. (The term job ceiling logically connotes a prescribed set of trades and/or occupations, restricted primarily to a group with an ascribed social and economic status, that rarely offer upgrading.) The easing of the labor shortage, through the increased volume of foreign immigrants after the wars and their accompanying preferential treatment in hiring, caused the Afro-American to become persona non grata in former "black" trades. A white teacher in New York's African Free School found little occupational mobility in the apprenticable trades, in manufacturing, or in professional employment available to educated Afro-American youth. For example:

> A young man of age, who two and a half years ago, left this school with a respectable education, . . . was taken on as an apprentice to a blacksmith's business in this city, served about two years with satisfaction to his master. Depression of business rendered little opportunity of his obtaining a thorough knowledge to the trade, his father making arrangements with his master to release him, with a view to the lad's serving his time elsewhere; every place that appeared suitable to his object was closed against him because he was black.[30]

The oral tradition that no black shall work side by side with a white man in most trades was also witnessed by E. S. Adby during his residence in New York City.[31] Even the Rev. J. W. C. Pennington, a former slave, was aghast to find so much "misery, ignorance and wretchedness of the free colored people," when he arrived in New York at the end of the 1820's. He decided to devote his life to raising the level of his people.[32]

The depression that followed the War of 1812 brought a heavy influx of white immigrants into the field of domestic service; a field that had been predominantly Afro-American since Colonial days. The files of the New York Society for the Encouragement of Faithful Domestics recorded that for the period 1826–1830 it had on file applications for employment from 8,346 Irish, 3,601 white Americans, and 2,574 colored Americans.[33] Professional opportunity for the blacks was even less than that found in industry, trades, or domestic service. An examination of graduates from the African Free School covering a 10-year period revealed that three had become ministers, two had entered the teaching profession, and the rest had found little solace in having an education.[34]

Despite the low correlation of educated Afro-Americans to economic mobility, the New York Abolition Societies continued to insist that abolition without education would be meaningless. Thus, at their 1821 Convention the delegates stated that one must "not forget how much depends on the careful instruction of all who are free." [35] Once more at the 1828 Convention the societies proudly presented a report stating that the level of education offered Afro-American children at the African Free School was equal to, if not higher than, that given to whites.[36]

Litwack summarized the double standard employed by the abolitionists:

> Of what use, was the right to vote, attend school, and to enter the homes of the abolitionists if it was still impossible to gain access to any but the most menial employment. The economic condition of the Negro was at best deplorable, and the new waves of immigrants, competing for many positions which Negroes had long monopolized, only made matters worse. Although some white abolitionists had agitated vigorously in the areas of civil rights and educational opportunities, little had been done in the way of economic assistance, except to call upon Negroes to improve themselves.[37]

Since economic status—a correlate of economic mobility—was one of the middle-class values in the dominant white society, the Afro-American stressed his need for economic opportunity to raise his own economic status. He requested the abolitionists to practice what they preached—greater economic opportunity for the colored community. Still, the abolitionists themselves practiced the same type of employment discrimination as did the racists. A *Colored American* survey revealed that not even one local abolitionist had placed a colored American in any responsible position in his business.[38] Even New York's Anti-Slavery Society's work force had no Afro-American on its payroll.[39]

During the 1820's economic opportunity for the educated Afro-American was summarized as follows:

A few [former] students, educated as well as white students
have obtained trades of the following descriptions: *viz;* sail-
makers, shoemakers, tinworkers, tailors, carpenters, blacksmiths,
etc. In almost every instance, difficulties have attended them
on account of their color, either in obtaining them, in finding
employment in good shops. . . . Many of our lads go to sea as
stewards, cooks, sailors, etc. Those who cannot procure trades,
and do not like to go to sea become waiters, coachmen, barbers,
servants, laborers.[40]

Messers Andrews and Adby's observations were reinforced by numerous articles in the *Colored American,*[41] a New York colored weekly
published during the years 1835–1841.

The 1830's revealed a further deterioration in the Afro-American's economic status, leading to the possible conclusion that the
circle of discrimination (or vicious circle), had become institutionalized. Since the Afro-American had little or no political power,
it was not conceivable that the political sector of society would fail
to discriminate against him. Thus, the municipal government
created various licensed monopolies. In itself licensing was not new;
it was a carryover from Colonial times and originally was intended
to prevent fraud. Now it was used for purposes of political patronage. For example, in the City of New York, the common council
appointed or licensed butchers, grocers, tavern and porterhouse
keepers, cartmen, and others. One writer asserted that in 1828 the
city's patronage list included nearly "seven thousand persons, more
than three-fourths of whom were in these [patronage licensed]
categories." [42]

Two instances of blocked economic opportunity based on the
lack of political power occurred in 1835 and 1836, respectively.

In 1835, Anthony Provost, an upright, industrious and sober
man, of New York City, applied for a license to drive a cart.
He was refused because of his color. He worked with his horse
and cart, a short time [unlicensed] and was fined $20.00; but on
application of his friends the fine was remitted, on payment of
[court] costs, and engagement to use his cart and horse no
more.[43]

[Again] in 1836, William Hewlett, of New York, a well known
and respectable colored man, for whom some forty firms
[mostly booksellers] petitioned, was likewise refused a cartman's
license, merely because he was colored.[44]

One authority contended that the reason for the city fathers' failure
to issue licenses to Afro-American cartmen and porters was that

> the prejudices of white labor and the fear of violence, [which]
> would bring them [colored American cartmen and porters]
> into collision with white men of the same calling, and the
> [colored men] would get their horses and carts "dumped" into
> the dock, and themselves abused and beaten.[45]

This comment coincided with the experiences of many Afro-Americans in Northern cities. As a result of this treatment many fled to
Canada. To exemplify, "One, John Moore, sought to raise his
economic status above his lowly station in the new world of unlimited opportunity and found himself mobbed and burned out." [46]
In such instances the lack of police protection and the Afro-American's failure to pressure elected city officials into protecting his
economic mobility revealed the impotence of his second-class political status.[47] (Afro-Americans were required to own a freehold plus
three years residence to be eligible to vote.)

The same period (1834–1846) was covered by two reports, both
of which arrived at a similar economic conclusion: Afro-Americans
were moving down the economic ladder in New York. One report,
written by a colonization promoter, contended that colored Americans were no longer able to succeed in their struggle with white
laborers. Negro Americans were being displaced in the higher
economic pursuits by white immigrants. Specifically, the colonization report alluded to economic conditions prior to 1846, when it
was common to find a large body of colored laborers in the city.
Now (1846) "none can deny that they [Afro-Americans] have
sunken much lower than they were years ago and are compelled to
pursue none but the meanest avocations." [48] Although the colonization societies were known to be biased, this promoter's conclusions
coincided with that of an Afro-American historian. For the period
1834–1846, the latter stated:

> Negroes had boldly asserted themselves during this period, but
> found themselves losing ground and sinking into meaner oc-
> cupations. The day was not far off when every desirable business
> in the city would be entirely monopolized by whites because of
> the rapid influx of foreigners who had to labor and knew how
> to toil to advantage.[49]

Demographic data for the years 1825–1835, by wards and by wealth per capita in each ward, tended to reinforce the thesis that Afro-American masses were experiencing an economic decline and being limited mainly to domestic service. This hypothesis was sustained by a shift in Afro-American residency from the first three wards to the fifteenth ward.[50] The first three wards were losing population because many affulent old merchant families moved uptown and took with them their servants—most of whom were Afro-Americans. (The employment of colored servants among upper-middle and upper-class white families was a status symbol in the 19th century.[51]) This high rate of domestic servants may be a factor in explaining the concentration of Afro-Americans (about 25 per cent) in the five wards with the highest average of income per capita in 1840.

The sliding economic status of the Afro-American was further elaborated upon by A. Dyson when he summarized the colored American labor situation from the time of legal manumission (1827) until about 1840.

Most Northern men still object to granting Negroes economic equality. When the supply of labor exceeded the demand, the Free Negroes, unable to compete with these foreigners, were driven not only from respectable positions, but also from the menial pursuits. Measures to restrict to whites employment in higher pursuits were proposed and where they were not actually made laws, public opinion, to that effect accomplished the same result.[52]

In dealing with the Afro-American's "struggle for equality," a 20th-century historian was even more outspoken.

When the militant phase of abolitionism began in 1831, the status of Northern Negroes was deplorable. Shut out from white schools and churches, forced to live in city slums and ghettos [*Five Points*, formerly common land is one area referred to], denied equal civil and political rights, . . . confined to menial occupations, almost universally despised as members of an inferior race, the Northern Negroes' lot in 1830 was a harsh one. In some respects their *status actually deteriorated* [further] *in the next thirty years* [1860]. The huge influx of immigrants in the 1840's and 1850's drove colored people out of many of their former occupations and subjected them to the mob fury of socially and economically insecure immigrants.[53]

By 1840 the Afro-American's job ceiling was limited mainly to those occupations usually described as irksome, dirty, heavy on the muscle, and light on the brain. Among others, they included long-shoring, hod carrying, whitewashing, coaching, and bootblacking. The *New Moral World*,[54] an Owenite newspaper published during the middle 1840's, ascribed a virtual colored American monopoly in these occupations.

Afro-American females found their job environment equally circumscribed. They, too, were restricted to menial occupations, such as maid, cook, scullion, laundress, and seamstress.[55] Like their male counterparts they discovered that this circumscribed economic circle was gradually being narrowed, because in the 1840's Irish women were already displacing colored women in domestic service [56] and in other occupations as rough washer, coarse sewer, and many other types of unskilled work.[57] Thus the concept of Afro-American jobs gradually became a fiction, and was destroyed with each wave of white immigrants that invaded what had formerly been considered "Afro-American jobs." [58] In the 1840's and 1850's the German and Irish immigrants took over the black jobs of porters, dockhands, waiters, barbers, and cooks.[59]

During the 1850's, both inside and outside of New York City, various reports emphasized the gradual decline of the Afro-American's occupational status. Outside of New York, for example, the *Maryland Colonization Journal* [60] stressed the fact that whites were preempting jobs usually reserved for the Afro-American in the South. Similar in its conclusions but less prejudiced was J. G. Speed's article in *Harper's Weekly*, which described the Afro-American's economic status as follows:

> The Negro is not a newcomer to New York. He has been here for two centuries and a half. . . . Free Negroes continued to live in New York from the time of abolition until now [1900], but they have always kept very much to themselves: [they had been involuntarily segregated], . . .[61]

> living in colonies and engaged in a few special occupations in which they were reasonably prosperous. In 1850, when New York had a population of 515,547, there were 13,815 Negroes in the city. This was . . . only 2.7 percent, but the Negroes in the city were in many regards better off [relatively] than their successors [were] fifty years later. At that time [*circa*, 1850], the chief caterers of the city were Negroes, [these included, among others, Delany, Downing, and Ten Eycks]. There were many

barbershops manned by colored men. The white-washing trade belonged, almost exclusively, to Negroes. Negroes were also the private coachmen of the town, and not a few drove public hacks. The bootblack business was theirs, and very many, if not most, of the hotel dining rooms and restaurants had Negro waiters.[62]

There was a small Afro-American middle class, which resided apart from the colored masses, mainly around Brooklyn's Fulton Street area. This group consisted of small merchants, clergymen, and their offspring, who either followed in their fathers' businesses or became professionals—physicians, lawyers, or teachers. But the group was close knit and was almost inbred, with little social contact with the masses of black folk. To contend that this group constituted a "middle class" in the modern sense, would be contrary to M. W. Ovington's description. In referring to them, she stated that "had they been white, they would have slipped into the population and been lost." [63]

In 1851, Dr. James McCune Smith, a member of New York's Afro-American elite, described the economic status of his ethnic group.

City life shuts us off from general mechanical employment; while journeymen in the cities refuse to work with us, and colored bosses have either too little capital, or too little enterprise to bring up and employ apprentices and journeymen. The enormous combination of capital, which is slowly invading every calling in the city [a primary reason for the decline of Afro-American hegemony in the catering business], from washing and ironing to place steamers must tend more and more to grind the fact of the poor in the cities, and render them more and more slaves of lower wages and higher rents.[64]

Doctor McCune's statement had added substance when it was recognized that nowhere "in the North were Negroes and abolitionists more hated than in New York City," especially by immigrants.[65] By 1852 the Irish, "who had to toil and knew how to toil to their advantage, furnished at least half of the machinists, shipwrights, carpenters, cabinetmakers and other men of manual skill in New York"; [66] also, they laid claim to nearly all of the officers positions in New York's Tailor Trade Association [67] and by the middle 1850's had gained control over longshoring. However, in spite of the

Irish monopoly of many former Afro-American strongholds, they still feared colored American economic and social competition.

The 1850 Federal Census [68] reinforced the thesis of Afro-American exclusion from most trades by reporting that of the 3,337 Afro-Americans gainfully employed, 2,615, or about 79 per cent of their number, were confined to five occupations: laborers (1,144); servants (808); mariners (434); barbers (122); and coachmen (107). Again in the middle 1850's one authority on the City of New York wrote:

> As tradition of servitude and the continuing stigma of inferiority prevented most Negroes from pursuing skilled trades, they followed the only course open to them: common labor and various service trades. . . . Some two thousand colored persons were servants, laundresses, cooks, and waiters—over half of all the gainfully employed Negroes. Negroes who were waiters or coachmen invariably competed with the Irish, and they sometimes competed with foreigners in menial occupations, as whitewashers, carpet shakers, chimney sweeps, and bootblacks.[69]

At the beginning of the 1860's, Afro-American employment was summarized as being at least 87 per cent concentrated in menial and/or unskilled jobs.[70]

For the 40-year period 1820–1860,[71] the federal government prepared a special statistical compilation of occupations held by immigrants prior to their entry into the United States. These statistics revealed that, aside from laborers and servants, the bulk of the immigrants living here had plied none of the "Afro-American occupations" in their own country. However, when economic necessity forced most of these foreigners to accept any job, many became porters and sweepers. To help maintain the household, the wives and children of these immigrants entered domestic service and took in sewing and laundry.[72] Thus, "blocked economic mobility," heightened by the arrival of white immigrants, made it "extremely difficult [for the colored American] to rise above manual labor and domestic service prior to the Civil War." [73]

Doctor Charles Wesley, a persuasive Afro-American historian, summed up the anti-slavery movement's failure to assist the Afro-American in becoming economically integrated.

> The anti-slavery movement would destroy slavery, but it neglected the more practical task of creating an economic

future for the free Negro population in industry. Many Negroes were physically free, and yet, they were enslaved and placed in degraded economic positions by the apathy of their friends and the hostile attitude of their fellow workers. Racial toleration in industrial occupations was rare. In the majority of places where Negroes and whites worked together there was a sullen suspicion which soon gave opportunity to the whites to force the Negroes out of employment, either by means of economic pressure, or by legislation. The conditions of Negro free labor which were brought out by the Civil War did not end economic strife between the races. They served only to increase the struggle between white and black labor in the United States.[74]

THE IMMIGRANT AND AFRO-AMERICAN DISPLACEMENT

Although some authorities may differ as to the degree of occupational displacement experienced by the Afro-American between 1820 and 1860, they do agree that an *Afro-American job ceiling did exist.*

The advent of the Civil War saw a marked rise in Afro-American displacement by white immigrants in such occupations as porters, tobacco stemmers, waiters, barbers, or cooks.[75] When jobs were at a premium, especially during cyclical downturns, whites invaded colored American occupations: a policy definitely in accord with "racism." To wit: in 1862, after many years of employment as stemmers in the Lorillard tobacco factory, Afro-Americans were forced out of their jobs by whites.[76] A white delegation threatened to walk off the job unless all employed Afro-Americans were released from employment. The ultimatum did not cease here; it included a demand for a promise on management's part that no colored Americans would be hired in the future.

Another example of white racism was given in a New York newspaper.[77] A group of Irish longshoremen informed their employer that all Afro-American longshoremen, dockhands, and other types of workers must be dismissed summarily, otherwise the Irish would tie up the port. Another muscle field—construction—was predominated by Germans and Irish. By 1865 the "shanty population of about 20,000 [Germans and Irish] were firmly established on the upper west side of Manhattan." [78] The majority of this "shanty population" were unskilled laborers engaged in grading, sewering of streets, and rock removal.

Preemption of Afro-American trades was not confined to those listed. In 1862 Henry Ward Beecher,[79] while serving as minister of Plymouth Church in Brooklyn, stated that Afro-American barbers and waiters were being driven from their trades as fast as white immigrants could be found to replace them. There was "not a foundry, machine shop, a ship yard, a carpenter shop, a cabinet shop, . . . in which the Negro could enter."

Enactment of the 1863 Conscription Act sparked the disorders during the week of July 11, 1863, commonly referred to as the "draft riots." Abolitionists, the American Missionary Association, and the Committee of Merchants for the Relief of Colored People Suffering from the late Riots in the City of New York [80] combined their financial resources to alleviate the Afro-American's plight resulting from the riots. The Merchants' report depicted the attitude of most white classes toward the colored American as one of contempt. However, it was the lower social and economic class that resorted to brutal murder and the hanging of Afro-Americans from trees and lampposts. During this internecine conflict, one foreign observer remarked that some whites would not hesitate to "shoot a blackman with as little regard to moral consequences as they would a wild dog." [81] Afro-Americans, beaten, robbed, and driven from the streets during the riots, sought refuge on Blackwell's Island and at various police houses on the outskirts of the city.

Following the week-long riots, about 5,000 women and children were left homeless and destitute.[82] Many wealthy white families were so conscience stricken that in retaliation they substituted Afro-American servants for their Irish servants. In the weeks and months ahead, a more Christian spirit was proclaimed toward colored folk.[83] However, time eased the "guilt complex," and the Afro-American's condition regressed to what it had been prior to the riots.

In 1860, New York City had 12,574 Afro-Americans; [84] constituting about 1.6 per cent of its total population. Following the race riots, well over 50 per cent of the black population applied for relief to the Committee of Merchants.[85] In addition to administering relief, the committee tabulated the occupations of its applicants, a listing that revealed a marked imbalance favoring menial work.

Restricted economic opportunity was not limited to those not in the white-collar segment of the Afro-American community. Professionals found their horizons curtailed when they were refused association in white organizations. Frequently this meant a practice limited to their own ethnic group. To illustrate the point, in 1867 the New York *World* stated that New York had two Afro-American

Of the 2,450 men relieved or assisted, their occupations were

Laborers and longshoremen	1,267	Tailors	4
Whitewashers	177	Artists	3
Drivers and cartmen	176	Music teachers	3
Waiters	250	Coopers	3
Porters	124	Engravers	2
Sailors and boatmen	97	Janitors	2
Coachmen	72	Measurers	2
Cooks	45	Oystermen	2
Barbers	37	Undertakers	2
Chimneysweeps	34	Landlords	1
Tradesmen	25	Flour inspectors	1
Butchers	20	Teachers	1
Ministers	11	Farmers	1
Bootblacks	15	Copyists	1
Shoemakers	11	Botanists	1
Tobacconists	11	Physicians	1
Woodsawyers	11	Bookbinders	1
Carpenters	8	Tinsmiths	1
Basketmakers	7	Upholsterers	1
Scavengers	6	Blacksmiths	1
Carpet shakers	5		

Of the 3,942 women relieved or assisted, their occupations were

Day's work women	2,924	Hucksters	13
Servants hired by month	634	Teachers	4
Seamstresses	163	Artists	1
Cooks	106	Boardinghouse keepers	1
Tobacco workers	19	Basketmakers	1
Nurses	13	Infirm	32

attorneys with a practice limited to their own kind. Furthermore they stood outside their profession since they were refused membership to the New York Bar.[86]

Afro-American doctors found themselves equally restricted, because they were refused affiliation with hospitals. Thus their practice was limited to office and house calls, and they could not refer their patients to a hospital for surgery or other needed medical care. To be admitted to a hospital, the patients had to seek out white doctors who had an affiliation with a hospital that would accept colored patients. Since medical science was predominantly associated with hospitals affiliated with medical schools, Afro-American physicians lost contact with current advances in medical knowledge. This discouraged patients from continuing their relationship with these physicians, causing a loss of income and acting as a deterrent to future Afro-Americans who might consider entering the profession.[87] This helped to maintain the white man's stereotype of the colored man. In the field of education, some Afro-Americans did find some employment as teachers in public schools. However, their professional mobility was restricted to segregated schools in Kings, Queens, and New York counties.[88]

William E. B. DuBois depicted the situation in 1865 for the masses of colored American workers:

> Before the Civil War the Negro was certainly as efficient a workman as the raw immigrant from Ireland and Germany. But, whereas, the Irishman found economic opportunity wide and clearly growing wider, the Negro found public opinion determined to keep him in his place.[89]

Like the previous decades, the 1870's saw no easing of Afro-American occupational displacement, even though the Irish were classified frequently on the same, if not lower, social level as the Afro-American. Doctor R. T. Berthoff [90] reported:

> The name Ireland has become a hissing and a by-word among the nations of the earth, that of Irishman a synonym for the lowest caste in the social scale—a badge of servitude as marked as was for so many years, a black skin.

There were many local ads in newspapers that capitalized the phrase, "Irish People Need Not Apply." [91] Despite this social stigma the Irish gained economic strongholds in many trades,[92] leading to upward economic mobility.

Although the Irish were assigned a "badge of servitude" akin to the black man, other ethnic groups must have shared this "honor," since in 1870 some 42 per cent of New York City's population were foreign born.[93] (The percentage would have been much higher if first generation offspring had been included.)

No matter how low any white ethnic group's social status was, it was usually higher than that of the Afro-American, with the former being given economic preference in the labor market. In other words, "the newcomers from Europe had to be provided for," [94] even if it was to be at the expense of the indigenous colored American. This was the case even when the bulk of immigrants had little or no prior occupational skill for the jobs. This contention has

merit when viewed longitudinally. Thus, the 1870 Census of Occupations for New York City [95] revealed that foreigners constituted
at least 50 per cent of the mariners, 90 per cent of the laborers, 74
per cent of the launderers, and about 80 per cent of the shoemakers.

During and after the Civil War, white job preference, or intensity of discrimination in employment, was again manifested, but
in a new form. (This is designated as *indirect, or oblique, displacement.*) During the antebellum period, industry had been skilled for
the most part, and it had been controlled by the Americans, the
English, and the Scots.[96] The post-bellum period brought a deskilling
of many sewing operations (section work) that lowered their social
and economic status. These jobs were now filled mainly by the Irish
and Germans,[97] who constituted about 66⅔ per cent of the clothing
industry's total work force following the Civil War.[98] If there had
been no influx of immigrants, the principle of supply and demand
would have forced employers to hire Afro-Americans.

Before the 1880's, the Irish and Germans in particular were able
to elevate their economic status in the trades and in municipal employment. This upward economic mobility opened up the lower
rungs of occupational mobility. But these "older immigrants" were
replaced in the late 1880's by a wave of "new immigrants," comprised chiefly of Eastern and South Europeans. Thus the Italians,
Hebrews, and others replaced the Irish and Germans in the needle
trades.[99] This is not to imply that there were no clashes between the
Irish and the "newcomers" in many employment areas. The classic
case was the conflict between the Irish and the Italians on the waterfront. Throughout it all the Afro-American remained the "outsider." [100]

Until World War I the upgrading of Irish and Germans in the
trades and in municipal employment brought an infiltration of
many "new immigrants" into the lower status jobs. Thus in the late
1880's and early 1890's there was revealed a heavy influx of new ethnic groups in such trades as longshoring, barbering, shoeshining,
catering, and paving. The Italians first gained a strong foothold in
longshoring during the middle 1880's,[101] and in numbers rivaled the
Irish. Italians also took over such Afro-American occupations as street
paving and shoeshining.[102] Always race conscious, the Afro-American fought back by resorting to "scabbing," a method that rarely
offered him permanent entry into any trade.[103]

J. G. Speed offered some perspective with regard to the colored
American's relative economic status during the 1880's, when compared with earlier decades.

By 1880, the number of [Afro-Americans] had increased to 19,963, which was little in excess of 1½ percent of the total population of 1,206,299. This was the period when the decline in industrial opportunities for Negroes in New York became very apparent.[104]

The same opinion was held by the New York *Globe* in 1884.[105]

Time was when colored people largely monopolized such positions as: coachmen, footmen, valets, chefs, waiters, etc.; but they have been superseded in these employments by foreign white help.

It was the vogue to hire foreign domestics and coachmen. The Afro-American had to close shop when the Germans and Italians invaded barbering.[106]

In addition to Speed and the New York *Globe* there were others who subscribed to this thesis.[107] One statistical survey covering the 1890's described the situation as follows: A total of 14,000 Afro-Americans, 10 years of age and over were employed, constituting 8,000 males and 6,000 females. A representative sample of those employed showed

		Males	
Barbers and hairdressers	111	Messengers and porters	559
Janitors	336	Common laborers	882
Servants	3,647	Draymen and teamsters	476
		Females	
Laundresses	1,526	Servants	3,754

The Afro-American's employment situation in the 1890's was described by one historian as follows:

Most of the Negro population . . . worked at varieties of unskilled and low-paid jobs. The Negro middle class was quite small. The largest number, some 450, were clerks, followed in descending order, by actors, and actresses, musicians, music teachers and small businessmen. . . . More than 90 percent of the community, male and female, were employed as menials or laborers: servants, porters, waiters, waitresses, teamsters, dressmakers, laundresses, janitors and "laborers not specified." [108]

After June 30, 1896, the new immigrants assumed a preponderance when their total rose to 57 per cent; [109] and continued to hold a clear majority over immigration from northern and western Europe. Thus, during the period 1890–1910 [110] the total percentage of new immigration in New York never fell below 76 per cent.

From the middle 1890's through 1910 many of the newer immigrants who settled in New York—such as the Italian peasants—were "so unskilled that they could be put only to pick and shovel in another country . . . ,[111] or like the Greeks, whose proportion of unskilled rose from 66 percent in 1900 to 91 percent in 1907," [112] could easily take over the unskilled jobs vacated by the mobile Irish and Germans. Italians took over the paving of streets. When an asphalt paving company was awarded the contract to pave the square around Cooper Union in downtown New York,[113] it "began to fill the places of Afro-American pavers and rammermen with Irish and Germans . . . , to be followed in succession by Italians." Other ethnic groups, for example the Slavs, took over much of the heavy work in brickmaking plants along the Hudson River.[114]

Prior to this influx of new immigrants, it was traditional for Southern Afro-Americans to perform this seasonal type of work. Colored Americans were displaced by Greeks and Italians in the shoeshining and catering trades. During this same period, young Germans and Frenchmen joined the ranks of Italians and Greeks in taking over diningroom service.[115] Likewise, in every city of considerable size along the lines of the New York Central Railroad, Italians and Germans were fast monopolizing the barber trade.[116] The invasion was penetrating further and further into Afro-American territory when the white housepainter, decorator, and paperhanger took over the colored American trade of whitewashing.[117]

After white immigrants had accommodated themselves to their new conditions and found segments of a trade no longer economically and socially advantageous, they permitted the Afro-American to enter. For example, Afro-Americans were admitted to the needle trades around 1900. Many colored American women applied, but they were limited to the waist industry,[118] a branch of the needle trades so low in skill and pay that even white immigrant girls shunned it. In 1906, Miss Ovington [119] did a survey of Afro-Americans in New York City's needle trades. She found no colored American garment cutters or operators and only a few finishers and thread cleaners. Commercial laundries followed the same pattern of stratification of occupations based on color. The better paying jobs, such as drivers, markers, and sorters, were reserved for whites; Afro-Americans were assigned the heavy and unskilled jobs as wringers, pullers, and assistant washers.[120]

Those Afro-Americans proficient in the construction industry, who had been trained largely in the West Indies, found work assignments limited to repair or alteration work. Those in the catering industry were sent out to second-class "houses" rather than to first-class dining halls.

Miss H. Tucker's survey of New York City's craftsmen for the years 1907–1908 [121] revealed that Afro-American mechanics did not share the available work on an equal basis with their white counterparts. Frequently, when the Afro-American found his trade insufficiently remunerative because of lack of work,[122] he shifted to menial work. (Miss Tucker stressed the irregularity of work because of discrimination rather than seasonality.) The gradual diminution of employed colored craftsmen dried up one possible source of sponsorship for Afro-American apprentices. This oblique or indirect displacement made eventually for "lily-white" unions.

Economically speaking, another impact of a serious nature was the differential in annual earnings between white and colored American in the same craft and union, resulting from the dependency of the Afro-American on the white business agent for employment. This type of discriminatory practice was especially prevalent in catering, waitering, and longshoring (the shape-up).[123] One survey reported that whereas Afro-Americans were high in proportion to the total group—200 colored waiters out of every 1,000—the colored waiters rarely competed with the other 800 for jobs. In other words, the Afro-American was restricted to a certain type of house (restaurant or hotel). These offered the lowest income in the trade, because gratuities, which form a key element of earning, were low and they in turn affected annual earnings. To put it another way, the Afro-American working the same number of hours or even longer hours than his white counterpart would still wind up with lower weekly and annual earnings.

Longshoring had a peculiar quirk to it—the shape-up.[124] Each pier had a regular gang, or gangs, assigned to it, and members of the gang were given priority in hiring. The stevedore, the company's representative, did the hiring at a "shape-up," held as often as three times a day. A shape-up consisted of men forming a semi-circle and the stevedore's pointing to the men who were to work for him. The Irish controlled most of the local unions and stevedoring in the city; thus, hiring was mostly along ethnic lines. Since the Afro-American had no assigned pier, he was an extra and had to depend upon a shortage of longshoremen to be placed. Although hourly rates would be the same for all workers regardless of ethnic affiliation, the irregularity of work for the Afro-American meant lower annual earnings.

In 1907, Samuel Scrottron, a member of the Board of Education, described the Afro-American's occupational status in a manner reminiscent of earlier observers.

> Negro waiters, and hotel employees were giving way [as they had in the past] before the inroads of whites. Throughout the entire North and West most of the best hotels and restaurants [continued] to replace Negro waiters with whites. . . . The Italian, Sicilian and Greek foreign to America's institutions occupy what was confessedly the Negro's forty years ago [*circa* 1860]. They [the Greeks and Italians] have bootblack stands, newsstands, barbering, waitering, janitors and catering businesses.[125]

Relatively speaking, there was continuous displacement of the Afro-American, first by the singing Irish and stolid Germans and later by the new immigration, revealing a pattern changed little since the plateau of intensity reached in 1860.[126]

In 1905, Miss Ovington's study revealed conclusions similar to those of Scrottron. Her study, based on some 2,500 New York City Afro-American families in New York, covered 9,788 persons. She excluded those under 15 years of age and 82 persons who were either self-employed or in the professions. Her total sample consisted of 7,847, or 23 per cent of New York City's black population in 1900. (The 1900 Census listed 38,616 persons.) [127] Her sample, broken down by sex, consisted of 3,802 males and 4,045 females, all predominantly employed in domestic and personal service. A statistical breakdown by occupation showed that 40.2 per cent of the male and 89.3 per cent of the female black population were in domestic and/or personal service.

Covering the period 1865–1910, the *Annals* of the American Academy of Political and Social Science devoted an entire issue to the Afro-American and in dealing with his economic status, it stated:

> Fifty years ago, the waiter in New York . . . was usually a man of color, as was the barber, the coachman, the caterer, or the gardener. True enough, he had little opportunity to rise above such menial occupations, but with the growth of a humanitarian, if rather apologetic, attitude toward the Negro engendered by the great conflict which had brought about verbal abolition of slavery. . . . it [was] possible that the Negro's status in New York . . . would have been rapidly and permanently improved, industrially, as well as in civic recognition, had not the current immigration which had been retarded for a decade or two during the Civil War and preceding the agitation, started with the renewed force on the cessation of conflict. . . . The European immigrant soon outstripped his Negro rival for employment and the respect of the American, . . . [the white immigrant] looked and still looks upon the Negro with the contemptuous eye of an easy victor over a hopelessly outnumbered weak and incompetent foe.[128]

The 1910 Census for New York City reinforced what the *Annals* and Miss Ovington and Scrottron had said. The census reported that over two-thirds (some 70.1 per cent) of all colored American workers were employed in domestic and/or personal service trades. The majority of the remainder were concentrated in manufacturing and in mechanical industries (porters and general utility men),[129] with a few scattered in trade, professional services, transportation, and communication. "It was quite evident that the occupations of Negro workers were not far removed from the traditional Negro jobs akin to the work they did as slaves." [130]

Although the "ubiquitous porter" remained the fulcrum of Afro-American employment during the 1910 decade, there were some occupational changes in work formerly held exclusively by white immigrants. There were at least two reasons cited: the cessation of European immigration, and the extreme shortage of laborers because of heavy induction into the armed forces. The nonmilitarized immigrant found upgrading readily available, and the result proved economically advantageous to the Afro-American. (The drop in immigration during the years 1913–1918 is given in the following table.[131])

VOLUME OF IMMIGRATION INTO THE
UNITED STATES, BY YEARS, 1913–1918

Year	Volume	Year	Volume
1913	1,197,892	1916	298,826
1914	1,218,480	1917	295,403
1915	326,700	1918	110,618

A comparison of the census data for 1910 and 1920 buttresses the contention that a decline in immigration was reflected in the changed industrial composition of New York City's Afro-American labor force. The most radical change took place in the category of clericals, rising from 1,528 in 1910 to 3,659 in 1920.[132]

In some respects the 1910 decade resembled the Colonial period: both periods had a marked labor shortage, and the principle of supply and demand in a capitalistic economy temporarily surmounted other odds. Thus between 1914 and 1918, formerly blocked occupational mobility in such fields as trade, transportation, and manufacturing was eased for the Afro-American. Granted that his entry was limited to the lowest levels, it did offer him a new lease on life.[133] Despite these new avenues of employment, the bulk of New York City's Afro-Americans were employed as longshoremen, draymen, or teamsters, and in the trades, "laborers, porters and helpers in stores, while in the division of public service, the greatest number were classified as laborers." [134] Closer examination reveals that the majority of the Afro-Americans in new occupations had little to look forward to, because many of the jobs were deadend. Supervisory posts were held by recently upgraded whites, and the end of the war would see the former employees returning to their posts.

A private survey corroborated the delineation mentioned in the 1920 Census.

In New York City the majority of Negroes [were] engaged as personal and domestic servants, elevator operators, porters, and laundry workers. Although the number of colored males in domestic and personal service [was] still large, the concentration in this field [was] being broken and many men [had] entered industries of the City. They [were], however, largely confined to the unskilled occupations [mentioned above], in such industries as [had] been opened to them.[135]

Negro women . . . found their lot even more restricted than the males. Before 1915 the number of colored women employed in Northern industries were negligible; almost 80 percent of Negro workers in the North were limited to domestic service. Since that date, they have appeared more frequently in such positions as unskilled processors connected with the garment trades [in the shirt, collar and cuff division of the garment industry, women jumped from 2 to 61 persons in this industry], . . .[136]

paper box factories and meat packing houses, and to some extent in clerical occupations connected with mail-order houses.[137]

G. E. Haynes in his doctoral dissertation, other authorities, and federal governmental surveys substantiated these conclusions.[138]

The "immutability" of the principle of supply and demand, which forced employers to hire Afro-Americans in spite of social prejudice, was again confirmed by various surveys covering New York City and other large industrial centers. When interviewed, Northern employers stated that *they had hired Negro Americans only because of an existing acute labor shortage.* Most employers conceded that they would release their Afro-American employees as soon as the labor shortage eased.[139]

In summarizing the period covering 1777–1920, we find that the Afro-American did make economic headway during World War I. Since this rise was due to an emergency that created an acute labor shortage, the Afro-American masses still remained at the bottom of the economic ladder. Secondly, when the supply of immigrants was heavy, the Afro-American's occupational status regressed in spite of an increased need for semiskilled and unskilled help. Ira A. Reid arrived at a similar conclusion, although for a shorter historical period.

During the period prior to World War I, the repeated efforts of Negro spokesmen and interested white persons to entrench Negro workers in industrial positions, with such increments as might accrue to them from those positions, were futile. America had relied for over one hundred years on European immigrants to fill industrial needs. The sudden cessation of immigration found many unfilled demands for labor. The activities of labor agents were bringing Negro workers into

Northern industries. . . . *They went into those industries
needing masses of unskilled workers.* . . . These new industrial
opportunities were in no small way responsible for the migration 1,200,000 Negroes who moved from South to North.[140]

Focusing on the displacement theory: the need for social and
economic discrimination stemming from social prejudice (white
racism) strengthened the need for the continuation of a circle of
discrimination. Hence the newly arrived immigrant had to be given
priority in employment, even at the expense of the Afro-American,
since in the American class society his was the lowest group in the
socioeconomic hierarchy. Put another way, the artificially ascribed
status assigned to the Afro-American formed a three-way prong: (1)
Being restricted to the lowest class on the social and economic
ladder, he had to make way for the immigrant, who, without previous skills, took over such trades as barbering, catering, and longshoring. (2) Being above the Afro-American on the socioeconomic
ladder, the immigrant frequently upgraded the social image of former black occupations. Once the occupations were upgraded socially
and economically, they were closed to the colored man. (3) Being
low man on the scale, the Afro-American discovered that what
had been his "monopolized" jobs were subject to change in times
of economic stringency. In toto, this prescribed a set mode of life
for the Afro-American. Inherent in this way of life was the establishment of standards repugnant to white middle-class society. This
repugnance was reinforced by the immigrant, since his anticipatory
status depended upon his acceptance of the dominant group's value
system. In combination, the dominant group and the immigrant
helped to foster the continuation of the circle of discrimination by
offering each other a higher rung in our class society.

CHAPTER 3

Discrimination in Employment Against the New York Afro-American, 1920–1965

Each class and each strata or group of each class in America has had, at one time or another and to one degree or another, to face economic restrictions and difficulties in the process of achieving social betterment. But the Afro-American has had the dubious honor of having had the longest period of economic restrictions imposed on him with the least to show for the time and effort he has expended in his struggle for social improvement. This is best illustrated by a study of one economic area: the factors affecting Afro-American employment during the years 1920–1965 in New York.

In our analysis of this period, the major emphasis will be on the final three decades, since institutionalized discrimination—blocked economic and social mobility established during Colonial times—continued to exist in substantially unchanged form during the 1920's and the 1930's. However, the pattern that connects all five decades is the sustained low economic-social status hereditarily linked with the Afro-American and its maintenance through the differential controls that will become apparent in our study. The mechanisms of this control are: full restrictions in employment, or complete denial of Afro-American employment in an industry or workplace; partial restriction in colored American employment, or confinement of blacks to menial, arduous, or dirty jobs; and discriminatory retrenchment, or the principle of last to be hired, first to be fired, irrespective of length of service (unless strict union seniority is practiced).

In a decade associated with the "new capitalism," "the beginning of a new epoch," and what General Hugh Johnson, administrator of the National Recovery Administration under President Franklin Delano Roosevelt, called a "new era" and a "high level of prosperity," the Afro-American found himself treated as a pariah of old and locked out of this "new era." In a study of employment patterns in Harlem between 1920 and 1930 by T. J. Woofter, it was found that the white businessman of that community rarely hired colored Americans except for menial posts, even though the black man domiciled there accounted for over 25 per cent of the total consumer trade in the area.[1] The survey, involving 258 stores and their 2,000 employees, revealed that only 163 of the employees were Afro-Americans, and all of them were engaged in menial occupations. Woofter did a followup study in which he asked Harlem businessmen if they would hire Afro-Americans. Where the answer was "yes," invariably the caution was added, "but only for the positions of porters, maids, and like work." [2]

The findings of the Woofter study were typical for the period and similar to conditions prevailing in other major cities, as the studies of Spero and Harris (*The Black Worker*) and Cayton and Mitchell (*Black Workers and the New Unions*) demonstrate. In the following decade—marked by the depression and the corrective measures of the New Deal—the position of the Afro-American in employment can only be summarized in the remark of an official commission, that the "Negro had one-half of a bad chance to get a job." [3] More characteristically, the plight of the colored American seeking employment during the 1930's is revealed by the comment of the largest single employer in Harlem, the owner and operator of a large department store, who categorically asserted that he would hire Afro-Americans only for "Negro jobs"—porter, maid, and elevator operator. This was the employment situation in an area where the Afro-American held his greatest economic power as a consumer,[4] and, we may add, the most frequent control practiced by white employers for the 1920's and 1930's: full restriction of Afro-American employment, not merely in Harlem but also in the other metropolitan centers of New York State.

Our analysis of Afro-American employment patterns, for which there are considerable empirical data, begins with the years associated with World War II. The three basic control patterns serving as lines of cleavage in the study of discriminatory employment practices against the black man in New York will be most clearly seen with the beginning of the 1940's.

FULL RESTRICTION IN EMPLOYMENT

Employers have utilized four evasive devices to deny employment to the colored American—with, or without previous experience: (a) a claimed lack of experience, (b) discriminatory employment agencies, both private and governmental, (c) special qualifications for Afro-Americans, and (d) collusion between employer and union.

In 1943, Miss Ruby Bell filed a complaint with the Fair Employment Practices Committee (FEPC), against the U.S. Weather Bureau. She alleged that the bureau had failed to hire her because of her color. Miss Bell, a Hunter College graduate with graduate work in geology and meteorology, had been referred to the Weather Bureau by the U.S. Civil Service Commission. A personnel officer of the bureau did interview her and informed her that if she were accepted for training she would be notified within a few weeks. When she had received no notification after a reasonable period of time following her interview, she did a bit of private investigating, and her findings formed the basis of her complaint.

The FEPC's findings substantiated Miss Bell's allegations. First, the FEPC's investigating team found that no Afro-Americans were employed by the Weather Bureau. Secondly, they noted that the bureau had hired white applicants from the same list that included Miss Bell and that these girls were less academically qualified than was Miss Bell. Also, these white girls, who were for the most part high school graduates, had no previous experience in this vocation. With this evidence before it, the FEPC requested the regional office of the Weather Bureau to appoint Miss Bell to the job of junior observer. The agency refused, and the case was then referred to the national office of the FEPC. A conference was arranged between FEPC officials and G. Swain, chief of the Division of Personnel of the U.S. Department of Commerce, to discuss the matter. After Mr. Swain examined the evidence, he agreed that this was an instance of discrimination because of color.[5] However, Miss Bell was never hired.

Public transportation was another area where Afro-Americans found an outright refusal to hire fairly common, even in areas outside the operating trades. Miss Thelma Williams' case is but one example of this practice. In October, 1943, she was referred to the Pennsylvania Railroad by the U.S. Employment Service (USES) for the job of file clerk. Following her interview, she was told that the company's policy was not to hire Afro-Americans for white-collar jobs.[6] The FEPC's investigation confirmed the fact that no colored Americans were employed in white-collar positions by the railroad, and that the employment blank required the applicant to answer a question on race.[7]

Also, there is evidence that refusal to hire Afro-Americans was prevalent in the manufacturing sector. One example was that of E. Leitz and Company, manufacturers of tools, dies, and optical equipment. In February, 1944 the company had a total of 123 employees on its payroll. None was colored. A review of the company's hiring practices showed a pattern of outright refusal to hire on account of color. During the period covering July, 1941 through August, 1943, the company added 109 employees. None was a Negro American. This information, derived from Form No. 270 of the USES, was used as the basis for a visit to the company by a representative of the Labor Utilization Section of the War Manpower Commission (WMC). The commission's report substantiated the pattern found on Form 270: "No Negroes are employed; when nonwhites do apply, they are automatically refused employment." [8]

The 1950's appeared little different from the 1940's. If in the past long-established companies were guilty of full denial of employment opportunities to the Afro-American, the newer industries continued in the same tradition. Concerning air and surface transport, where it was the practice not to hire Afro-Americans, Ramon Rivera, formerly industrial relations director of the Urban League of Greater New York, made the following allegation in July, 1955:

> Not a single scheduled air-line in the metropolitan area employed Negroes as pilots, co-pilots, flight engineers, navigators, hostesses, or in any other flight capacity. The point was made that even though air-lines recruited from the pool of former air-force personnel, they consistently by-passed former Negro air-force officers.[9]

Mr. Rivera's charges were never refuted.

As in the air, so on the ground. The Afro-American found himself excluded in the field of transportation. In 1945 a pattern of employment discrimination in transportation was disclosed in a joint study made by the New York State Commission Against Discrimination (SCAD) and the New Jersey Division Against Discrimination.[10] As late as 1958, the followup studies of these two commissions revealed little or no abatement of discrimination in the hiring of Afro-Americans. The studies covered 19 railroads on both sides of the Hudson River. The commission's classification broke down jobs as follows: office and general work, operating transportation, other transportation, and maintenance. In the office and general work category, 16,836 were employed, 627, or about 3.7 per cent, of whom were Afro-American—almost an insignificant percentage. Closer scrutiny revealed that more than a third of these 627 were working either as janitors or cleaners.

> None [of the 627 Afro-Americans was] employed in an executive, professional, or chief clerk position, nor as a traffic or claim agent, travelling auditor, inspector, investigator, ticket agent, or police officer.[11]

In 1965, as in the past, the category of operating transportation offered very little employment to Afro-Americans. Of the 20,099 persons employed in operating transportation, 118, or less than 1 per cent, were colored. Again looking behind the figures, we find that all but five of the 118 were employed by a single railroad, and all 113 were in yard positions.[12]

The same pattern was found in the field of public accommodations. SCAD made two studies of the New York City hotel industry, one in 1951 and another in 1957, to see what change, if any, had taken place in the hotel industry's employment pattern of minority groups. Although both studies were made of the same group of hotels, the first study covered some 35 hotels; the second, only 33,[13] since during the 1951–1957 period two hotels included in the original survey had gone bankrupt.

The 1957 survey found 20,996 persons employed in various capacities. This number included 2,327 Afro-Americans, or about 11.1 per cent of the total. The commission grouped these hotels into four categories. Viewing each category as a whole, it was found that some colored Americans were employed in each category. In its analysis of each category, the commission used the hotels' departmental employment breakdown: food preparation, food service, bar service, front service, and housekeeping and cleaning service. Since three of the 33 hotels included in this survey had leased food preparation departments, they were excluded from the analysis. The remaining 30 hotels employed 3,428 persons, and of this number there were 223, or 6.5 per cent, colored. Four of the 30 hotels surveyed had no Afro-American employee.[14] Of the 39 clerks employed by the 33 hotels, only one hotel had an Afro-American, although over 50 per cent of its help was classified as colored Americans.[15]

The commission's classification of hotels included one group of better-type hotels, referred to as Group I, comprising 12 hotels employing 1,858 persons. Of this total, 1,064 were waiters and waitresses, five of whom were Afro-Americans. These five were employed in three of the 12 hotels as waiters; three were in one hotel and each of the other two was in a different hotel. Thus, Group I hotels had no colored Americans in about 75 per cent of their service departments.[16]

An examination of the 33 hotels surveyed showed that 29 had food service departments, which together employed 58 Afro-Americans. Twenty-seven, or almost half of the total colored, were confined to one hotel: four were in room service and 23 in two dining rooms were mixed crews. To summarize, excluding waiters servicing banquets, employee cafeterias, drugstore fountains, or room service, it was noted that 45 Afro-American waiters were employed in some type of regular dining room service in 11 out of 29 hotels. Incidentally, all 33 hotels excluded Afro-Americans from their bar service and front service departments.[17]

At the end of the 1950's, in a revealing cross-section study of the principal areas of business in New York City, the great cosmopolitan center of the nation, a SCAD report stated:

> The lineaments of discrimination [were] not difficult to discern. Where the race and color or religion [were] determinants of employment, the pattern of employment will reflect the areas of resistance [exclusion]. It may assume various forms—complete exclusion. In varying degrees this [was] the pattern of employment which [had] categorized the hotel industry. . . . The pattern was not dissimilar to that which the Commission encountered in the principal areas of business enterprise—banking, insurance, department stores and public utilities.[18]

The first half of the 1960's still found institutionalized discrimination in most of New York's economic enterprises. For example, East Side hotels confined Afro-Americans mainly to housekeeping trades. Rarely did one find colored Americans in front-end services, such as bartender or barman, on either the East or West side of town. A similar situation existed among waiters. "All-whiteness including rooms staffed by crews restricted to one national

group in order to create a particular atmosphere," remained the prevailing mode of operation.[19] Occasionally, one found a few Afro-
Americans waiting on tables in the newest West Side hotels, a
change brought about through pressure by various colored and white
integrationists.[20]

The situation was no different in many manufacturing plants.
An independent agency survey made in 1958 of 10 General Motors
assembly plants, covering noncontiguous geographic areas throughout the United States, disclosed that there was no Afro-American
in a salaried classification in any of the plants surveyed.[21] The report
criticized the apprenticeship training program (a controlled management program until 1962) as "completely [disregarding] Colored
employees in the bargaining unit who have the necessary qualifications." In many instances the company failed to offer any on-job
training opportunities to Afro-Americans.[22]

Of particular importance in promotion and upgrading at General Motors were two programs: "Employees in Training" and "Apprenticeship Training." The successful completion of either course
meant the transfer of an individual to the "Skilled Trades Department," which in turn led to journeyman status. At the time of the
survey, the Skilled Trades Department had 775 employees, only
10 of whom were colored. All 10 were in the Chevrolet Gear and
Axle Division. In 1963 the "Employees in Training" program, covered in 11 plants in the Greater Detroit area, had 11,125 persons in
training; of this number, 67 were colored.[23]

A similar pattern existed in the apprenticeship training program. In 1961 the program had 289 apprentices in the Detroit area,
one of whom was black.[24] About three years later a survey was
conducted covering General Motors plants in three states in the
Central Atlantic region. There were 171 apprentices in the tri-state
area, and two of them were Afro-Americans. Incidentally, both
Afro-American apprentices were in plants in the same state.[25] The
pattern was similar in the tri-state survey with respect to the skilled
trades. The total employed in the three areas was 11,314, which
included 230 Afro-Americans. New York had about 25 per cent of
the tri-state total in skilled trades and boasted some 17 nonwhites.[26]

The advertising field, until recently described as having "no
stated policy" against the hiring of colored Americans, had "almost
never hire[d] Negroes, except as messengers and porters." [27] In 1961
the Urban League of Greater New York, which alleged that seven
of the "Top Ten" advertising agencies employed no Afro-Americans in creative and/or executive positions,[28] charged that the re-

fusal to hire colored Americans resulted from a long-established policy, a policy that was reaffirmed after review by the top agencies.[29] The New York advertising field was summarized as follows:

> The most optimistic reports of individuals in the agency field estimate a total of 50 Negroes employed in all capacities. A careful survey of 15 experienced advertising personnel, both colored and white, [disclosed] that to the best of their knowledge admittedly incomplete, a maximum of 16 Negro artists, writers, account people, media and research workers [were] employed by advertising agencies in New York City, the remaining 34 [included] clerical and messenger help who work directly for agencies.[30]

A strategic source of employment discrimination is the employment agency. These agencies have been used to practice covert discrimination. Even though it is against the law to advertise for "white only," employment agencies can circumvent the law very easily.[31] In March, 1944, SCAD investigated the Holland Employment Agency,[32] typical of a group employing discrimination in this area. SCAD found that the agency's résumé requested race designation; an entry contrary to New York State law. When the manager of the agency refused to delete this question from its form, the case was turned over to the State Industrial Commissioner's office, which set a hearing for Jan. 22, 1945. The manager appeared, but neglected to bring the materials requested in the original subpoena. A second subpoena, *duces tecum*, was served, which stipulated that the manager was to produce her books and records covering the period from September, 1941 through Feb. 1, 1945. She appeared, but again failed to bring the evidence cited in the subpoena, claiming that all her records for the past four years had been destroyed.[33]

Similar violations of the law were attributed to the Federal License Officers Association, a private employment agency that serviced requests from private and government shippers for sundry maritime personnel. The director of the agency limited membership to whites only. To fill his employee lists, he often received assistance from various governmental agencies, one of which was the U.S. Employment Service. There, someone had written on one of its reports: this association places only white personnel.

A formal complaint was filed with the FEPC, and the findings revealed that the association did indeed employ only whites. Furthermore, the complaint alleged that certain shipowners specifically used the association to recruit workers in order to be certain that only whites applied for job openings. The FEPC's report, with recommendations, was forwarded to the USES. The latter thereupon issued a directive effective on Sept. 25, 1944,[34] to discontinue all USES services to the association.

It was not uncommon for employers to use public and private employment agencies to circumvent the law. Some federal agencies like the USES and later the New York State Employment Service (NYSES) apparently cooperated with employers by filling their "white only" requests. In 1949 and again in 1950, when the author was doing a field study in New York, he was apprised of this practice by an Afro-American interviewer at NYSES, who explained the situation as being inherent in the merit system used by the state government to grant wage increases and promotions. Some years later the allegation was further substantiated by a SCAD investigation, which revealed that in 1950 and 1960, state employment interviewers were coding applicants by color, a device employed to comply with employers' requests for "white only." [35]

~ Shortly after the 1960 investigation the state set up a special employment office in the Bedford-Stuyvesant area to assist Afro-Americans and Puerto Ricans in finding employment. Again the allegation was made—this time by members of the American Federation of State, County and Municipal Employees Union—that a special coding system was employed "to show [which] applicants were Negro." Sponsors of the project, a group of Brooklyn Negro ministers, felt strongly enough to withdraw their support.[36] ~

It was not surprising to find that, if an agency in New York State practiced discrimination in employment, there would be similar instances in other states. Thus the U.S. Civil Rights Commission reported in a volume entitled *Employment* (one of a number of studies published by this federal agency) that many states were utilizing similar discriminatory procedures in their employment agencies.[37]

Private employment agencies found it lucrative to fill employers' requests for white only. On Aug. 9, 1962, Office Temporaries, Inc., a large and well-known employment agency filling some 7,000 positions a year, admitted that the notation "NFU" ("not for us"), was intended to distinguish Afro-Americans from whites.[38] The officers of Lynhall Placement Associates were summoned before License Commissioner J. O'Connell on the grounds that they violated the law. They were charged with using the code "POK" to distinguish "persons of color" from whites on their application forms. When

the firm's employees were questioned about this code, they first
informed the investigators that their instructions were to say that
the letters stood for "OK." [39] The commissioner suspended the
agency's license for 30 days.[40]

There was evidence that even the "liberal" sector of our society—colleges, universities, and churches—bowed to employers seeking "WASPS" only. One survey, covering 41 colleges and universities, reported:

> Almost half of the placement officers reported receiving dis-
> criminatory job orders. . . . [A] general discussion [with these
> officers] revealed that practically every placement official was
> inclined to process discriminatory job orders. Job orders dis-
> criminating on the basis of race were twice the number of all
> other discriminatory specifications combined.[41]

PARTIAL RESTRICTION IN EMPLOYMENT

~ Even those firms that practiced complete restriction in skilled
occupations occasionally permitted some Afro-Americans to fill
menial jobs. Other firms made it their policy to restrict colored
Americans to deadend, and/or hazardous, dirty, or low-status jobs
that whites refused to accept. Restriction of Afro-Americans to
specified occupations was rampant throughout the 1930's in the
hotel and restaurant trades, department stores, banking, and needle
trades.[42] This discrimination continued throughout World War II,
even though the economy experienced extreme labor shortages. Such
discrimination did ease slightly during the 1950's and early 1960's.

Illustrative of these practices in New York City was the policy
of the Arma Corporation during the 1940's. In 1943 the regional
chief of placement for the War Manpower Commission, charged
the corporation with discriminatory hiring practices. The allegation
was forwarded to the head of the New York regional office of the
FEPC. The charge read:

> Although we have recently come to the conclusion that our
> own experience with the employer [Arma] indicates that the
> firm is managing its hiring practices of applicants just sufficiently
> open to minority groups as to preclude a formal charge of
> discrimination by us, we think . . . the ES. 270 reports would
> be sufficient justification for a visit by a member of your com-
> mittee.[43]

Involved with the Arma Corporation was the USES, which had been a recruiting source for the company. An examination of USES records revealed that the company had consistently rejected non-whites. This evidence formed the basis for a conference between company officials and a USES representative. Simultaneously, but independently of the USES, a Mr. J. Doyle, representing the State Commission on Discrimination, was studying the company's hiring practices, and he submitted his report to USES officials on Aug. 27, 1942. Doyle's report stated that he had met with the personnel assistant for Arma, and that he had been assured that equal treatment would be shown to Afro-American applicants from approved vocational and technical schools. On Feb. 10, 1944, less than two years after the Doyle report was filed, the state commission reopened the case.

> We do so mainly on the basis of its pattern of rejections. Our figures indicate that an unduly high percentage of Negroes referred to Arma are turned down. . . . We found . . . and still feel . . . that while they employ Negroes, they are, nevertheless, following a pattern of rejection which closely resembles discrimination.[44]

The FEPC became an interested party to the case on Jan. 25, 1945. Its findings disclosed two pertinent data: (1) An examination of the company's requisitions to the USES showed that the company had placed orders for eight junior and 37 experienced Afro-American draftsmen, but none was hired. The USES records indicated that a Charles Bingham, an Afro-American draftsman, was on the Arma payroll, but an examination of the payroll disclosed that no such person had ever been employed by this company. Also, shortly after placing a requisition with the USES in 1944 for ten clerical employees, the company reduced its request to two clericals. Neither job was filled by a colored person. (2) An examination of Arma's private recruiting sources showed that they had no Afro-American clientele.[45]

This pattern of employment restriction had become so customary (institutionalized), that even when a colored American did prove his qualifications, he was rarely granted the post. One typical example was the case filed with the FEPC in 1945 by a white college student on behalf of a colored woman, alleging that the Charlton Company not only limited Afro-Americans to menial jobs but also refused to upgrade them in the shop. She used the example of a college-trained colored woman who took the place of a regular mechanic on a machine when he failed to appear for work, but was soon replaced. The foreman, when questioned about the incident, admitted that the woman had performed efficiently; still, she was not allowed to operate any machine again in the shop.[46]

Partial restriction in employment frequently meant that there was no chance for upgrading, despite seniority on the job. Whereas,

> under a strict seniority system promotion tends to be automatic, because even gross differences in skill or performance may be disregarded. Average performance at each assignment may be enough to warrant promotion where there is sufficient seniority.[47]

That many Afro-Americans were not covered by the usual seniority clause was illustrated in the case of Mary Veale.[48] In 1942, Miss Veale joined Lerner's as its first woman packer. After three years of service, she entered her bid for promotion based on posted vacancies. When she was bypassed, she consulted with her coworkers. They in turn suggested she take the matter up with the union's organizer. The latter studied the company's past practices and discovered that no colored Americans had ever been promoted to clerical positions. Later, the same union organizer noted that it was personnel policy to bypass Afro-Americans regardless of qualifications and/or seniority in upgrading.[49]

There was a bright side, however, and this time it took place in department store policy. Since the law of supply and demand asserted itself in times of critical labor shortages, Gimbel's department store broke with tradition during World War II and hired some 750 Afro-Americans. However, these colored workers did not anticipate promotion to section manager, or even supervisor, even though they might be qualified through ability and length of service.[50]

Another type of employment restriction, employer-union cooperation or collusion, usually resulted in the restricting of Afro-Americans to deadend jobs. Two instances are offered to illustrate the point. In one situation, the assistant special counsel for the National Association for the Advancement of Colored People (NAACP), alleged that the Pennsylvania Railroad and the Brotherhood of Shop Crafts of America of the American Federation of Labor (AFL) discriminated against its Afro-American members. In June, 1946 she presented to SCAD a charge against the company and the union, alleging that they colluded in demoting colored mechanics to the status of laborers. She based her allegation on the company's and union's misinterpretation of the "escalator of seniority clause" in the G.I. Bill of Rights. The misinterpretation was contrary to the U.S. Supreme Court's interpretation of the bill. The NAACP's interpretation of the court's decision was that "all returning veterans . . . be placed where they would have been [on the seniority list] had they not entered the armed forces." [51] However, union-management interpreted the clause to give white employees superseniority.

Furthermore, the NAACP counsel alleged that until 1941 all colored employees were denied upgrading to mechanic's helper or mechanic. After 1943 some Afro-Americans managed to become eligible for upgrading. The change was short-lived, however, since a new contract, effective Jan. 24, 1945, gave white employees superseniority. Theoretically, Afro-Americans were eligible for upgrading; in reality, whites with less seniority were given preference.

In the second instance, Herman Boykin, a worker at the New York Navy Yard, alleged that officers of the yard had refused repeatedly to upgrade him to a supervisory position. To justify his complaint, Boykin cited the fact that many white employees whom he had trained and who had less seniority than he, had been promoted. The regional director of the New York FEPC paid a visit to Rear Admiral Kelly, on Feb. 14, 1944. Throughout the interview he sought to establish the yard's criteria for promotion. Later, he summed up the interview as one of total evasion by the admiral of any and all questions put to him. However, a month later the director received the following note from the admiral's office:

In the ordinary course of events he [Boykin] is reasonably sure of being included in the next group promoted to Mechanical Instructor.[52]

Although the 1940's and the first years of the 1950's saw some alleviation in discriminatory employment patterns against colored Americans, institutionalized employment restrictions still continued to exist; exceptions took the form of "tokenism." The hotel industry remained one of the chief practitioners of such discrimination. Although in 1951 the New York Trades Council and the Hotel Association had signed an agreement stipulating that all employment would be handled by the New York State Employment Service, one

year after the agreement 12,958 persons were placed out of 20,576
referrals, with nonwhites accounting for 23 per cent of the total.
The significance of placement becomes manifest when examined in
the light of SCAD's statement.

> Almost two out of every three non-whites were referred and
> placed in housekeeping, laundry and maintenance jobs. White
> applicants were referred and placed in a greater diversification
> of jobs.[53]

Furthermore, SCAD emphasized that nonwhites had a better chance
of referral and hire as elevator operators and uniformed staff than
as clerks or telephone operators. What should be stressed is the fact
that the elevator jobs invariably were for freight elevators, and this
group had its own seniority list. This meant that no amount of
seniority could lead to front service jobs. Seldom were nonwhites
placed in maintenance work, and almost never as bartenders.[54] Yet
three years after the agreement (1954), the situation remained substantially the same in New York City, where about three fourths of
the state's 45,799 workers in the hotel industry were employed.[55]
There were attempts to break the circle of discrimination, but the
commission's files summarized the experiment as follows:

> Occasional break-through in employment of Negroes as waiter,
> busboy and bartender, but the overall picture [was] not one of
> major, or extensive advance.[56]

Dress manufacturing was another significant industry in New
York City that employed low-paid workers, chiefly women. In 1948
the dress industry encountered a decided shortage of skilled sewing-
machine operators. Recruitment forced the industry to turn to Afro-
American and Puerto Rican women, and it hired about 50 per cent
of its operators from these two groups. Yet, in the middle 1950's
colored American women in the industry were still in

> the less skilled, in the lower paid crafts and shops and [were]
> making the lower price lines. In this industry their advance-
> ment to higher skills was not proceeding very rapidly.[57]

Department stores similarly limited Afro-American employment. Even when a Afro-American managed to make a break-

through, mobility was usually blocked. For example, in 1940 Gimbel's signed a union contract with District 65, and a colored American woman was hired as a waitress. She worked for about seven years in the basement restaurant. When management decided to close this restaurant she had greater seniority than many of her white colleagues employed on the 11th- and main-floor restaurants. However, she was transferred to a nonwaitress job while her white coworkers were assigned to other restaurants in the store.[58]

A representative picture of Afro-American women in employment at the beginning of the 1950's, as compared with white women, was summarized as follows:

> Non-white women aged 18–24, . . . [revealed] a quite different occupational pattern from their white contemporaries. Fewer than a sixth of those employed held clerical jobs in 1950, about 40 percent were employed as operatives, and about a third were [still] in household or other service jobs.[59]

In 1960, despite various assertions by the hotel industry in New York City that integration was taking place, little progress was visible. The union's newspaper illustrated this contention on its front page.

> Two Negro waiters have gone to work in the Savoy-Hilton's "The Columns," another has been taken on in the hotel's Savoy Room. Two rooms that have a history of all-whiteness have started to acquire the blend of skin hues that we find satisfying.[60]

Shortly after this statement, it was announced that the Savoy was to be demolished to make way for a new office building.

The above citation reveals "tokenism" at best on the part of the employers. (Ironically, it may be noted that by 1962, the union's antidiscrimination clause, found in all its contracts, was 25 years old.) Additional evidence establishes the fact that partial restriction in employment pervaded the industry. The October, 1963 issue of *Hotel and Motel Worker* disclosed that housekeeping was still predominantly nonwhite.[61] A union official of a sister union, contended that the positions of bellman, waiter (especially banquet waiter), and other front services were generally restricted to whites. There was some "tokenism," but, as mentioned previously, it was found in the newer West Side hotels.[62]

A broader view of the employment situation was offered by two surveys entitled "Plans for Progress." These surveys disclosed that the majority of the companies that were signatories to the voluntary pact had failed to carry out their moral responsibilities. A *Fortune* magazine survey, dated September, 1963, stated that

> in the aggregate, corporations' voluntary actions have fallen desperately short of what needs to be done to increase employment. . . . The Plans for Progress program of the President's Committee on Equal Opportunity provides a perfect case. . . . Over 100 corporations have signed Plans for Progress, promising to "undertake a program of affirmative action" to recruit Negroes and train them for employment and promotion. . . . While total employment for Negroes has increased since the program began, only a few contractors account for the bulk of the increase. . . . A *Fortune* survey in July (1963) of Plans for Progress signers in twelve cities around the country revealed the same pattern. . . . They "applauded the lofty ideals and worthy goals of the program," but they haven't done much to reach these goals.[63]

Julius A. Thomas, formerly of the National Urban League and now a private consultant to many firms in the field of integration, alleged that less than 5 per cent of some 50 firms with which he had contact—all members of Plans for Progress—actually implemented their personnel policies to fulfill their moral obligations.[64] Although, both studies overlap, they tend to reinforce the idea that *voluntarism* has failed to carry out its goal.

Another form of partial restriction in employment was lower income for Afro-Americans with equal or higher education than whites. Thus,

> there were proportionately as many non-white doctors as whites, but average earnings of non-whites were only half that received by whites. [This was due, partly, to restricted affiliations with hospitals.] [65]

The same pattern existed in other areas of Afro-American employment, since "non-white men earned less than whites with the same number of years of schooling because they were employed in lower-paid jobs, and were paid less even when they did the same kind of work." [66] Again a study, based on 1960 census data restricted to New

York State, revealed the same disparity in annual earnings between white and colored graduates. This study compared white college graduates with white males who had not completed one year of high school. White college graduates could figure on an additional income of $6,277 per annum over their nonschooled fellows. The disparity was revealed when the comparison was made between colored college graduates and their nonschooled counterparts. "On the same scale, the non-white college graduates had the advantage of $2,918" per annum.[67] This differential in median income between whites and nonwhites with comparable education, was ascribed to the disproportionate concentration of nonwhites in such relatively low-paying professional jobs as medical technicians and social workers.[68] Most nonwhite medical technicians were employed in hospitals. Two union officials, both connected with the same hospital union, estimated that about 80 per cent of the medical technicians in voluntary and proprietary hospitals were nonwhite. White technicians with comparable skills usually found employment with private doctors or in research areas where the salary was much higher for the same job.[69]

DISCRIMINATORY EMPLOYMENT RETRENCHMENT

Since the Afro-American is the last hired, he is fully cognizant that he will be the first to be laid off. The reason is that with the lowest seniority in the workplace he becomes most vulnerable to lay-off during periods of retrenchment.

During the severest depression to date—that of the 1930's— the Afro-American was again reminded of his ascribed status. Almost everywhere he found employment preference extended to the white man. For example, the Federal Emergency Relief Administrator's report of 1935 revealed that colored Americans were displaced from private employment at twice the rate of white workers. Also, Afro-Americans were "being re-employed at only one-half the rate —in other words, Negroes [had] one-half of a bad chance to get a job." [70]

An isolated instance, but not atypical, may help to define the Afro-American's employment situation. In 1937 a bus company in New York City had 97 colored "bus service stewards" in its employ, 55 of whom handled passengers' luggage. Early in 1938, 91 of the 97 were summarily dismissed. Their release had no relationship to their work performance, because their white supervisors had graded them as excellent workers. They were replaced by released bus drivers, whose job title was changed to "baggage checkers" and their rate of pay set at $90 per month. The Afro-American stewards had been receiving $35 per month for the same job.[71]

The 1940's also revealed a practice of preferential employment release. Many Afro-Americans with greater seniority than their white fellow workers often found themselves outside looking in on their former "buddies," because of another type of bumping that ignored seniority. Classification was the main source of job retainment. The higher one's job classification, regardless of seniority in the plant, the less possibility of lay-off, and whites usually monopolized the upper classifications.

Thus in 1944 a cutback at the Brooklyn Naval Clothing Depot caused the summary release of all colored females on the night shift. (Black women were arbitrarily refused employment on the day shift.) Many of these released women had greater seniority than their day-shift counterparts. It was only after the intervention of the Federal Workers' Union of the Congress of Industrial Organizations (CIO) that a halt was brought to this inequity.[72]

In 1945, Seymour Wolfbein described Afro-American discriminatory employment retrenchment as being related to past discrimination in employment.

> The Negro had made his greatest employment gains in those occupations, especially, semi-skilled factory jobs, which will suffer the severest cutbacks during the post-war period.

> Finally, it should be noted that in those occupations and industries in which the Negro had made his greatest employment advances, he was generally the last hired. Therefore under the seniority rules he is more likely to be laid-off than the average worker in these occupations.[73]

Wolfbein's prophecy was realized between Aug. 15 and Sept. 16, 1945, when the FEPC reported that in New York City Afro-American dismissals were 44.7 per cent, as opposed to the overall city percentage of 21 per cent.[74] This meant that there were approximately over two Afro-American releases from employment for every white release.

The 1950's continued the tradition of discriminatory employment retrenchment and added an ingenious device to the pattern. In interviewing a score of persons seeking help in employment at the

New York Urban League, this author perceived a consistent pattern of discrimination. These persons, who were registered with the New York State Employment Service, were invariably sent out on temporary jobs. In some instances the individuals interviewed were non-union craftsmen with many years of experience in areas of extreme labor shortage. In checking out this hypothesis with the Urban League's interviewer, the author was told that this pattern had been going on for many years.

A number of years later (in 1960), the author returned to New York and found Afro-Americans still being sent out as temporary help, this time in office work. One midtown office, which had need for temporary help several times during the year, was most often given colored help. Conversations with these temporaries revealed that the practice was not uncommon. Such referrals were listed as preferential employment release, since the applicant could not hope for a permanent post. This meant that the individual could not acquire seniority, and he was most vulnerable to lay-off and economic insecurity. Obliquely, this practice was substantiated by the ratio of unemployed colored workers to white job seekers. During the booming 1950's, Afro-American unemployment, although at an all-time low, was still one and one-half times that of whites.[75]

Conversely, during recessions, preferential employment release should show intensification, and it did. Studies of the second quarter of 1950 revealed that Afro-Americans were unemployed at approximately twice the rate of whites: 11.8 and 6 per cent for colored and white, respectively.[76] In the second quarter of 1954, during the postwar recession, it remained two to one, or 11 and 5 per cent, respectively.[77] In March, 1958, during the middle 1957–1958 recession, Afro-Americans had a 15 per cent rate of unemployed as compared with 8 per cent for whites. Although some recovery had taken effect at the end of 1958, Afro-American unemployment was still approximately twice the rate of whites; percentagewise it was 11.4 and 4.8 respectively.[78] What held true for the short run was equally true for the 1920–1965 period; in other words, Afro-Americans maintained an average ratio of twice the unemployment rate for whites.

Even when Negro American employment increased at a faster rate than that of whites during the period from 1955 to 1965, Afro-Americans still constituted "a smaller proportion of the employed [10.7 per cent], and a much larger proportion of the unemployed" [20.3 per cent].[79]

Of interest in terms of employment was the fact that there was an increase in the absolute number of colored American workers, yet they remained concentrated in occupations with limited growth prospects. This occurred because the colored infiltrated into jobs vacated by whites who had moved up the economic ladder. The consequent lack of immigrants to fill these jobs had made it necessary to offer them to nonwhites. Thus it was found that more than one fifth of the colored Americans were non-farm laborers, "in contrast with about one-fifteenth of the white males."

Afro-American females had a worse situation than that of their male counterparts. Colored females constituted over 50 per cent of all employed nonwhite women in private household and other service occupations.[80]

J. L. Russell summed up the prospects of Negro American employment for the period 1965 to 1975 as follows:

> If nonwhites merely continue to hold the same proportion of jobs in each occupation that they held in 1965, nonwhite employment will increase from 7.8 million in 1965 to 9.1 million in 1975. Despite this growth, however, the nonwhite proportion of total employment would decline, simply because of the slower growth of occupations in which nonwhite workers are now concentrated.[81]

Based on the slower growth in Afro-American employment, Russell projected unemployment rates into 1975 and arrived at the conclusion that unemployment would be in the ratio of five to one for colored and whites, respectively.[82]

To recapitulate: the following practices prevailed in the economy with respect to Negro American employment.

I. Full Restriction in Employment:
   A. where the Negro applicant has equal, or more, academic qualifications than white applicants, but is refused employment on account of color;
   B. where the employer has had one or more bad experiences with a Negro employee, he stereotypes the entire group;
   C. where the Negro applicant has the experience but is rejected because whites, with whom he would share employment, allegedly will walk off the job;
   D. where the policy of an employer is not to hire Negroes for white-collar positions;

E. where different physical requirements are used between white and Negro to disqualify the Negro;

F. where the employer uses the employment agency to screen out Negroes.

II. Partial Restriction in Employment:

A. where the employer hires a sufficient number to be inside the law—"tokenism";

B. where the employer restricts the Negro to the least desirable jobs—deadend jobs;

C. where the employer refuses to upgrade, even though the employee has sufficient experience and ability to do the job;

D. where both Negro and white persons perform the same task, frequently, there is a wage differential in favor of the white;

E. where the employer, in collusion with a union, restricts Negro occupational mobility.

III. Discriminatory Employment Retrenchment:

A. where the employer disregards seniority in employment releases;

B. where the Negro is confined to temporary jobs so that he cannot acquire seniority.

We recognize the fact that the above categories are not mutually exclusive nor are they organized on a uniform basis; rather the statement is presented as a working schema.

CHAPTER 4

Job Entry, Occupational Mobility, Income, and Economic Security

While recognizing the fact that many groups in American society have suffered from job and occupational immobility, it should be noted that the specific limitations placed upon Afro-American job entry and occupational mobility have been continuous. Therefore, their devastating effects plague each generation anew from childhood to death. Virtually all colored Americans are affected: from those adolescents searching for their first job to older colored Americans who try to retain a job until they are eligible to retire.

It should be mentioned that the economic aspects of this process are primary. Still, the psychological aspects do complement the economic and sociological process in reinforcing an equally vicious pattern of subjective relations. These relations begin with disappointment in job seeking and lay the foundation for life-long bitterness, hatred, and apathy.[1] A depression study specializing in Afro-American youth after they left school, stated that the colored youth were unemployed from 50 to 100 per cent of the time. The study went on to stress the economic immobility of colored youth when compared with white youth of equal education. In conclusion, the authors said that Afro-American youth were always shunted into part- and short-time jobs and they had to accept this pattern of employment or remain idle.[2]

JOB AND OCCUPATIONAL MOBILITY

The Afro-American's unfavorable job pattern of the 1930's was still evident in the early 1960's. In 1962, in a special labor-force report, the Bureau of Labor Statistics of the U.S. Department of Labor stated forcefully that nationally, nonwhite graduates and high-school dropouts held an "unfortunate position with respect to educational and economic attainment—despite [nonwhite] advances in these areas in recent years." [3] Thus,

> nonwhites failed to improve their economic position over time as much as white youth. Comparing the October 1962 jobs of young people who last attended school before 1960 and those who left school between 1960 and 1962, the proportion of graduates and dropouts in service and laboring jobs dropped off noticeably for the older white youth, but remained approximately the same for the older as for younger nonwhites. . . . Rates of unemployment for nonwhite graduates and dropouts remained relatively high even after they had been out of school several years, while the rates of the older white graduates and dropouts declined sharply.[4]

HIGH SCHOOL GRADUATES AND SCHOOL DROPOUTS AS A PERCENTAGE OF THE UNEMPLOYED IN THE CIVILIAN LABOR FORCE [5]

	Last attended school during 1960–1962	Last attended school prior to 1960
High school graduates not enrolled in college		
Nonwhite	17.2	14.5
White	10.0	5.3
School dropouts		
Nonwhite	21.3	18.0
White	19.8	10.2

Again in 1964 the "Manpower Report of the President and a Report on Manpower Requirements, Resources, Utilization and Training" by the U.S. Department of Labor confirmed that there had been no change in the institutionalized pattern of disad-vantaged Afro-American youth. Such youth averaged at least twice the rate of unemployment experienced by white youth between the ages of 14 and 24.

Moreover, rates of unemployment of young nonwhites, both high school graduates and dropouts, remain relatively high even after they have been out of school several years, *but unemploy-ment drops sharply among white graduates and dropouts as they gain experience.*[6]

UNEMPLOYMENT RATES FOR THE UNITED STATES, BY COLOR, SEX, AND AGE, 1963 [7]

Sex and age	White	Nonwhite
Male	4.7	10.6
14–19	14.2	25.4
20–24	7.8	15.6
Female	5.8	11.3
14–19	13.6	33.1
20–24	7.4	18.8

When compared with the national pattern, New York City's employment pattern was equally disadvantageous to Afro-American youth and to all Afro-Americans.[8] The following data illustrate this thesis.

UNEMPLOYMENT RATES FOR NONWHITES COMPARED WITH TOTAL LABOR FORCE IN NEW YORK CITY, 1960 [8]

Age group	All races		Nonwhite	
	Male	*Female*	*Male*	*Female*
Total 14 and over	4.4	5.1	6.8	6.5
14–19	11.2	7.1	19.0	14.7
20–24	7.0	5.3	9.7	9.2
25–34	3.9	5.1	6.6	6.7
35–44	3.1	4.8	5.3	5.8
45–64	3.8	4.8	5.6	4.7

The U.S. Civil Rights Commission reinforced the idea that Afro-American youth were not alone in their state of high unemployment, since employed Afro-Americans were generally found to be concentrated in the less skilled jobs,

> and it is largely because of the concentration in the ranks of the unskilled and semi-skilled, the groups most severely affected by both economic layoffs and technological changes, that Negroes are also disproportionately represented among the unemployed. The recent recession [1958] made this all too clear. But even now [1960] Negroes continue to swell the ranks of unemployed as technological changes eliminate the unskilled and semi-skilled tasks they once performed. Many will be chronically and/or permanently unemployed.[9]

Again in 1964 the similarity between the national situation and New York City was enunciated in a special report issued by Mayor Robert F. Wagner's council. The report stated that the Negro male unemployment rate was almost 50 per cent greater than the rate for white workers and the Puerto Rican male rate, 100 per cent greater.[10] Historically, the Afro-American's unemployment ratio to whites has averaged about two to one.[11] Since averages tend to cover up blight in individual areas, an examination of one such nonwhite area, Bedford-Stuyvesant, showed that the male unemployment rate was about 17.3 per cent, which was three and one-half times the citywide average rate of 5 per cent.[12]

Directly related to economic and social mobility is the factor of job entry. An analysis of some empirical evidence indicates that limited job entry and mobility were either the result of purposeful planning or at best an absence of planning, making the Afro-American on the whole a noncompetitive individual.

Different in degree but not in kind was the case of Herman Boykin, mentioned earlier. Because of his color, his employer had refused to upgrade him to preferential employment status. This denial curtailed Boykin's chance to acquire occupational seniority. When an Afro-American is refused job entry or is released because of color, two repercussions affect his future job and occupational mobility: (1) He has to counteract the "usual aversions" to hiring a man of color; and (2) he is denied the opportunity of acquiring additional skill because of the constant refusal to upgrade him.

The New York State Commission's 1944 report offered supporting evidence when it stated:

> The investigations conducted covered practically every area in the state, and almost every type of industry engaged, directly or indirectly, in war production. More than 350,000 employees were reported working in plants visited. Of this total approximately 346,000 were white and about 6,000 were Negro.[13]

What was true for the state as a whole was equally the case in city government. Thus for comparative purposes, two reports issued by the office of the mayor of New York revealed the difficulty of job entry in municipal government. One report gave the overall picture of employment in municipal government, the other broke the figures down by departments. The report for the city at large made the general comment that the

> occupational distribution of nonwhite and white workers in New York City [was] sharply different. Three times the proportion of white males as nonwhite males were employed as professional and technical workers, managers, officials, proprietors and sales workers.

> On the other hand, nonwhites were more heavily employed at the lower levels; 25.1 percent of the employed nonwhite males worked as operatives [apprentices, assemblers, attendants, railroad brakemen, and switchmen, bus drivers, manufacturing checkers, packers, wrappers, taxi drivers, etc.], and only 18.1 percent of the white males were so employed. Twice the proportion of nonwhite males as whites were employed as laborers in 1960—9.6 percent compared to 4.4 percent for white males. Nearly twice the proportions of nonwhite males as white males were employed as service workers—18.7 percent, compared to white males, 9.6 percent.[14]

The U.S. 1960 Census for New York City revealed a similar distortion in nonwhite and white females by occupation.

> Twelve percent of white females were employed as professional workers, [whereas], 7.8 percent of the nonwhite women were so employed. More than twice the proportion of white women were employed as clerical and kindred workers [40.5 percent], as compared to 16.8 percent nonwhite women.[15]

To ascribe the above differencies in occupational distribution to education alone would be difficult, because the proportion of New York City's whites, age 25 and over, with at least eight years of schooling, was almost equal to that of nonwhites.[16]

A second study was initiated by Mayor Wagner after he had held office for about eight years. The study, which was assigned to the City Commission on Human Rights, was to ascertain what effect the mayor's campaign had on increasing equal employment opportunities in city departments. Like the census data, the study revealed that blocked occupational mobility was an integral factor in the city's bureaucracy.

> Negroes within the City's plant actually are underrepresented in terms of percentage as Officials, and notably so in the entire Craftsmen category. Also [1964] City employment of Negroes show[ed] a disproportionate bulge in the Service, Clerical and Operative categories *and a tendency to cluster in agencies of a special type.*[17]

Illustrating what the commission meant by the bulge in the service area was the fact that it had over 42 per cent of all Afro-Americans employed by the city.[18] The studies cited demonstrate that occupational mobility is an adjunct of income level and economic security, and that occupational mobility cannot take place without job entry.

New York City's employment distribution at large, and the employment distribution practiced by New York City's municipal administration—perhaps the most liberal in the nation—offer one view of the full circle of discriminatory employment practices against the Afro-American.

Historically, this institutional imbalanced employment pattern dates back to the Afro-American's original slave status. As a slave he ministered to white society but was never a part of it. Following his manumission, the Afro-American was linked with his slave past, a condition easily maintained by his high visibility. With the combination of high visibility and chattel status under slavery, it was possible to continue assigning him a subordinate social and economic status which in turn limited his economic chances. This lack of economic mobility was still apparent some three hundred years later in the New York State's commission report.

> Nor have Negroes been upgraded to the highest skills for which many of them are qualified, a situation to be taken seriously

when considered in connection with the critical shortage of skilled labor in many occupational categories.[19]

In 1964, some twenty years after the state's report, the "Manpower Report of the President" deviated little from the above conclusions.

Although the higher rate of unemployment for nonwhite in part results from their concentration in the less skilled blue collar and service occupations, it is notable that in every occupation their rate of unemployment exceeds that of white workers. Furthermore, the difference tends to be relatively greater in the occupations with higher skill demands—such as clerical, sales workers, craftsmen and foremen—than in the less-skilled ones, for example, farm laborers and foremen, and non-farm workers. While the Negro has advanced slowly into the more skilled occupations, where unemployment is a lesser hazard than in the unskilled ones, *he is obviously hired reluctantly into these occupations and is the first to be discharged from them, perhaps in part because of his lower seniority.*[20]

Although the Afro-American has made some absolute gains in his occupational status, the myth that he has enjoyed a relative advance in his occupational mobility was dispelled by Dr. Herman Miller, special assistant in the Office of the Director, Bureau of the Census.

There is a general impression that the relative economic position of the Negro—particularly with respect to employment opportunities—has improved in recent years. The Department of Labor states that occupational differences between Negroes and whites are still large, but Negroes have raised their occupational levels appreciably faster, in the past 22 years, than whites. *This conclusion is valid as a generalization for the country as a whole.* It can be shown, however, *that most of the improvement in the occupational status of the Negro since 1940 has been due to his movement from the rural south to the urban industrial areas, rather than to any major improvement in job opportunities.*[21]

There has been a general upgrading of occupational skills for both whites and Negroes as the American economy has moved away from agriculture and become more complex and industrialized. . . . [But], *the real question is whether the relative upward movement has been faster for nonwhites than for whites. . . . The results . . . show that there have been few significant changes in the occupational distribution of nonwhite males relative to whites during the past 20 years* [1940–1960].[22]

INCOME, ECONOMIC SECURITY, AND STANDARD OF LIVING

Perhaps the intense effect of discriminatory employment practices on economic security with its components—job and occupational mobility—can best be demonstrated by a comparison of parallel black and white group incomes. In 1935–1936 the U.S. Department of Labor reported that the median income of native-born, non-relief Afro-American families was approximately 64 per cent of its comparable white group ($1,350 and $2,110, respectively). An aggregation of relief and nonrelief colored American families revealed a median income of $980.[23] In 1939, New York State's temporary commission supplied the following figures, covering both Afro-American and white families on relief, including such of these families that had one or more of its household employed. This time the lower half of the Afro-American group, when compared with its white counterpart, received less than one half the latter's income.[24] Expressed in dollars the white group averaged approximately $1,814 per annum, and the Afro-American group, less than $837.

An examination of median wages and salaries for males 14 years and over, by color, for the years 1947–1962, revealed almost no relative advance in income for the colored American. There was a reduction in the income ratio during the war years. However, it cannot be viewed

as part of a continuing process, but rather as a phenomenon closely related to war-induced shortages of unskilled labor and government relations such as those of the War Labor Board, designed generally to raise incomes of lower-paid workers, and to an economy operating at full tilt.[25]

To reiterate, whatever Afro-American gains were made in income were not the result of massive occupational upgrading but rather the effects of a transfer from rural to urban employment,

MEDIAN WAGE OR SALARY INCOME OF EMPLOYED
MALES, 14 YEARS OLD AND OVER, 1947–1962 [26]

Year	White	Nonwhite	Nonwhite as per cent of white
1947	$2,357	$1,279	54%
1948	2,711	1,615	60
1949	2,735	1,367	50
1950	2,982	1,828	61
1951	3,345	2,060	62
1952	3,507	2,038	58
1953	3,760	2,233	59
1954	3,754	2,131	57
1955	3,986	2,342	59
1956	4,260	2,396	56
1957	4,396	2,436	55
1958	4,596	2,652	58
1959	4,902	2,844	58
1960	5,137	3,075	60
1961	5,287	3,015	57
1962	5,462	3,023	55

from South to North and West, where wage rates were normally
higher and racial wage differentials less marked than in the South.[27]
At the same time, white workers were experiencing both absolute
and relative occupational upgradings. Thus they were moving
rapidly into the expanding white-collar occupations and into other
relatively well-paid jobs. It was this upward shift of whites that
made room for nonwhites to move into the passed-over jobs.[28]

Indirectly, the income status of nonwhites in New York may
be gauged by examining the ethnic stock (race) distribution of
poverty. Utilizing 1964 budget requirements for various sized
families ranging from one to seven persons, nonwhites constituted
29.2 per cent of the poor; almost twice their representation in the
city's total population. Poverty stricken families were concentrated
in 16 out of the city's 74 communities.

Geographically, "cultures of poverty" reveal a tendency for the
poor to congregate, regardless of color, in certain areas. Unlike
earlier periods in American history, it was not uncommon for af-
fluent groups to live side by side with poverty groups in New York
City. Thus,

just under 30 percent of the city's population resides in the 16 areas of poverty. What is consistent is the remarkable comparability [of these "cultures of poverty"], in degree of concentration of nonwhites and Puerto Ricans in the [same geographic areas].[29]

Converting this general remark into statistics: 73.3 per cent of the city's nonwhites and 73 per cent of its Puerto Ricans resided in the 16 areas.[30] The impact on the family was different for nonwhite and white. Among the nonwhites, the poverty problem primarily affected the young; whereas, among the whites, the aged were most affected, and these aged were primarily of immigrant stock.[31]

The Afro-American's employment tangle can also be illustrated by the quality of his economic security and standard of living. Since the Afro-American is confined to the lower status jobs and he is the "last hired and the first fired," it follows that his economic security is at best precarious. Economic security consists of two parts: job security and occupational status. However, *economic security depends upon more than merely having continuous employment,* unless the term is used in a restricted sense. By itself, continuous employment fails to disclose the relationship between earning power and occupational status; the latter a desideratum for economic security. Thus, the higher the occupational status, the higher, usually, is the earning power. Frequently, high occupational rank affords greater job mobility. In turn, the standard of living, a normative level of consumption, represents a goal of living that people try to maintain. Obviously, the latter is related to economic security. And, as we have shown, the Afro-American's standard of living is dependent upon a low economic status and security.

CHAPTER 5

Afro-Americans and the Trade Unions, 1866–1910

Prior to and during the period from 1866 to 1910, craft unions contended that they were not acting with any special malice toward the Afro-American; however, in a new form they re-articulated a position suitable to conditions in an industrial society; conditions that had pervaded the social structure and social consciousness of society in the United States. Since black inferiority was sanctioned "socially," unions employed exclusion as an economic weapon to maintain and raise their members' economic and social status. The acceptance of colored subjugation was linked in part with economic preservation; the latter, with the doctrine of job scarcity. Thus artificial restriction served a twofold purpose: it enhanced the bargaining power of the union, and it increased the union's economic power over its membership.

Even though economic historians contend that the United States suffered from a relative labor shortage between 1866 and 1910, craft unions operated on the premise that there was a job scarcity. Thus, to preserve this doctrine the union's economic power —in practice, craft unions—stressed job property rights, restriction of union membership, and a nepotistic apprenticeship system. Since the majority of the craft unions' members did sanction colored exclusion to some degree, they added a link to the circle of discrimination. In combination with other related factors, the craft unions' policy of blocked Afro-American economic mobility assisted in the formation of an atmosphere conducive to the social and economic subjugation of the black man.

In part, the Afro-American's low occupational status stemmed

from closed apprenticeship systems. (Even when he did have the
requisite skill, unions refused him membership.) Thus, the colored
American's low occupational status, or restricted economic mobility with respect to skilled jobs, tended to reinforce the white
man's need to rationalize the status quo. In a class society someone
has to be at the bottom—and the colored man was so assigned.

Historically, organized labor's attitude toward acceptance of
the Negro in the labor movement rested upon three levels; usually,
the higher the rung on the hierarchy (the National Labor Union,
the American Federation of Labor, the international union, and the
local union), the more likely was officialdom inclined to accept the
Negro. Thus, early in its short historical life-span (1866–1872) the
National Labor Union sought to have its international affiliates
organize the Negro, pressing them to set up all-Negro locals. On the
international level, some unions were willing to charter separate
all-Negro locals; others were willing to accept separate all-Negro
national unions; but the local unions of the various internationals
usually had sufficient power to stop their national unions from
carrying out such a program. Resistance to Negro union admission
on the local level may be linked to a fear of direct job competition
and its impact on the white man's job security.[1]

UNION BEGINNINGS OF A VICIOUS CIRCLE

With the first attempts of labor to form unions in the United
States, we find craftsmen seeking economico-social security in
diverse ways.[2] In addition to warding off competition from "green
hands," organized labor accepted the prevailing attitude of race
prejudice;[3] utilizing race prejudice, labor employed economic discrimination to bar Negroes from union admission to safeguard their
market monopoly.[4] Thus, during the first quarter of the 18th
century we find many transitory trade societies explicitly or tacitly
denying the Negro union membership.

The earliest trade societies to practice color exclusion included
the Caulkers of Boston in 1724,[5] the Shipwrights of New York in
1802, the Carpenters of New York in 1806, and the New York
Typographical Society in 1817.[6] These discriminatory practices
against the Negro were deeply embedded in the social structure.
Thus, it was logical to extend discrimination into the economic
sphere, as witnessed by the practices of such later labor organizations as the Workingman's Convention in 1830, the General Trades

Union of New York City in 1833, and the National Trades Union in 1835. In practice this meant overall discrimination. Thus, the degree of physical segregation in our social structure—a measure of social segregation impinging on economic life—may be gleaned from the fact that by 1840 over two thirds of New York City's Negroes were corraled into six wards.[7]

The formation of the present national labor unions began during the 1850's. The first national union was the Journeymen Printers, formed in 1852.[8] It was followed by the Iron Molders and Machinists in 1859.[9] These unions and others employed various devices to bar the Negro from their fraternal organizations. The action of the Cigar Makers' Union is illustrative: in 1864[10] a specific provision was incorporated into its constitution barring Negroes from possible membership.[11]

On the other hand, those international unions that were not so blatant in their policies used equally effective devices. To wit: the National Typographical Union (name changed in 1869 to International Typographical Union), in its 1852[12] and 1857[13] constitutions had in its by-laws a reference to the "Union Card" that stated: "This is to certify, That [name inserted] . . . is entitled to the friendship and good offices of all Unions under the Jurisdiction of the National Typographical Union."[14] Since these constitutions also contained the article that "any union within its jurisdiction refusing to abide by its laws and decisions shall be expelled,"[15] the national union had the *paper power* to enforce the acceptance of the travel card by all of its subordinate unions. However, as late as 1869 a special committee appointed by the national union's president recommended that "the question of admitting or rejecting colored printers be left to the discretion of Subordinate Unions."[16] Instead of enforcing its constitution, the union, on occasion, would lightly admonish some of its locals[17] for not adhering to the constitution.

The Iron Molders Union,[18] the National Carpenters' Union,[19] and the Bricklayers' and Masons' Union[20]—the latter two were formed in 1865—also employed devices similar to those practiced by the printers. The Knights of St. Crispin formed in 1867,[21] originally a secret society, also practiced Negro exclusion.

Of some 32 unions in existence during the early 1860's, none accepted the Negro into its fraternity.[22] Professor F. E. Wolfe's study reinforces this contention: "Indeed, all available evidence supports the conclusion that Negroes were seldom admitted into a union in any part of the country."[23] To implement control over the labor supply where exclusion (Caucasian clause, ritual, and tacit consent) failed to achieve its purpose satisfactorily, many unions encouraged the use of measures that included segregated and auxiliary locals.

NEGROES AND THE NATIONAL LABOR UNION

In 1866, when the first National Labor Congress (NLU) convened in Baltimore, Md., labor leaders such as A. C. Cameron,[24] editor of the *Workingman's Advocate*, and W. H. Sylvis, first president of the Iron Molders Union, and their confreres, tried to have organized labor accept the Negro as an integral part of the labor movement. However, most union delegates reasserted their traditional position by emphasizing that race prejudice was not the issue; the issue was a limited market. They argued that race prejudice is part of our way of life and existed long before unionism and collective bargaining were incorporated into our economy; therefore, organized labor was not responsible for discrimination.

A. C. Cameron managed to have the Negro question included on the congress' agenda. In addition, he had himself appointed chairman of the congress' first Negro labor committee. In this capacity he was responsible for the committee's report, which emphasized that "his [the Negro's] interest as a workingman . . . has as yet received no consideration. . . . The committee feels that it would be a sad dereliction to pass it by unacted.

"What is wanted from them is for every union to help to inculcate . . . the idea that the interest of labor is one; . . . the interest of all on our side of the line is the same. . . . If these general principles be correct, we must seek the cooperation of the African race in America." [25]

The need for cooperation and unity between black and white workers was placed on an economic level when the committee stated that "the question . . . is, shall we make them [Negroes] our friends, or shall capital be allowed to turn them into an engine against us? . . . A practical illustration . . . is afforded in the recent importation of colored caulkers from Portsmouth, Virginia, to Boston, Massachusetts, during the struggle on the eight hour question." [26]

Apparently, Cameron and his colleagues on the committee were convinced that their economic logic would prevail over prejudice. They decided to let the next convention decide on the time and place: "The time when such cooperation should take effect, we leave to the decision and wisdom of the next congress [1867]. . . . We believe that such enlightened action will develop as to resound to the best and most lasting interests of all concerned." [27]

In 1867 the second National Labor Congress convened in Chicago, and was presided over by J. C. C. Whaley. In his presidential address he referred to the Negro question and also offered a possible solution: "The emancipation of the slaves has placed us in a new position. What labor position shall they now occupy? . . . They will soon resort to mechanical pursuits and thus come in contact [competition] with white labor. It is necessary that they should not undermine it, therefore, the best thing that they can do is to form [separate] trades unions and thus work in harmony with whites." [28]

A second committee on Negro labor was appointed, with A. W. Phelps as chairman. Phelps' union, the Carpenters and Joiners of New Haven, Conn., was known to bar Negroes. This committee's report tabled the Negro issue saying: "We realize the danger in the future competition . . . , yet, we find the subject so involved in so much mystery . . . and so wide a diversity of opinion among our members, . . . that it is inexpedient to take action on the subject during this National Congress." [29]

There seemed to be more agreement than disagreement on the Negro question, since the majority of the delegates believed that either the problem would solve itself or that it did not belong in the house of labor. On the first point, Mr. W. Cathers [30] insisted that there was no need to discuss the Negro question, because the Negroes would "combine of themselves and by themselves without the assistance of white workers." On the second point the secretary to the convention [31] argued that the Negro issue should be deferred. Finally a resolution was adopted that "they [the Committee] found that the Constitution already adopted prevented the necessity of reporting on the subject of Negro labor." [32]

The attitude of the majority of the delegates at the 1867 Convention was revealed to some degree when Mr. Phelps raised the question of Negro membership. He started with the statement that there were many colored mechanics in his home city and that each one was denied union membership. The question, Is there a single union in the United States that "would admit these people?", was greeted by an ominous silence.[33]

Between 1867 and 1869 the Negro issue was pressed by some

National Labor Union (NLU) delegates, and finally at the 1869 Convention in Philadelphia some colored persons were admitted as delegates. The change in attitude may be ascribed partly to Whaley's 1867 presidential address and partly to the impact of Negro competition.

This was the first time in American labor history that a national convention of white workingmen *advocated the formation of labor unions by Negroes, separate but equal,* and authorized the admission of Negro delegates to its annual session. The spirit that must have pervaded the group can be felt in reading the resolution sponsored by Horace Day and adopted by the 1869 Convention: "The National Labor Union knows no North, no South . . . and urges our colored fellow members to form organizations in all legitimate ways to send their delegates from every state in the Union to the next Congress." [34]

This spirit moved one New York *Times* correspondent to eulogize the congress in his article. "One peculiar fact stands out in bold relief, *viz.,* that the barriers of class and caste have been broken down so far as the laboring classes of the country are concerned, *if we take the solemnly avowed sentiments of this body as indicative of the feelings that exist among the constitutents therein represented.* For the first time in the history of this nation a convention has been held in which workingmen and working women, white and black . . . have met together on terms of *perfect equality,* for the purpose of taking deliberate action on vital questions affecting equally the interests of all.

"The great wall of caste and color, which has hitherto divided the laboring classes is no longer insurmountable." [35]

The Negroes referred to were from two states, Maryland and Pennsylvania, and represented all-Negro trade unions. The Maryland Negroes, four in number, represented the Colored Caulkers Trade Union, the Colored Engineers Association, and the Colored Painters Society; the remaining five colored delegates from Philadelphia were members of the United Hod Carriers Association.[36]

Obviously the Negro artisans did not share the pleasant expectations held by the New York *Times* correspondent, nor did they accept at face value the separate but equal resolution adopted at the 1869 Convention, since they formed their own Colored National Labor Union only two months after the National Labor Union adjourned.[37]

In addition, the Negro's distrust of the white man's statements was founded on the belief that a line of demarcation existed be-

tween the NLU's adopted resolutions and its application by NLU
affiliates, since each affiliate had complete autonomy. Furthermore,
most subordinate unions of each NLU affiliate held sufficient local
autonomy to block any attempt by its international to close the gap
between pronouncement and practice. Finally, the Negro's distrust
of organized labor was linked to the white man's social antipathy;
an antipathy so overwhelming that even Negroes with trades were
rarely organized.[38]

As late as 1862 the New York Negro felt the white man's
deeply rooted antipathy when Irish workers rioted against the
Lorillard tobacco factory, which employed 50 Negroes and 25
whites.[39] These unorganized workers reflected the attitude of the
general populace toward the Negro, and we must remember that
this upheaval took place before the riots associated with the 1863
Conscription Act. The mores accepted by society were used by craft
unions to further their own ends. The Cigar Makers' 1865 Constitution was illustrative. It included Article IX, which stipulated that
"unless said person is a white practical cigar maker," he cannot belong to any local union.[40] This provision was upheld at the Cigar
Makers' 1868 Convention.[41] During the 5th annual session of the
Carpenters Union in 1869, the prevailing attitude toward the Negro
was revealed. The carpenters' committee on colored labor reported:
*"We believe that the prejudices of our members against the colored
people are of such a nature that it is not expedient at present to
admit them as members or to organize them under the national
union."* [42]

Again in 1869, President George, at the International Typographical Union's Convention, mentioned the difficulty a colored
printer, L. H. Douglass, had in being admitted to the Columbia
union (in Washington, D.C.). President George appointed a special
committee to study the Negro question. Its report recommended
that the prerogative of admittance or rejection of colored printers
be "left to the discretion of Subordinate Unions." [43] When
Douglass' case came before the local union, a member of the union
questioned the charges with the comment that "he was a colored
man." [Since this was the basis for rejection], "was contrary to the
letter and spirit of the Constitution of their National Union." The
local's membership tabled the entire matter when it voted 56 to 28
not to deal with the question.[44]

In 1870 the problem of Negro competition finally forced the
carpenters to change their attitude. At their 6th convention, Pres.
A. W. Phelps informed the delegates that they could no longer

shut out colored mechanics, since "we must strike hands in a common cause." [45] In response to Phelps' statement the delegates agreed to invite all carpenters and joiners, regardless of color, "to form new local unions under the charter granted by the national union," but each local was to retain the power "to admit such colored members as it deemed best." [46] In essence, this meant that separate but equal all-Negro locals could be established only with the consent of existing white locals.

In 1871 the Cigar Makers' Convention delegates voted unanimously to eliminate Article IX, or Negro exclusion, from the union's constitution. [47] However, the rescinding of Article IX did not mean "perfect equality," [48] since Article I still left the final decision of union admission in the hands of the local union. [49]

On the other hand, where the international union's constitution neglected specifically to exclude the Negro from membership, and the question was raised at an international convention, the delegates usually referred the issue back to the local union. Typical of this action was the International Typographical Union's case cited above.

Other international unions seeking the power to organize the Negro found their local unions blocking every step of the way, unless Negro competition forced a change in their attitude. Thus, in 1870 at the Bricklayers' International Convention, the proposal to grant power to the international to issue separate charters to all-Negro locals failed of adoption, [50] as it did again in 1871. [51] The anti-Negro feeling was so intense at the Bricklayers' 1871 Convention that two New York locals fought openly against admission of Negroes into either the national union or any of its locals and even against the establishment of separate Negro locals. [52]

The bricklayers' attitude persisted throughout 1874, since the delegates to the national convention continued to deny membership to any skilled Negro. [53] To insure that the international union would not be able to bypass the locals, the delegates to the 1875 Convention succeeded in amending the constitution so that no international charter could be granted in any locale without the consent of the existing local union. [54] When the question of organizing the Negro was raised at the 1877 Convention, the bricklayers rejected it. [55]

The social antipathy toward the Negro between 1869 and 1878—a period described by some writers as one of Negro acceptance into the fold of organized labor—was demonstrated by various contemporary reports. One authority summed up the situation by stating that "all available evidence supports the conclusion that Negroes were seldom admitted into a union in any part of the country." [56] In March, 1869 a report appeared in the New York *Times* denying that there was a meeting of white and black on terms of "perfect equality." In addition to union exclusion, white society sanctioned physical violence against the Negro. Furthermore, white nonunionists refused to work side by side with the Negro, another indication of the deeply rooted white antipathy toward the black man.[57] Another report appeared in 1871 in the New York *Tribune,* stressing the Negro's continued lack of economic mobility.[58] In 1879 an international union's president stated: "That there exists strong prejudice against the admission of colored printers into many unions I will not attempt to deny; but I trust that this matter will receive your earnest and thoughtful consideration, so that a conclusion may be arrived at in conformity with the principles upon which our organizations are based and *in consonance with the enlightened spirit of the times.*" [59]

During the period 1866–1878, union admission was left to the discretion of the international union and/or its locals.[60] Hence the top rung of the union hierarchy, the National Labor Union, welcomed any resolution that would admit the Negro into labor's family, but national and local union policy, usually contrary to the NLU's advocacy, prevailed. Thus, for all practical purposes, unless Negro competition forced a change in policy, the Negro was excluded from unionization. By 1872 the National Labor Union ceased to function as a pure labor union and became a political entity.

THE KNIGHTS OF LABOR

The Knights of Labor existed in juxtaposition with the National Labor Union. The Knights opened their rolls to Negro union membership in 1869. Initially, it was Uriah Stephens, a man of God, who established the union's policy toward Negro acceptance. He said: "I can see ahead of me an organization that . . . will include men and women of every craft, creed and color.[61] His successor, Terence V. Powderly, accepted Stephens' Labor philosophy, not on religious, but rather on economic and sociological, grounds. On economic grounds, Powderly thought that the free Negro would be used to exploit white organized labor: "The Negro is free. . . . His labor and that of the white man will be thrown upon the market side by side, and no human eye can detect a difference between the article manufactured by the black mechanic and that manufactured by the white mechanic. . . . Both mechanics must sink their differences, or fall prey to the slave labor now being imported to this country." [62]

There is some evidence that this economico-social philosophy had filtered down to the level of the district and local assemblies, as evidenced at the 1886 Convention held in Richmond, Va., F. J. Ferrell, representing New York's District Assembly No. 49, stated: "When D.A. 49 of New York made arrangements for hotel accommodations, . . . the agent of D.A. 49 did not state that there would be any colored men among them, and when . . . [they] appeared at the hotel selected, they were told that Mr. Ferrell would not be admitted because of his color. . . . The representatives of D.A. 49 withdrew in a body, and secured quarters where there would be no objections to any one of their number." [63]

The general master workman of the Knights of Labor, Terence V. Powderly, again demonstrated his belief in social equality when he asked J. E. Quinn, master workman of the Richmond District, to let him introduce Governor Lee of Virginia. Following the governor's address, Ferrell was to present Powderly.[64] In his introduction Ferrell stated: "One of the objects of our Order is the abolition of those distinctions which are maintained by creed or color." [65]

Also in the same vein was a letter written to John Swinton that included this statement: "[My] Assembly of Knights of Labor which contains 450 members, 25 of whom are colored, . . . has not [had] a single outburst of feeling on account of color. I am a colored man myself, and am Worthy Treasurer, an office which was forced upon me for the third time." [66]

In addition to the above citations, there were numerous newspaper accounts attesting to the acceptance of the Negro by the Knights of Labor. Even when the Negro represented a minority in a particular branch of the Knights, he could hope to be elected to positions on all levels of the order—the local assembly, district assembly, state convention, and General Assembly.[67]

In spite of the prevailing antipathy toward organizing the Negro, tens of thousands were brought under the union banner of the Knights. Although we have only estimates of Negro membership in the Knights, they did reveal that during this period the Negro was interested in affiliating with the labor movement. In 1887 the New York *Sun* reported that there were over 400 all-Negro locals in the order, with an estimated total Negro membership in both mixed and all-colored locals in excess of 90,000.[68]

Thus, during the period 1870–1876, which includes the rise, progress, and rapid growth of the Knights, this organization did modify substantially some white workers' anti-Negro attitude. Although there were at least 400 all-Negro locals that did not meet the test of "perfect equality," as stressed by Stephens and Powderly, the Knights were moving in that direction. Again, as in the case of the National Labor Union, the top echelon appeared to be more liberal than the lower echelons in the union hierarchy.

THE AMERICAN FEDERATION OF LABOR

The decline of the Knights of Labor in May, 1886 followed the loss of the Southwest strike, the failure of the eight-hour-day movement, the prosecutions that followed the Haymarket bombing, and the growing dissatisfaction with trade unions.[69] After 1886 the American Federation of Labor (AFL) won a leading position among organized labor. Once more the top echelon of the new federation expressed a need to organize all workers regardless of color or creed. This was expressed forcefully in the preamble to the constitution: "Whereas a struggle is going on . . . between the capitalist and the laborer, which grows in intensity . . . [it] will work disastrous results . . . if [it is not] combined with mutual protection and benefit. *The history . . . of constant struggle and misery* [is] *engendered by ignorance and disunion.*

"The history of the non-producers of all ages proves that a minority, thoroughly organized, may work wonders for good or evil. . . . [Therefore] *the formation of a Federation embracing every trade and labor organization in North America, a union founded upon a basis as broad as the land we live in,* [must necessarily be even more effective]. . . . Trades unions . . . have accomplished great good, yet their efforts have not been of the lasting character *which a thorough unification of all different branches of industrial workers is bound to secure."* [70]

Despite the lack of any reference to the Negro in the AFL Constitution, the federation's officials required a pledge from all national unions seeking affiliation that they would not exclude craftsmen solely on account of color, creed, or nationality. Samuel Gompers, president of the AFL, like his predecessors, Cameron, Sylvis, Powderly, *et al.,* recognized the need for total organization of the working class in order to achieve labor's goal—economic, social, and political strength: "If we don't make friends of the colored man, he will of necessity be justified in proving himself our enemy (echo of Cameron and Powderly). They will be utilized . . . to frustrate our every effort for economic, social and political improvement." [71]

When the National Association of Machinists sought affiliation with the AFL, its constitution contained a Caucasian clause. John B. Lennon, treasurer of the AFL, stated that so long as the machinists' constitution contained "provisions excluding from membership persons on account of race, or color, [admission was impossible]. When the National Machinists Union removed from their constitution such conditions, so that all machinists shall be eligible for membership," [the AFL would accept them].[72]

Again in 1891 Gompers reiterated the AFL's stand on the Negro question: "Organized labor . . . is decidedly in favor of maintaining and encouraging the recognition of the equality between colored and white laborers, [and to this purpose] the Federation will call a convention of all machinists unions for the purpose of forming a [rival] national union which shall recognize no color line." [73]

Although both the National Association of Machinists (name changed later to International Association of Machinists), and the International Brotherhood of Blacksmiths were threatened with rival unionism unless they expunged the Caucasian clause from their respective constitutions, the AFL failed to effect compliance. At a later date both unions were admitted into the AFL when the machinists substituted ritual for the Caucasian clause and the blacksmiths substituted the auxiliary local. For all practical purposes, both remained "lily-white."

In the one year (1894) that Gompers was not reelected president of the AFL the machinists were admitted into the Federation. John McBride was elected president of the AFL in 1894, but when he was taken ill, James Duncan became acting president. The latter made a distinction between a national union's constitution and local union practices. This was a bit of casuistry, since Duncan implied that the federation was not concerned with local practices. Thus, local unions could ban Negroes so long as the national union's constitution had no specific restriction on Negroes. Duncan said: "as long as you have the word 'white' establishing the color line as part of your constitution either your action must be changed or your lodges and your national body must stand debarred. . . . Yours [IAM] is the only national union, that at present has the color line as distinctly formed, *while at the same time many crafts refuse to admit a colored man without having such a provision in their constitution, the matter being left absolutely with the local unions.*" [74]

The IAM substituted ritual for the "lily-white" clause,[75] and the blacksmiths circumvented the issue by setting up auxiliary locals, with members of auxiliary locals barred from craftsman status. By 1895 the AFL's officialdom rationalized its failure to enforce nondiscrimination as a prerequisite for affiliation and in 1896 national unions with "lily-white" constitutions were granted charters.[76] By 1900 the AFL's officialdom recognized that the federation's structure lacked sufficient power to enforce its nondiscrimination policy. Therefore, to include all workers, Article 12, Section 6, of the AFL Constitution was revised to read: "Separate charters may be issued to Central Labor Unions, Local Unions, or Federated Labor Unions, composed exclusively of colored workers where in the judgment of the Executive Council it appears advisable." [77] Technically, this would create jurisdictional problems if the newly created colored unions were to operate on a par with their white counterparts.

The AFL's action has been interpreted by some writers as a "signal that the AFL had abandoned even the formality of equal status for Negro workers." [78] Furthermore, P. S. Foner interprets several of Gompers' letters as implying that segregation was the only solution to the problem.[79] Although this is a possible interpretation, closer examination of how Gompers might have viewed the complexity of the problem reveals at least two aspects that he had to resolve: (1) How to eliminate race prejudice, since exhortation had failed to change union admission policies and (2) how to prevent a schism in the labor movement, since the AFL's official policy was to embrace all workingmen.[80] Gompers straddled the issue; he fought on both sides of the fence.

Thus, in 1897 the AFL reaffirmed its earlier declaration that "the working people must unite and organize irrespective of creed, color, sex, nationality, or politics." [81] In accord with this philosophy, the AFL discouraged Negro exclusion by taking positive measures. It introduced the Federal Labor Union as part of its structure in an attempt to remedy the structural weakness inherent in the AFL, where its internationals had complete autonomy. In this instance the only thing the AFL could do would be to revoke the charter of its affiliate or refuse to issue a charter to potential affiliates. The issuance of charters to central, local, and federal labor unions meant direct affiliation with the parent body.[82]

However, such extraterritorial bodies as federal labor unions could offer the Negro only uncertain and temporary entry into the labor movement. Since such unions are temporary by nature, they are usually raided by existing international unions, or they may form the nuclei of new internationals. Once the latter are formed, the federal union's direct relationship with the federation is terminated.[83] This posits two issues: (1) Should the new international union accept the Negro, it would probably take the form of either an auxiliary or a segregated union, and should an existing international union have jurisdiction over some of the federal labor union's membership, it is not obligated to accept the Negro on an equal basis with its white membership. (2) Should the new international union refuse to accept the Negro, he could remain in the federal labor union within the community. The latter issue only raises another question: the relationship between the international union's locals and the federal labor union within the same locale. Where more than one local exists within a given community, a district council, joint council, or similar unit usually has the power to assign a specific territory to each local, a factor essential in the crafts for employment purposes. This would leave the federal labor union with no assigned territory. In other words, the federal labor union could at best, afford the Negro acceptance in name only.

At least until 1910, if not later, the federation encouraged the formation of separate Negro unions in localities where otherwise the Negro would have remained unorganized. It was the hope of the AFL that its policy would be accepted, and that the labor movement would accept the Negro as a full fraternal brother. Secondly, the federation advocated, in speeches and publications, that the Negro should be admitted to unions subject to the discretion of each individual national union.[84] Thus the AFL thought that its own open policy and the acceptance of Afro-Americans by some individual national unions would act as a wedge to open the way for the Negro into the labor movement.

When Gompers was addressing those unions that were antipathetic to the Negro's cause, he would state that the AFL did not compel its affiliates to accept colored workmen into their organizations. On other occasions he went so far as to advise that Negroes should not be accepted into the house of labor because of their strikebreaking activities.[85] (Gompers' earlier prophecy did come true. "If we don't make friends of the colored man, he will be justified in proving himself our enemy." However, when addressing labor groups antipathetic to the Negro, Gompers reversed cause and effect.) Here, Gompers' own behavior illustrates, in miniature, the rationale for the vicious circle. The Negro was barred from white organizations and consequently tried to break the union's stronghold by strikebreaking. But when he did scab, he no longer could hope to be admitted into a union. Thus, no matter which way he turned, he appeared to be doomed.

In 1910 the unions affiliated with the AFL whose constitutions explicitly excluded the Negro through ritual, tacit consent, or "lily-white" and other clauses included: the wire weavers,[86] the switchmen,[87] the maintenance of way employees,[88] the railroad telegraphers,[89] the railway and steamship clerks,[90] the commercial telegraphers,[91] and the boilermakers, and iron ship builders.[92]

To this list must be added the Railroad brotherhoods, all independent unions until 1960. It was contended that the Brotherhood of Locomotive Firemen and Enginemen remained outside of the AFL because it refused to delete its Caucasian clause and use a subterfuge.[93] On the other hand, the bulk of those unions that refused to admit Negroes did not object to the Negroes' setting up separate and/or independent organizations. This attitude was expressed in an editorial in the *Electrical World* as late as 1903.

We do not want the Negro in the International Brotherhood of Electrical Workers, but we think that they should organize in locals of their own, affiliated with the American Federation of Labor as that organization knows no creed or color.[94]

The AFL's advocacy of Negro union admission, as espoused in official speeches and publications, is difficult to measure either quantitatively or qualitatively. However, these exhortations in combination with the AFL's policy of admitting all-Negro federal labor unions and central labor councils,[95] and the gradual development of Negro competition, especially in the trowel and woodworking trades, showed a forced change in some international unions' policies. When the change did take place, it was primarily to control Negro activities.

Prior to 1881,[96] the Bricklayers' Union permitted its subordinates to flaunt acceptance of any travel card held by a Negro. At its 1881 Convention the official policy was changed to an insistence that all locals must recognize the travel card of a colored bricklayer in good standing.[97] Following this concession by its locals, the national executive board acquired in 1883 the right to charter separate colored subordinates.[98] By 1886 increased Negro competition in the woodworking trades, controlled by the United Brotherhood of Carpenters and Joiners, resulted in a change in the brotherhood's constitution. Henceforth, the national union had the power to charter more than one local within the same community, *provided that the existing local offered no reasonable objection.*[99] It was not until 1893 that the Cigar Makers' International Union was granted discretionary power to form new local unions in areas where a local was already in existence.[100]

Other national unions granted the power to establish new local unions had a *caveat* attached to their discretionary power. The *caveat* meant: (1) that national unions did not have to accept the AFL's official policy toward Negro membership; and (2) that national unions with only paper power to establish new local unions could be stopped by their local unions, which had sufficient autonomy to establish policy. These unions included the painters, sheet metal workers, plumbers,[101] coopers, and tailors, since all of their national unions had to obtain the consent of the local within the community where an additional local was projected.

The case of the operating engineers illustrated two points developed previously: (1) The power of the local union to bar the formation of all-Negro locals and/or at the local's discretion to accept the travel card of a Negro. (2) The need to control Negro craftsmen when they were able to compete for the same job.

The operating engineers were established as a national union in 1896 (their original name was the National Union of Steam Engineers). The color question was first raised at the 1910 Convention and rejected on pragmatic grounds. "The union was essentially a stationary engineers organization with no control over the labor supply. *The Negro engineers could not be excluded from employment. Therefore, it was considered preferable to include them in order to control them.* Negro members of stationary locals are not uncommon today [1963], but they are rare in hoisting and portable locals. The *matter has remained in local hands,* and there is no doubt that considerable discrimination exists." [102]

To summarize, during the 1866–1910 period we found that as early as 1869 an attempt was made to include the Negro into the organized labor movement, but the autonomy held by international unions and their subordinates permitted continued exclusion. Even in the early 1870's when some national unions, saw the need to control the total labor supply brought on by competition from nonunion men, the locals still refused to grant this power to their internationals. In other instances where the international had acquired the right to establish separate Negro locals, or where a particular local did accept the Negro, the Negro's travel card was usually rejected by a sister local.

The rise and impact of the AFL's philosophy and policy both directly and indirectly influenced the attitude of some national unions toward Negro acceptance, at least in principle. Thus the AFL was able to "coerce" the IAM into eliminating its "lily-white" clause; it did "coerce" the blacksmiths into offering the Negro second-class union membership—in auxiliary locals. In a manner of speaking this was a form of "breakthrough," a process facilitated and spurred by growing Negro competition and the union's need to control the Negro craftsman. What is of importance is that many national unions actually did set up all-Negro locals.

Although the new structure's function was aimed at control of the Negro's economic mobility and security, it had an unanticipated consequence: the formation of the mixed local. Theoretically at least this new union structure contained the possible means for changing all-white, to mixed, locals. We emphasize the word *theoretical*, since local unions still have many ways of circumventing their national union's edict that each local had to respect the travel card of a sister local. For example, the local's officials can question the competency of a Negro craftsman or use an employer to perform the same act. On the local level, it was the business agent who had almost exclusive power of job placement, and it made a difference whether he placed a worker on the deck of a job or at the tail end.

Nevertheless, once the Negro did become an accredited journeyman he had the privilege of sponsorship; a privilege essential to maintain and to increase the number of Negro apprentices (father-son, or relatives) in a particular craft union. Secondly, once the Negro became an accredited journeyman he could become a small independent contractor. Finally, once the Negro became an accredited journeyman, even though he was restricted to "repair work," his economic status was higher than that of the common laborer.

The AFL's exhortations and the international's need, did little to alter the local white craft union's antipathy toward the Negro. White craftsmen still thought in terms of a limited job market and job security. This concept included the idea that the number of workers in a trade must be kept to a minimum to insure against a decrease in wages and steady employment. To secure wage increases and to win negotiations it was essential to control the total labor supply or at least a sufficient number of workers to keep the job from being done. This was realized by some internationals, and they in turn proceeded to set up separate all-Negro locals to control the labor supply.

In review, it can be seen that the farther men were removed from the threat of job insecurity—that is officials of the NLU, the K. of L., the AFL, and the international down to the local—the less antagonistic were they to Negro acceptance. Of course each echelon in the hierarchy held a different frame of reference: the central federation was interested in organizing all workers the national viewed organization in terms of trade control; and the local business agent thought in terms of reelection or jobs for his members. In turn, the individual craft union member related his job security, overtime, and other benefits to numbers in the trade. Thus, in the past the strongest link in the formation of the vicious circle was the local union. The international had been less firm in its effort to organize the Negro. Finally, the complete autonomy of international unions and the control many locals had over their internationals permitted blockage of the AFL's efforts to enforce its nondiscrimination policy. The AFL's only recourse was expulsion or the setting up of rival unions; both of these, historically, have proven ineffective.

CHAPTER 6

Afro-Americans and the Trade Unions, 1910–1965

The outbreak of World War I offered the Afro-American, temporarily, many unanticipated opportunities to upgrade his occupational status, insure his economic security, and possibly raise his social status. Among the events that led to a critical labor shortage in the United States were: (1) the emigration of aliens back to their mother country, either for nationalistic reasons or because of unfilled military obligations to their country of birth; (2) the drying up of new immigration; (3) the increased industrial activity created by the belligerents' orders for military supplies from the United States; and (4) the entry of the United States into the war in 1917. Conscription also siphoned off many semiskilled and unskilled workers. Such factors, plus others, caused a critical labor shortage, and with the shortage, a need to tap neglected labor resources—Afro-American labor. To meet wartime and peacetime orders many Northern industrialists recruited Southern colored people to fill the void.[1] Even though these special Afro-American social and economic opportunities petered out during the demobilization period, the war period created difficulties within the American Federation of Labor (AFL).

During the 1910–1920 decade, AFL president Samuel Gompers continued to straddle the Afro-American question. Whenever a group attacked his policy of

> reading the Negro out of the labor movement, [invariably he responded that the] AFL [was] trying to bring them into the organized labor movement.[2]

To reinforce his position, Gompers pointed to the federation's policy of directly sponsoring "separate but equal" local and federal labor unions. Continued union discriminatory admission policies failed to keep his federation from expanding its membership, which increased from 2,072,700 in 1916 to 4,078,700 by 1920.[3] This increase took place primarily in all-white trades: building, metal, machinery, shipbuilding, and clothing.[4] Although the Afro-American was barred from most craft unions affiliated with the AFL, the federation's policy of chartering directly all colored locals and federal and central labor unions did permit the Negro American to apply pressure on the AFL's executive council. Also, Negro American forces outside the AFL tried to apply pressure by having the executive council effect a change in its policy. Thus, at the AFL's 1918 Convention, the National Urban League [5] raised the colored question and even met with the executive council to discuss the problem. The league, in conjunction with other Negro American groups, was permitted to present a resolution to the convention.[6] This resolution acknowledged that the AFL's official policy was welcome to the colored American; but the question was raised: Why did certain international unions exclude Negro Americans from their rolls? If the AFL acknowledged that many of its affiliates were "lily-white," why were they permitted to remain affiiliated with the AFL?

Although the resolution was adopted at the convention, the delegates failed to establish any machinery to study and/or to eliminate the continuation of its affiliates' "lily-white" practices.[7] This type of administrative action, or inaction—let time heal the breach—was in accord with Gompers' straddle position. Undeterred, Negro American delegates to the AFL's 1919 Convention again offered suggestions and made a direct complaint against the International Union of Metal Trades, a union that barred Negro Americans from its organization.[8]

At the 1920 Convention the Negro American again protested. This time the protest was spearheaded by Negro American locals and federal labor unions directly chartered by the AFL. The protest was phrased in terms of four demands: That the AFL (1) initiate an educational program among white and Negro American workmen that would convince them of the necessity of "bringing into the ranks of labor all men who work regardless of race, creed or color"; (2) institute periodic conferences of white and black leaders with the executive council at which the Negro American labor question would be discussed; (3) appoint an executive secretary or a special committee for organizing the colored American; and (4) hire Negro American organizers in all crafts, whose duties would be to build up Negro American membership. When the resolution was acted upon, sections 1 and 3 were deleted, and section 4 was amended so that the appointment of Negro American organizers became optional. It was further watered down by having section 4 referred to the executive council for possible action, only if funds were available.[9]

What remained of the emasculated original resolution was subjected to at least two further reservations: (1) Since the executive council's membership represented many international unions whose policy was to bar the Negro American from equal membership, the verbal acquiescence of many international union officials would in no way pressure their unions to discontinue the practice. Furthermore, many local unions practicing discrimination had sufficient autonomy either to block suggested changes in, or to ignore, their international union's constitution. (2) Since the appointment of Negro American organizers depended upon the executive council's proclaiming the availability of funds, the council could easily circumvent the issue by merely stating that no funds were available at this time. This would be administratively feasible since Negro American organizers expressly hired to organize the Negro American would, if successful, put additional pressure on many craft unions that practiced discrimination. This influx of potential colored membership would intensify an existing problem.

At the end of the 1910–1920 decade it could be stated with some certainty that the top officials of the AFL did express good intentions, but they failed to put them into practice. Thus the AFL's ineffectual Negro American policy was ascribed to the inherent weakness of its structure—a confederation of unions whose affiliates held almost complete autonomy. Although the AFL did have recourse to expulsion or rival unionism, its power hierarchy felt that this could lead only to a Pyrrhic victory. On the other hand, left-wingers contended that Gompers and his colleagues had sold the Negro American out of the labor movement, because the AFL's leadership had failed to adhere to the principles clearly enunciated in its constitution by its unwillingness to force affiliates to accept the colored American into the ranks of organized labor.

Left-wingers did not fail to point out the fact that the federation did request cooperation, but rarely if ever threatened to expel any of its "wayward affiliates." They noted that at various constitutional conventions during this decade, resolutions were presented condemning various affiliates, but the council never acted upon them. The federation did request "the Railway Clerks to remove the words 'white only' from their Constitution [in 1920]. When the clerks refused to comply, the parent body neglected to enforce its request." [10] The AFL did expel the clerks in 1926, but for jurisdictional reasons. Leo Wolman summarized the federation's ineptness on the colored question when he stated:

> The AFL as a central organizing machine [had] fallen into disuse for this purpose, [organizing the Negro American even into Federal Labor Unions], several decades ago, and as it grew older, it lost, with its youth, its energy. [11]

The spirit of Gompers continued to pervade the federation's policy on the Negro American issue after his death. The leadership still retained his straddle position. When the Brotherhood of Sleeping Car Porters was organized in 1925 by A. Philip Randolph, AFL President William Green freely and constantly offered Randolph expert advice on union organization. Green even permitted Randolph to attend the AFL's 1926 Convention as a visitor. Although there is no question of Green's sincerity as an individual, there was evidence that he feared the unorganized Negro American worker. If the Negro American were not admitted to the federation *on some basis* (possibly second-class membership), in the words of Gompers, he would "be utilized to frustrate [labor's] every effort for economic, social and political improvement." [12] Hence, the "segregated organization of Negro workers in certain occupations through local and federal labor unions," [13] was a method of control over potential strikebreakers and at least a possible stopgap against such Communist-inspired organizations as the Negro Labor Congress. Green was sufficiently concerned with the threat of the left-wing labor movement to write an editorial on the issue.

> Negro Wage Earners, I deplore the misrepresentation and deception . . . used to promote the World Negro Congress. . . . [The latter would] take advantage of the weaknesses of those who have a *moral right to our special care.* . . . The Negro World Congress is quite outside the pale of decency and ethics. . . . The AFL offer[s] Negro wage earners the protection and experience of the trade union movement. [14]

The condescension was implicit in Green's phrase, the "moral right to our special care." No mention was made of the economic right as being necessary to mutual protection. Furthermore, the editorial implied that the Negro American was helpless without the aid of his organized benefactor. Thus, Green neglected to mention that the Negro American had tried to form national labor organizations in the past, and even at the time that he wrote his editorial, Negro Americans had organized all-colored independent unions.

The federation continued to issue resolutions bidding the Negro American to join the traditional labor movement, even though its affiliates continued to bar him from their organizations. Those Negro Americans who did heed the plea of the AFL formed 109 Negro locals in 1919, all directly affiliated with the AFL. The federation's success in fulfilling the needs of Negro Americans who did affiliate was revealed in time. Ten years later only 21 of the 109 Negro locals remained within the AFL.[15] The Negro American's distrust of the AFL was so entrenched that Randolph had to make public denials that the brotherhood entertained any notion of affiliating with the federation.[16] Furthermore, Randolph knew from experience that there was considerable hostility toward his minority group, and that an independent organization would generate additional opposition to possible Negro American success.[17]

Actually, Randolph faced two major problems in launching the brotherhood: (1) How to get the Negro American to accept the AFL as his union's sponsor in spite of the colored American's distrust of the federation, and (2) how to get the federation to charter the brotherhood as an international union on a par with white international unions. Since the first problem was internal in scope, it need not detain us here. The second was consequential because it did reflect upon the AFL's past policy toward the colored American. One of the difficulties Randolph had to face was a jurisdictional one: the Hotel and Restaurant Employees International and Bartenders League of America (Hotel Alliance) claimed jurisdiction over the brotherhood.

The Hotel Alliance's jurisdiction over "sleeping and parlor car employees"[18] extended from 1920 and formed the basis for the union's raising the question of jurisdiction when in 1928 the Brotherhood of Sleeping Car Porters sought an international charter. Instead of dealing directly with the question of jurisdiction, the federation's executive council requested the Hotel Alliance to respond to two queries: Did the union accept colored workers? and Did the union grant equal membership rights to the Negro American? The alliance responded in the affirmative to both questions.[19]

Not satisfied with these answers, the executive council decided to hold a hearing and invited both President Flore of the Hotel Alliance and A. Philip Randolph to be present. During the proceedings the executive council announced that it was inviting Randolph's brotherhood to join the ranks of traditional labor. The jurisdictional issue was bypassed when the council stated that since the executive council of the AFL has the power to issue separate charters to federal labor unions when it serves "the best interests of the trade union movement to do so," [20] it had the power to offer the Brotherhood of Sleeping Car Porters individual local affiliation with the federation. But, since the "objections of President Flore of the Hotel Alliance [were] considered sufficiently meritorious," no national charter would be issued to the brotherhood.[21]

It was interesting to note that the council asserted itself by claiming higher jurisdiction over its affiliates, because the international had failed to organize the workers under its constitutional jurisdiction. (One reason for the Hotel Alliance's previous failure to organize the Negro American was that it maintained segregated locals.[22]) Furthermore, the council's action fitted well into the straddle position established by Gompers. Thus the brotherhood was not granted an international charter and had no equal standing with other internationals in the labor movement; rather, it was split up into many federal labor unions. On this basis the Hotel Alliance claimed paper jurisdiction over the brotherhood under its charter. Actually the alliance continued to claim *de jure* jurisdiction over the brotherhood in the years that followed.[23]

Randolph had cleared his first hurdle: the AFL had recognized his organization as part of the traditional labor movement, even though it was splintered into a series of federal labor unions. He now focused his attention on how to get an international union charter with its own jurisdiction and equal status with other internationals in the AFL.

In the jurisdictional conflict between Randolph and Flore, Green followed in Gompers' footsteps by failing to threaten the expulsion of the Hotel Alliance. Unlike Gompers, he also failed to raise the question of rival union sponsorship. Green managed to prevail upon the executive council to issue federal labor union charters to the brotherhood, because the majority of the council's members were presidents of international craft unions, and the admittance of these all-Negro American federal locals posed no threat to their "lily-white" craft unions. On the other hand, it was politically expedient, since this type of affirmative action could be used to stave off left-wing domination of the colored American. Green's action left the officers of the Hotel Alliance at least two alternatives: to disaffiliate and turn independent, and/or to continue their jurisdictional fight by carrying the issue to the convention floor. The alliance decided against leaving the fold of organized labor.

Negro Americans also managed to get into some other unions based on their competitive position. A group of New York Negro American motion picture operators tried to affiliate with Local 306, International Alliance of Theatrical and Stage Employees and Moving Picture Machine Operators, between 1920 and 1924 but were consistently rejected. They formed a rival union called the United Association of Colored Motion Picture Operators, who were employed in at least eight theaters in greater New York. When Local 306 found that the colored motion picture operators were blocking their power to negotiate favorable terms with theater owners, the colored union was invited to join Local 306 as an auxiliary. It refused, and further negotiations found it obtaining full membership.[24] (The 1930's saw a repetition of the same problem, thus the acceptance of the 1920 group was mainly to control the trade rather than to change admission policy.)

The second instance resulted from the advice of Frederick Douglass, who had stated in the 1850's that the way to break the circle of discrimination was to "Learn Trades or Slave!" This instance involved a single individual, Edward Doty, a colored American, who refused to accept the closed door to apprenticeship. He started a self-study course, aided by a tutor, mastered the trade by passing a technical examination administered by the City of Chicago, and eventually gained full union membership in Local 130 of the plumbers' union. Eventually, before his retirement in 1960, he was elected business representative of his local.[25]

These two examples illustrate Douglass' thesis that the Negro American could break out of the vicious circle; that the Negro American did not seek preferential treatment; and that the Negro American did not fit the stereotype of being lazy or indolent. It also illustrated the fact that the Negro American wanted an equal opportunity to learn a trade and to be accepted on his merits in the trade union movement.

The AFL's inability, unwillingness, or ineptness to coerce its affiliates [26] into including the Negro American as a member of labor's family during the 1920's can best be illustrated by the following classification:

I. Unions excluding Negro Americans by constitutional provision.
    A. AFL affiliates:
       Switchmen's Union of North America, National Organization of Masters, Mates and Pilots of North America, Order of Railroad Telegraphers, Commercial Telegraphers Union of America, Railway Mail Association, Brotherhood of Railway Carmen,[27] Brotherhood of Railway Clerks, American Wire Weavers Protective Association, Order of Sleeping Car Conductors, and American Federation of Express Workers.
    B. Unaffiliated organizations:
       Brotherhood of Dining Car Conductors, Order of Railway Conductors, Grand International Brotherhood of Locomotive Engineers, Order of Sleeping Car Conductors, Order of Railway Expressmen, Neptune Association, American Federation of Railway Workers, Brotherhood of Station Employees and Clerks,[28] American Train Dispatchers Association, Brotherhood of Railroad Trainmen, Railroad Yardmasters of America, and Railroad Yardmasters of North America.

II. Unions excluding Negro Americans by tacit consent and/or ritual.
    A. AFL affiliates:
       International Association of Machinists, International Brotherhood of Electrical Workers, International Association of Sheet Metal Workers,[29] Operative Plasterers and Cement Finishers International Association, Flint Glass Workers of North America, International Brotherhood of Boilermakers, Shipbuilders and Helpers of America, International Association of Journeymen Plumbers and Steamfitters of the United States and Canada.

III. Unions affording Negro Americans segregated and/or auxiliary status.
    A. AFL affiliates:
       International Brotherhood of Blacksmiths, Iron Shipbuilders and Helpers of America,[30] American Federation of Teachers, United Textile Workers, Cooks and Waiters

Union,[31] Hotel and Restaurant Employees,[32] Journeymen Barbers International Union of America, Laundry Workers International Union, Brotherhood of Carpenters and Joiners of America.[33]

IV. Unions nominally affording Negro Americans "equal status": [34]
  A. International Ladies Garment Workers Union, International Association of Longshoremen, Motion Picture Projectionists Union, Journeymen Tailors' Union of America, Brotherhood of Painters, Decorators and Paperhangers of America.[35]

During the 1920's the AFL's "forced" amalgamations and mergers of various unions was done primarily to solve jurisdictional wars.[36] More often than not the merger was not based on "justice" but rather in favor of the union holding the most power. This consolidation gave a distorted view of the number of unions barring the Negro American from the organized labor movement. Thus, although the total number of internationals decreased, individual units within the internationals still practiced discrimination after their merger. This was the case even where the joint union that emerged had no constitutional ban on colored Americans. For example, when the railway clerks were merged with the International Brotherhood of Teamsters in 1926, the clerks' charter, which contained a "lily-white" clause, was revoked, since the teamsters' constitution had no such clause. The amalgamation did not mean that the newly formed locals of clerks under the jurisdiction of the teamsters abolished their former practice of banning colored Americans. The teamsters, without the benefit of a "lily-white" clause, also practiced discrimination in many of its divisions. There was evidence that the teamsters did not especially welcome Negro Americans as union members when the wagon drivers were replaced by truck drivers. Thus the shift from horse and wagon to motorized trucking saw a drop in Negro American membership from 6,000 to 313 between the years 1910 and 1928.[37] There was also the flagrant case involving the local of over-the-road drivers, which banned Negro Americans from driving a truck.

Large numbers in a union did not mean that the union maintained an open-door policy. Many craft unions have included semi-skilled workers in separate divisions, with the semi-skilled frequently outnumbering the craftsmen. The Brotherhood of Railway and Steamship Clerks, Freight Handlers, Express and Station Employees

Union, which resulted from a combination of various separate unions, found many of its former separate internationals with "lily-white" clauses in their constitutions now substituting segregated locals. (It was common in this international to denote all Negro American locals by the first digit, which was usually six.) There were other unions that restricted the Negro American to the competitive area of their trade. Thus, operating engineers had several divisions— including the stationary engineers, an old stronghold of Negro Americans. When the hoist and crane division [38] was introduced, the colored American was excluded. There was the instance of tacit consent, which continued to exist after the merger of the steamfitters and plumbers, now making one union that practiced discrimination where formerly there were two.

To summarize, amalgamation or merger offered the incorrect impression of a decrease in the number of unions discriminating against the Negro American, since such consolidation placed the total jurisdiction of two or more previous unions under a single banner but left discriminatory practices untouched. Thus the areas formerly closed to the Negro American continued, even though the number of unions decreased.

The 1920's ended with a decline in union membership and the enlargement of individual international union jurisdiction [39] because of changing materials and methods. A change of jurisdiction was also necessary for many unions to enable them to control the job market and to survive financially. This decade saw an increased control of the Negro American through the use of segregated and auxiliary locals.[40]

The advent of the 1930's with its National Industrial Recovery Act (NIRA, commonly referred to as the National Recovery Act, NRA) and the push by the AFL to organize the unorganized in mass-production industries seemed promising for Negro Americans. Many flocked into federal labor unions formed in such industries as steel, rubber, and auto. However the promise of equal recognition in the house of labor was short-lived. International unions with jurisdiction over crafts in these industries pulled out the craftsmen and left the unskilled and semiskilled to flounder. The AFL's craft union philosophy, including its attempt to organize workers into federal labor unions, failed and was partly responsible for the formation of the Committee of Industrial Organizations (CIO). Many writers felt that the formation of the CIO would be the Negro American's salvation. Mary Heaton Vorse wrote:

> Kept out of many AFL unions, the Negro worker will never again be isolated and friendless within the labor movement, for the CIO organizes without regard to color, creed or nationality.[41]

This generalization proved to be incorrect, as can be illustrated by the more obvious examples of the United Auto Workers' (UAW) Skilled Trades Department, which followed a policy very similar to that of the old-line AFL craft unions; the United Steel Workers with its separate seniority lists; and the Transport Workers under the leadership of the late Michael Quill in the privately owned BMT and IRT subway lines in New York City during the late 1930's and early 1940's.

During the 1930's there were at least two additional writers, H. Harris[42] and C. L. Franklin,[43] who thought that the needle trades unions were "hospitable" toward the Negro American. It was not to be disputed that both the International Ladies Garment Workers Union (ILGWU) and the Amalgamated Clothing Workers of America had Negro Americans in their New York locals; it was disputable as to whether these unions practiced "egalitarianism." Both unions accepted the colored American primarily as a means of controlling the trade, but they restricted him to the least skilled trades (finishers, cleaners, and pressers). Control over these workers was essential to carry on effective collective bargaining in the industries. Secondly, the ILGWU accepted the bulk of its Negro American membership during organizing drives, taking the Negro American into the union in order to make a union shop rather than to organize colored Americans per se.

Unionization of the colored Americans neglected a crucial issue: What occupations were open to these black Americans? What chance of upward economic mobility was available through a seniority system? The cutters' locals of both unions had no Negro American behind a pair of shears. It was little different in the Hat, Cap, and Millinery Workers Union (occasionally referred to as the "Headgear Workers"), which excluded its colored workers from hat blocking, a skilled craft. Although the leaders of these three unions had socialist beginnings and preached government ownership of the means of production, in the trade they practiced the usual business unionism associated with the crafts.

Doctor Franklin[44] cited two reasons for the "new position of Negro American workers during the NRA period":

(1) the more friendly attitude of white workers toward the acceptance of Negro workers into their unions, and (2) the new attitude of Negro workers themselves toward taking the risk involved in first steps of unionization of workers.

Franklin alleged that this "more friendly attitude" was built on the fact that many unions sought to build up their membership while the time was ripe for organization (the 7a clause in the NIRA), and they also sought "to control all workers in industries" under their jurisdiction. Furthermore, Dr. Franklin suggested that this new interest in organizing the Afro American was due to "a slight shift from race consciousness to class consciousness."

His conclusion was questionable. A primary reason for organizing the colored women—the latter predominated in the least skilled and lowest paying jobs in a low paying industry—was to obtain control over the shops and to hold on to the union's white membership. Negro Americans constituted about 6 per cent of the garment workers in New York City in 1934.[45] On the other hand there were some new unions that tried to organize the Afro American during the 1930's, like some locals of the Upholsterers Carpet and Linoleum Mechanics International Union of America and the Furniture Workers of America. These unions were dominated by a Marxist philosophy.

Miss E. Kine's [46] study of the needle trades during the early 1930's supported the contention that unions were more interested in controlling their trades than in accepting a change in race consciousness. She reported that before the summer of 1933 there were very few Afro-Americans organized in the garment industry. Most of the 5,000 colored—out of some 90,000 employed in the dress shops—had gained employment because of the labor shortage brought on by World War I and the cessation of immigration. These Negro Americans were hesitant to join unions because of their previously unhappy experience with union practices and a fear that unionization would mean the loss of their jobs. The grounds for their hesitancy were: (1) equal pay and working conditions would mean substitution of white for colored, and (2) equal status in the union would mean the preferential placement of whites.

Although Dr. Franklin was aware of the need for unions to control their respective industries, he believed that labor was really concerned with the colored worker, per se. He attempted to establish his point by comparing union membership between 1928 and 1934 and finding that Colored American union membership had jumped from 3.8 to 9.3 per cent.[47] Still, he acknowledged that this increase was to be found primarily in

> unskilled labor such as transportation and communication work and domestic service. . . . On the other hand, Negro membership in unions of the highly skilled workers [was] negligible.

In another part of his dissertation Franklin revealed that even the much eulogized ILGWU was organizing the colored worker in order to control the trade rather than to elevate the Afro-American's economic status. Colored Americans in the largest union of the needle trades were found mainly in locals consisting of semi-skilled and unskilled persons. The highly skilled crafts, such as the cutters and the operators, had no colored membership.[48]

A similar pattern was found in the domestic and personal service unions, as revealed by the membership of the International Union of Building Service Employees. The largest number were in the General Building Service Workers local, with some 9,000 Negro Americans out of a total membership of 31,800; the majority of these colored Americans were porters and clean-up men and women. In locals of the same international that had jurisdiction over the more highly paid occupations, such as the Hotel and Apartment Workers, there were two Negro Americans out of a total membership of 1,472.[49] Franklin failed to make an important distinction in the crafts between "A" Journeymen and "B" members, a distinction common in such unions as the plumbers, electricians, and carpenters.[50] He did recognize in passing that most craft unions banned the Negro American from membership, as was evidenced by Local 28 of the Sheet Metal Workers Union and Local 40 of the Ornamental and Structural Iron Workers Union.

During the 1930's and later, many craft unions did not expressly bar the Negro American from their unions by constitutional provision. Instead, they resorted to such means as tacit consent and ritual. *The Electrical World's* editorial stated:

> We do not want the Negro in the IBEW, but we think that they should be organized in locals of their own, affiliated with the American Federation of Labor as that organization knows no creed or color.[51]

Continued adherence to the sense of this editorial was illustrated in 1936. The New York *Times* reported that, following a successful strike involving Local 3 of the International Brotherhood of Electrical Workers (IBEW) and the Standard Equipment Company of Long Island City, the union refused to accept Negro Americans who had been asked to march on the picket line. The attorney for this minority group alleged that letters were sent to both the national headquarters in Washington, D.C., and to the local in New York requesting an explanation for this local's refusal to admit these former plant workers into the union. The president of Local 3 acknowledged receipt of such a letter and explained that he had turned the matter over to the local's business agent. The latter ignored the request for an explanation.[52]

To illustrate that labor had not shifted from race consciousness to class consciousness, a check of unions that were still discriminating at the end of the 1930's shows: [53]

I. Unions excluding Negro Americans by constitutional provision:
   A. AFL affiliates:
      Masters, Mates and Pilots, Locals 1 and 88; Telegraphers Union of North America, Commercial, Eastern Brokers Division; Brotherhood of Railway and Steamship Employees; International Association of Insulators and Asbestos Workers, Heat and Frost, Local 12; Wire Weavers Protective Association; Order of Switchmen's Union of North America; American Railway Association.
   B. Unaffiliated organizations:
      Order of Railway Conductors; Brotherhood of Locomotive Firemen and Engineers; Brotherhood of Railroad Trainmen; Order of Train Dispatchers' Association; Marine Firemen, Oilers and Water Tenders and Wipers Association of the Pacific.

II. Unions excluding Negro Americans by tacit consent and/or ritual.
   A. AFL affiliates:
      International Association of Machinists, District 15; Brooklyn Metal Trades Council, Local 132, Field Construction Lodge Local 295; United Association of Journeymen and Apprentices of the Plumbing and Pipe Fitting Industry of the U.S. and Canada, Locals 1 and 2; International Association of Bridge, Structural and Ornamental Iron Work-

ers, Local 40; Amalgamated Clothing Workers of America, Locals 246 (Shirt Makers, Cutters), Local 248 (Shirt Makers, Operators); United Neckwear, Local 251; International Ladies Garment Workers Union, Local 10 (Cutters), Local 82 (Examiners and Bushelers), Local 1 (Cloak and Suit Operators); United Garment Workers of America, Local 3 (Tailors, Coatmakers), Local 8 (Tailors, Pants Makers); United Hatters, Cap and Millinery Workers International Union, Local 7, (Hat Trimmers); International Union of Elevator Constructors, Local 1 (Elevator Constructors); Hotel and Restaurant Employees International Alliance and Bartenders International League of America, Local 1 (Waiters and Waitresses), Local 3 (Bartenders); International Association of Sheet Metal Workers, Local 28 and Local 137; International Brotherhood of Electrical Workers, Local 3 and Local 277 (Marine Electrical Workers); Journeyman Barbers International Union, Local 1 and 3.

B. Unaffiliated organizations:
Marine Engineers Beneficial Association, Local 33; United Licensed Officers of the U.S. of America.[54]

III. Unions offering some Negro Americans segregated and/or auxiliary status:
A. AFL affiliates:
United Brotherhood of Carpenters and Joiners, Local 1888; International Seamen's Union of America; Cooks and Stewards Union of the Atlantic and Gulf Marine; Hotel and Restaurant Employees International Alliance and Bartenders International League of America, Local 370 (Dining Car Employees—all Negro American).

IV. Unions offering Negro Americans "nominal equal status."
A. AFL affiliates:
Motion Picture Projectionists, Local 306; International Association of Longshoremen. (There was an all Negro American local in Brooklyn, but no permanent piers were assigned to them.)

One additional incident will help to illustrate that the AFL had not changed its attitude from race consciousness to class consciousness. Some 4,000 longshoremen, "mostly Negroes employed as freight handlers on railway piers in the port of New York," sought union membership in the railway union. Since this union by constitution did not accept Negro Americans, they remained unorganized. When the late president of the longshoremen's union tried to organize them into his union, Green told him: "You cannot organize them as longshoremen because they are railway employees." [55] This ended an attempt to bring the colored longshoremen into the fold of organized labor.

World War II, accompanied by a wave of patriotism and the need to keep the boys at the front properly supplied, found little amelioration of race consciousness. President Franklin Delano Roosevelt issued a special executive order creating the Fair Employment Practices Committee (FEPC). The committee found Afro-Americans being excluded by unions in wartime even as they had been in peacetime. One manifestation was segregated job placement, since integration in employment would mean close contact between whites and Negro Americans. The Oil Transfer Company was a case in point. G. A. Weston, a man with 21 years of culinary experience at sea, was referred to the company by the War Manpower Commission (WMC) as a sea cook. He passed the company's physical examination and was told to report to the captain of the tugboat. When Weston was refused permission to begin his work assignment, he reported back to the WMC, which filed a complaint with the FEPC.

On Feb. 14, 1945, the personnel manager of the Oil Transfer Company telephoned the FEPC's investigator and disclaimed any company responsibility for charges filed against it. Management maintained that the captain of the tugboat had been instructed to place the new colored cook. On the very day that Weston was hired, Captain Bradley, then president of the International Longshoremen's Association, Marine Division, telephoned the company's personnel manager and specifically informed him that the white crew would leave the boat if a colored cook was hired. [56]

At least two other unions, both in the airlines industry, banned the Negro American. They were the Airline Pilots Association, AFL-CIO, and the Flight Engineers International Association, AFL-CIO. [57] During the 1940's there were at least five other AFL craft unions that practiced "partial restriction in employment," a more refined method of controlling the Negro American's economic outlets. There were some unions that had all-colored auxiliaries for Negro Americans, even though the union's constitution had no specific color ban. The Brotherhood of Blacksmiths, Dropforgers and Helpers Union [58] and the International Association of

Sheet Metal Workers [59] had separate auxiliaries in accord with their by-laws. Article 28 of the Blacksmiths' Constitution read:

> Sec. 1. Where there are sufficient colored helpers an auxiliary is to be set up under the jurisdiction of a white local.
> Sec. 2. Members of auxiliary locals composed of colored helpers shall not transfer, except to another auxiliary local composed of colored members, and colored helpers will not be promoted to blacksmiths' or helpers' apprentices and will not be permitted to shops where white helpers are now employed.[60]

One union whose constitution made no mention of the Negro American, the Seafarers' International Union of North America (SIU), discriminated against the colored American by maintaining two hiring halls until late in 1944: [61] One was for the exclusive placement of whites and the other for Negro Americans. Furthermore, after both hiring halls were merged, the Negro American was restricted to two occupations: fireman and steward. Even in these classifications there was discrimination, since firemen were confined to coal-burning vessels and black stewards to all-Negro American sculleries.

Comments attributed to various union officials established the fact that the union practiced retrenchment in employment. John Hawk, secretary-treasurer of the SIU, allegedly made such statements, as cited in a letter sent by C. S. Vincent, the New York regional representative of Recruitment and Manning Operations of the War Shipping Administration (RMO), to his superior in Washington, D.C., Vincent stated:

> On several occasions, Mr. Hawk has called me to object to our policy of referring Negroes . . .
>
> The SIU maintain[ed] in the port of New York, a separate department and dispatcher for Negro seamen. Negroes [were] assigned to ships by this union only in the Steward's Department, although only a fraction of the total number of ships for which they hold contracts carry an all Negro Steward Department.
>
> On January 30, 1943, Mr. Hawk called me and stated: "You are interfering with our hiring hall." . . . Mr. Hawk [also] stated [neither] the President [of the U.S.] nor anyone else

[was] going to tell men with whom they [were going] to live
and to a seaman a ship is his home.[62]

That no collusion between the union and management existed
in this case was supported by at least ten letters on file with FEPC.
These letters were copies of ones sent to the union, and each
specifically stated that all hiring was to be done solely on the basis
of qualifications, not color.[63]

There were other unions that claimed to practice full acceptance of Negro Americans. However, investigation found that they
practiced employment retrenchment—preferential placement of
whites. One such union segregated its colored members by circumscribing their employment to a fixed geographic area. This type of
artificial restriction made equal employment opportunities a farce. In
the category of full acceptance it was found that there was a high
correlation between hiring and refusal to upgrade, making this category a misnomer.

The Garage Carwashers and Cleaners Union, as well as the
Motion Picture Projectionists Union, Local 306, maintained mixed
membership and claimed to offer "equal occupational status" and
equal placement of its employed on a seniority basis. Still, an official state investigation revealed that the garage carwashers consistently refused to send out an unemployed Negro American member as long as a white union member was unemployed.[64] Again in
1938, Local 306 of the Motion Picture Projectionists Union refused to accept qualified Negro American projectionists. Persistent
demands on the part of its former Afro-American members finally
brought about a partial change in the Union's attitude. This time
15 nonunion colored projectionists were involved, all of whom were
employed in Harlem. The union stipulated that nine would be accepted on the condition that three of them would relinquish their
jobs to whites. If the proposal had been accepted, it would have
meant that out of the 15 applying for membership, nine would become unemployed: the original six, who would not be accepted by
the union and thus forced out of their jobs; plus three of the nine
accepted, who would also have to turn over their jobs to whites in
exchange for union membership.[65]

Not satisfied with employment retrenchment, the Motion Pic-
ture Projectionists Union practiced segregation in employment—all
Afro-American union members were restricted to Harlem.[66] The
United Brotherhood of Carpenters and Joiners of America and the
International Longshoremen's Association employed similar devices.

When Local 1888 of the Carpenters Union was first organized shortly after World War I, it had a mixed membership; its white members had been refused membership in white locals. In time these white members were able to transfer to all white locals in the city, thus creating an all-Negro American local.[67] To maintain this type of segregation, colored American carpenters seeking union membership were referred to Local 1888.[68] To understand what this meant, it was necessary to examine the Carpenter's Constitution.

The constitution required that a district council be established where two or more locals existed within a given geographic area; in turn, the council would assign geographic jurisdiction to each local under its command.[69] Local 1888 was assigned to Harlem, an area that had little new construction and had to rely mainly on alteration work. This geographic jurisdiction was subject to gerrymandering, and it did occur. Despite the fact that each local has its own area, sister locals could call upon Local 1888 for mechanics when they deemed it necessary. Professor G. Peterson summed up the practices of the carpenters union as follows:

> The carpenters and painters usually admit them [Negro Americans] into separate locals and sometimes allow them to accept employment only under Negro contractors.[70]

The situation in the Painters Union, at least around New York, has changed considerably and will be commented on later.

Following the 1899 waterfront strike, the Italian local of the International Longshoremen's Association (ILA) opened its doors to Negro American membership.[71] However, this did not bring with it the usual perquisites—assignment to specific wharves.[72] Professor E. F. Frazier [73] stressed this inequality in the 1920's and as recently as 1960 believed that the problem still existed.

In 1944, Prof. Herbert Northrup reemphasized the fact that the ILA's Constitution made no mention of spatial limitation with respect to the employment of Negro Americans on the waterfront. Still, the bulk of colored longshoremen were confined to one Brooklyn local, and no specific wharves were assigned to them. (Anastasia, ILA president, merged his local 1814 with the Negro American local, promising that its members would be assigned permanent places on the waterfront.) Despite the practices of discrimination, various longshore union officials went on record as being opposed to discrimination in employment based on color.

Conversations with colored longshoremen in the early 1960's indicated that the situation was stagnant.[74]

At this stage in our history (1950), New York City locals
practicing discrimination against Negro Americans included:

I. Unions excluding Negro Americans by constitutional provision.[75]

   A. AFL affiliates:
American Railway Association; Commercial Telegraphers
Union, Local 16, Brokers Division, Marine Division, Tele-
graph Division; National Organization of Masters, Mates
and Pilots, Local 88; Order of Switchmen's Union of North
America, Railroad Telegraphers; Wire Weavers Protective
Association; Airline Pilots Association; Flight Engineers In-
ternational Association.[76]

   B. Unaffiliated organizations:
Locomotive Engineers; Brotherhood of Railroad Trainmen;
Brotherhood of Railway Conductors; Order of Train Dis-
patchers' Association; American Locomotive Firemen and
Enginemen; International Association of Machinists, Dis-
trict 15; Brooklyn Metal Trades Council, Local 132; Field
Construction Lodge, Local 205, . . .[77]

Marine Firemen; Oilers and Water Tenders and Wipers
Association of the Pacific.[78]

II. Unions excluding Negro Americans by tacit consent.

   A. AFL affiliates:
Asbestos Workers, Heat and Frost Insulators, Local 12; In-
ternational Brotherhood of Electrical Workers, Local 3 and
Local 277; Marine Electrical Workers; Plumbers and Steam-
fitters, Locals 1 and 2, and 374; Brooklyn and Queens County
Plumbers Apprentices Local 638; Enterprise Association of
Steamfitters, Local 639; Steamfitters' Helpers Local 711 of
the Brooklyn Navy Yard; Sheetmetal Workers Local 28;
Brewery Workers, Local 1345.[79]

III. Unions affording Negro Americans only segregated and/or auxiliary status.

   A. AFL affiliates:
Brotherhood of Blacksmiths, Drop Forgers and Helpers,
Local 28; Brotherhood of Boilermakers, Iron Shipbuilders,

Welders and Helpers, Locals 2, 21, 43, and 200; [80] Seafarers' International Union of North America; Brotherhood of Railway and Steamship Clerks, Freight Handlers, Express and Station Employees; Brotherhood of Express Division and the New York Central System, Brotherhood of Maintenance of Way Employees.

IV. Unions affording Negro Americans "nominal equal status."
Motion Picture Projectionists, Local 306; Brotherhood of Carpenters and Joiners of America; International Association of Longshoremen; International Ladies Garment Workers, Local 10.[81]

The list does not pretend to be exhaustive, but merely illustrative. Thus in the late 1950's some authors [82] gave the CIO a clean bill. Unfortunately, they failed to differentiate between the unions' formal constitutions and the everyday practices of local affiliates.

There were at least two international presidents who fought their own locals to eliminate discriminatory practices. They were Ralph Helstein [83] of the United Packing House Workers, and O. H. Knight of the Oil, Chemical and Atomic Workers Union; but the local practice of discrimination persisted.[84]

Changes in public opinion and the law did not deter many unions from circumventing the law and continuing to ban the Negro American from their jurisdiction. The 1950 list of unions given above illustrates how many unions evaded the Ives-Quinn Act, passed by the New York State Legislature in 1945.[85] This law banned unions from having "lily-white" clauses in their constitutions. To evade the law many resorted to ritual, or tacit consent; a few even to "tokenism."

To gain membership in most craft unions a person had to have completed an approved apprenticeship training program, and in some instances only programs sponsored by a particular craft union's local. The latter was the case with IBEW's Local 3. Another international, the bricklayers, had the classification of "Improver," a person who has had some experience in the trade outside an approved training program. The improver could take a qualifying test, pass it, and become a union member; however, this classification was not accepted by the New York Bricklayers Council. Thus the elimination of the "lily-white" clause did not open up the apprenticeship rolls to the Negro American. Even when a union was forced to accept a particular individual, it had means of making things so distasteful, that the man would leave the trade. Although the ILA in New York had Negro American membership, no Negro American gang had a permanent pier.[86]

The various laws in effect by the end of the 1950's forced the unions to seek a means of diverting legal and public interest from their discriminatory practices. To accomplish this, many unions either stepped up or initiated a policy of "tokenism." It soon became difficult to prove that a union had no Negro American members. Thus Local 2 of the plumbers had three "A" Negro American journeymen on its books, but rarely were they found employed on construction with other "A" men. More often than not these men were shunted into alterations, at a lower hourly rate and with less regular work.[87] There was the instance of a Negro American electrician with an "A" journeyman's card who was sent to the Riverton Houses when they were built in 1947. At first the foreman told him that a mistake must have been made: Negro Americans just were not employed on this project. After a few telephone calls from the union, the foreman accepted the colored worker, but subjected him to the usual treatment. He was placed in the "hole" to bend pipe all day, a task usually reserved for advanced apprentices, and was kept at this work for a whole month. At the end of this time the foreman, seeing that this worker would not quit, transferred him to regular journeyman's work.[88]

The point we are stressing is that even admittance to union membership was still a bar to equal opportunity in both craft and noncraft unions. Illustrative of a noncraft union employing similar tactics was the International Longshoremen's Association. When the all-Negro-American local merged with Local 1814—with the promise that it would get some pier it could call its own—some 1,500 Negro Americans gave up their independence. By the end of the 1950's they were still "casuals." The failure to have their economic status changed was illustrated by the fact that by the early 1960's only 700 Negro Americans held membership in good standing in Local 1814. The remainder were dropped for nonpayment of dues.[89]

Civil rights agitation was revived during the first half of the 1960's, reminiscent in kind if not degree of the late 1870's. The years 1960–1965 saw passage of the Federal Civil Rights Act and more intense activity on the part of New York State's Human Rights Commission and even the City of New York's Human Rights Commission. Also, increased verbal interest in civil rights was stressed by top officials of the AFL-CIO. Pres. George Meany admitted that the AFL-CIO had been ineffectual in coping with the minority problem in the craft union sector and publicly mentioned the need for federal intervention.[90] Meany's statement was subject to various interpretations: (1) He was addressing a skilled labor group when he made his speech and was probably hinting that unless organized labor changed its attitude toward colored minorities, the federal government might try new legislation; or (2) he was suggesting that the AFL-CIO was powerless to bring about any change because of its structural and other deficiencies, reinforcing the idea that federal intervention was necessary; or (3) he was making an effort to ward off public indignation.

Such comments are based on the fact that in at least three instances Meany tried to "coerce" his affiliates to modify their admission policies with respect to colored persons. One occasion involved his home local in New York, Plumbers Local 2. In this instance he worked behind the scenes but failed to prevail on the local leadership to change its policy. The other two instances involved the plumbers in Cleveland, Ohio, and the electricians in Washington, D.C. Finally, Meany realized his wish: the federal government passed the Civil Rights Act in 1964, and Section VII of the act affected unions; the act for unions took effect in September, 1965. In New York, as of 1966, this new civil rights act had only superficially achieved privileges for minority group members. The bulk of so-called new opportunities fell into the category of "tokenism."

On or about Aug. 2, 1960, the Negro American Labor Committee conducted a survey of nine unions, only three of which had Negro American membership, and one of these three offered only Class B membership. Although one local—Local 3 of the IBEW— claimed some 50 Negro American members in its "A" division, only about 10 were actively employed in construction. District 9 of the Painters Union had a large quota of colored Americans. Exploration in depth of this craft revealed that admittance was granted primarily to control unwanted competition, since the skill factor has reached a low ebb. Currently, very few of the mechanics know how to mix colors or do specialized work.[91] Many of the newcomers, chiefly Puerto Ricans, were taken into the union or into the apprenticeship training program because it was necessary to control the trade.[92]

In 1961, Negro Americans still found that many unions whose constitutions had no written clause banning them offered only second-class membership. Three Negro American members of the ILA give some evidence as to local practices. The work history of each [93] showed a pattern of constant transfer from one local to another in the hope that they would get equal opportunity to work. Each man's story revealed that New York City locals failed to follow even their own seniority rules. Two of the individuals exhausted the internal union machinery without gaining satisfaction. The third filed a formal complaint with the State Commission Against Discrimination (SCAD).[94]

The charge included the following facts: (1) The complainant first got his job as driver (fork-lift) after filing a complaint against the Grace Lines, whom he charged with a refusal to hire him because of his color. (Following the filing, Grace Lines hired its first colored American driver.) (2) The complainant shaped up for employment on Dec. 15, 1960, at the Waterfront Commission's Information Center and was told to report later in the day for employment. As was customary, he left his seniority card with the hiring agent. When he reported for work the timekeeper informed the complainant that his card had been picked up by the union's business agent. (3) The complainant telephoned the business agent, who informed him that his seniority card had been forwarded to the New York Shipping Association's ILA seniority board and that the latter had ruled that he was in the wrong work section. The board's action caused the complainant to initiate a series of grievance actions until he had exhausted the union's internal administrative machinery. (4) The complainant having failed to gain satisfaction, he resorted to the filing of a formal complaint with SCAD. About three years after the initial complaint was filed, the commission decided in favor of the complainant. Local 791 then appealed the commission's action in the courts.[95]

The Attorney General of the State of New York [96] undertook an investigation of longshoring, with particular reference to luxury-liner piers, commonly referred to as Section 7 area. Local 824 held jurisdiction over this area, with a regular membership of about 1,000 plus some 175 men on extra labor lists. There was not one Negro American in the entire group, even though there were about 5,000 Negro American longshoremen in the New York port. Incidentally, the president of Local 824 was an officer of the ILA's Civil Rights Committee.

The trowel trade, long known for its Negro American membership, has developed various techniques to discriminate against the colored craftsman. Illustrative of the situation was the allegation made by Waven O. Webb,[97] a member of Bricklayers Local 41, who claimed that the union's officials had failed to process his grievances against two employers and some of his fraternal brothers. After exhausting the union's grievance machinery, he filed a formal complaint with SCAD on Oct. 25, 1960.[98] He alleged that Negro American members of the union were generally restricted to rough work—flats, bowling alleys, and the like. Also he named an employer whose foreman had refused him a shift with the gang for finish work. Webb cited a second experience with a contractor for the construction of the Kew Gardens Criminal Court Building in Queens County. The complainant alleged that each company had released him from its employ when he requested their respective foremen to allow him to continue work with his regular gang—a shift from rough work to finish work.

Prior to Webb's filing a formal complainant with SCAD, he presented his case to the shop steward, and when the latter refused to act upon it, Webb contacted the business agent. The agent sided with the company foreman. Next, Webb sent a registered letter to the New York executive committee, which remanded the case back to Local 41. Following Webb's filing of a formal complaint with SCAD, he had more steady employment even though it continued to be rough work.

During a conference with Andrew Lawler,[99] secretary of the New York City's Executive Committee of the Bricklayers, Masons and Plasterers International Union of America, Webb's grievance was raised and Lawler neither affirmed nor denied that the committee had failed to process the grievance in accord with its by-laws. There was no reason given for Webb's being confined to rough work. Webb contended that he was well qualified to do finish work, and based his contention on the following: (1) He had had experience with finish work and had been a member of two other New York locals for at least 11 years prior to his current grievance; (2) had served his apprenticeship at Hampton Institute, whose standards are reputed to be at least equal, if not superior, to those of many formally recognized apprenticeship training programs in the trowel trades.

Negro American carpenters found a similar situation. Fred Andrews,[100] secretary of the all-Negro-American Local 1888, stated that his local's problem was a lack of Afro-American contractors to hire his men. This meant that the local's members could get employment out of sister locals only when the white locals' needs exceeded their membership. Four or five other Afro-American carpenters [101] agreed with the following statement by Andrews:

Negro American Carpenters get the harsh and roughest work, for example, work on subways, calling for the lifting of 12' x 12' and 8' x 10' supports. [Carpenter locals turn to Mr. Tumins, business agent for 1888, when] they need men for flat arch work, for finishing work they go to white locals.[102]

The number of Negro American carpenters doing finish work was limited to about two per local, and there were 26 locals in the Greater New York area.[103]

The total membership of the New York District Council was approximately 35,000; of this number about 2,835 were Negro Americans. The important factor was the markedly uneven distribution of Negro Americans among the 26 locals, a large percentage being in Local 1888. A random sampling of two locals showed further imbalance: Local 257 had a membership of some 3,000, which included a maximum of some 50 colored, or about 1.5 per cent of the total; and Local 2305, with a membership of some 700, had 35 Negro Americans, or approximately 5 per cent.[104] It should be reiterated that union membership did not mean equal opportunity in employment either in the construction sector (better known as outside work) or the shop (inside work). Furthermore, membership did not include continued employment when the gang shifted from rough to finish work.

Negro American employment in the construction sector of our economy between 1910 and 1960 was summarized by Rear Admiral R. K. James.[105]

(1) Open access to plumbing and pipefitting apprenticeship [was] controlled by the Plumbers Union; and (2) Similarly, Negro youth [was] almost completely excluded by the Sheet Metal Workers Union, the Lathers and Plasterers' Union, the Ornamental and Structural Iron Workers Union and from other craft unions operating in the construction industry. (3) [Among the most important of the building trades unions was the Carpenters and they] severely limited [Negro American employment] by organizing segregated Negro locals and giving them jurisdiction over areas where there was little or no construction, or prospect of construction.

Furthermore, Negro American locals were subject to jurisdictional raids by all-white units. Consequently, the restrictions in employment possibilities forced many Negro American carpenters to leave the trade.[106]

Restricted economic mobility of Negro Americans was not confined to minority men, as was demonstrated in the needle trades.

> Negro and Puerto Rican women who [were] on the lowest rungs of the city's economic ladder [became] important in the New York garment industry, but they [were restricted] mainly to the more standardized branches and with few exceptions . . . [did] not become highly skilled tailor-system workers on dresses or "cloaks."

The failure to upgrade these minority women caused a shortage of skilled sewing machine operators.[107]

Charles S. Zimmerman, a vice president of the International Ladies Garment Workers Union, conceded:

> We still have problems in our own ranks—but we are always working to fight discrimination in the ranks and fighting for legislation against discrimination.[108]

It should be noted that the same Mr. Zimmerman was chairman of the Civil Rights Committee of the AFL-CIO, and his statement reflected the views of George Meany. Both implied that the top echelons of organized labor sought relief through legislation rather than through internal control of organized labor.

Another member of the AFL-CIO's Civil Rights Committee, George M. Harrison, formerly grand president of the Brotherhood of Railway and Steamship Clerks Union, said: "In some places Negroes have their own charters. They do not want to be amalgamated. They feel they can get a better deal that way than in mixed locals." [109] Harrison implied that the power structure in mixed locals was stacked against the colored American, and that seniority was not always used properly. Many Negro American members of the union not only espoused this sentiment but also went further to say that colored members were kept in reserve and sent out only when there were no white unemployed union men. In his comment, Harrison neglected to mention that his colored membership was rather unhappy with union practices, and that intensified civil rights activity had caused the union to change its numbering system. Thus, for many years prior to 1960, all locals with the number

6,000 were known as segregated locals. This number was changed in 1960 to 3,000 to give the impression that desegation was taking place.

As in the late 1870's, so again in the 1960's, the civil rights movement attacked the craft unions, especially the construction trades, because they continued to neglect their minority group members. The revival of the underdog's cause was illustrated in a New York *Times* editorial. It stated that acceptance of Negro Americans and Puerto Ricans as "fringe members" by some craft unions was intolerable. "These low paid workers . . . merit primary attention." This contention was based in part on the extreme inequity between two divisions in the same local union. Thus, the hourly fringe benefits of division "A" members equaled the hourly rates paid to Negro American members of the manufacturing division. To make the case more extreme, the "A" division's members were guaranteed five hours of overtime each week, the latter amounted to about $33. This represented about 66 per cent of the manufacturing division's regular 40-hour weekly earnings. The ratio assumed that these "fringe members" worked full weeks.[110] The fact that the manufacturing division was subject to a "high rate of unemployment . . . chronically . . . through the years." [111]

The local's business manager addressed the 22d annual apprenticeship class in 1962 and gave substance to the above contention. He stated that "unemployment [was] a cancer on the economic and political body of our nation." [112] Incidentally, out of the total of 136 newly graduated journeymen, only one was a Negro American. Attitudes similar to that expressed in the New York *Times'* editorial must have put some pressure on this local, since it sought in 1962 to decrease the weekly work hours from 40 to 37 and increase the minimum hourly rate from $1.25 to $1.40 for its "fringe members." The local's belated interest in its underprivileged took on further significance when the same business manger stated that

> if, as expected, present trends continue, the manpower needs of the coming years will place a premium on skilled manpower, and those who lack adequate training will face increasing employment difficulties.[113]

Instead of trying to upgrade the local's "fringe members," the union sought to relieve the shortage of skilled manpower by importing journeymen from sister locals outside of New York. These men were referred to as "temps": persons with temporary work permits, who ordinarily could not transfer to this local. To effectuate a permanent transfer, these journeymen would have had to work out of the local for at least two years. However, the local's policy was to renew work permits for less than the required period of time. Hence, even though there was a labor shortage, the local did little to upgrade its union members. This local currently permits children of members other than "A" journeymen to compete for enrollment in its apprenticeship program if the father has been a member in good standing for at least ten years.

The renewed interest in civil rights was also evidenced by Stanley Lowell, who stated that

> the battle for economic equality and job opportunity [was] increasing in its intensity. . . . One out of every two Negro and Puerto Rican workers was unemployed at some time during 1961. . . . [thus] members of minority groups, were unemployed at two-and-a-half times greater than that of white workers.[114]

Lowell's remarks followed the announcement by Mayor Robert F. Wagner that the city's contract compliance program was to be enforced. This statement had no real significance, since legal prohibitions had existed in the administrative code for at least 20 years prior to the Mayor's announcement. Wagner's statement preceded his Executive Order No. 4, which was primarily a reiteration of Section 343-8.0 of the Administrative Code of the City of New York.[115] The governor of New York State, not to be outmaneuvered politically, sent a bill to the legislature outlawing discrimination in apprenticeship training by labor organizations.[116] Although both political announcements were intended to apply pressure on the labor unions, neither had its intended effect.

Public sentiment coupled with the President's Committee on Equal Employment brought further pressure on the unions. There was even a pledge on the part of 87 international unions to "abolish all racially segregated locals and to accept all eligible applicants." [117] This pledge failed to mention any extension of the apprenticeship rolls to minority groups. (It is the apprenticeship program that is the main source of craft union membership.) Furthermore, the abolition of racially segregated locals did not mean that minority group members would enjoy equal occupational mobility within the unions' jurisdiction. It was less than a fortnight later, at the White

House, that other international union officials "jumped on the band wagon." Now, 114 international unions, or

> nearly 90 percent of the membership of the AFL-CIO pledged to eliminate discrimination and unfair practices wherever they existed within labor's ranks.[118]

The agreement between top labor officials and government was similar to industry's program—"Plans for Progress." Both programs were voluntary, and both had failed to achieve their goals as of 1965. The Civil Rights Act with its Title VII especially relevant to labor unions, which was passed in 1964 to take effect in late 1965, again revealed the need to supplement the voluntary agreement.

There was at least one major dissimilarity between the two groups: whereas corporation officials had both the authority and responsibility to enforce nondiscrimination in employment and upgrading, top labor officials lacked the authority to carry out their pledge because their subsidiaries were largely autonomous. Still, the balance sheet did reveal a surplus in terms of an extremely healthy spirit. On occasion the spirit acquired corporeal being. For example, there was Local 3, of the IBEW, probably the only local in its international that opened a special apprenticeship program to minority groups in 1962.[119] However, further examination revealed that even this program had hidden gremlins. The 1962 group did not form part of the local's regular apprenticeship program. The special program was to be for four years, as opposed to the local's regular five-year apprenticeship program. Those completing the four-year program were to form a new division, "adequate-wiring"—rewiring homes inadequately wired to meet modern electrical appliance needs. Furthermore, it was meant to be a one-shot deal, since the regular apprenticeship program recruited each year. As of 1967 there had been no new four-year classes initiated.

The idea of the four-year program for minorities arose when the local sought a rather unique contract—a 25-hour week plus a guarantee of five hours overtime each week, with overtime at time and one half. The public outcry that resulted from the fact that there was already a shortage of men in the field and that the shorter hours would create a hardship, brought the union's agreement to an impartial survey of future manpower needs, a study conducted by labor mediator Theodore Kheel at the Mayor's request. Kheel's findings revealed that there would continue to be a shortage equal to, if not greater than, that which existed under the union's old contract—30 hours plus five hours overtime each week. It was therefore agreed to open the apprenticeship program. Recruitment was by special examination, supervised by the late Dean Carman of Columbia University. The total number admitted was about 1,020, with a goodly portion of Negro Americans and Puerto Ricans. The dropout rate reached about 65 per cent at the end of two years, a rate more than twice as great as that which prevailed in the local's regular apprenticeship program.

Another instance involved federal employees, members of the National Association of Letter Carriers. This association had had "Separate Charter Branches" since its inception. However, it was not until 1962 that the national organization abolished these branches.[120]

Although a combination of public, governmental, and civil rights groups pressured many unions to open their rolls to ethnic minority group members, with some degree of success, many unions still continued to employ both overt and covert discrimination. Those unions that had colored American membership usually restricted them to the lower occupations under the particular union's control. Local 6 of the International Typographical Union (ITU) was among this group, since its Negro American membership totaled only about 3 per cent, if retirees were excluded from total membership. Too, as late as 1962, almost none of its colored American members had gained admission to the union through its regular apprenticeship program. In addition, the bulk of its Negro American membership was employed in the book and job branch and not in the newspaper branch.[121]

On the other side of the picture it should be stated that the union has accepted all persons qualified in the trade who have passed a qualifying examination. Also to be noted is the fact that about 20 per cent of the craftsmen in the union have graduated from the union's regular apprenticeship training program; the rest picked up the trade outside the union before joining. Allegations made against other crafts in the printing industry such as photoengraving, lithography, and presswork were more telling, although the end of 1962 did see some results from pressures applied by Negro Americans and government and civil rights groups.

Interest in civil rights continued in 1963 and was manifested in increased governmental activity. The State Commission on Human Rights and the City Commission on Human Rights vied with each other for publicity, but they accomplished little. Even the staid Urban League of Greater New York accepted some responsibility for

backing mass picketing at Harlem Hospital, then under construction.
The National Association for the Advancement of Colored People
(NAACP), through its local chapters, in conjunction with the
Congress of Racial Equality (CORE) staged lie downs on bridges to
the World's Fair. Under the sponsorship of A. Philip Randolph,
the Negro American Labor Committee tried to pressure the AFL-
CIO and the President of the United States to curtail discrimina-
tion.

In 1963 the civil rights movement saw further progress on both
the legislative and organized labor fronts. First, President John F.
Kennedy paved the way for the enactment of the 1964 Civil Rights
Act when he dispatched a special message to Congress urging the
Justice Department to "participate" in National Labor Relations
Board (NLRB) cases involving allegations of racial discrimination.
He also informed the department to pressure the NLRB "to take
appropriate action against racial discrimination in unions." [122]

Coincidentally, the President's message appeared while several
allegations charging racial discrimination were pending before the
board. Two of these charges were against AFL-CIO affiliates; the
United Steel Workers of America and the Sailors' Union of the
Pacific, the latter affiliated with the Seafarers International Union.
Both cases had been under consideration by the general counsel for
the board for at least three months prior to the President's message
to Congress. The charge against the Steel Workers Union alleged
the use of separate seniority lists; the other involved the Sailors'
Union, which excluded Negro Americans from membership, thereby
refusing them the use of the union's hiring hall.

Secondly, during this period, George Meany contended that officially, trade union discrimination against Negro Americans was
now a "bootleg product sneaked in by the back door and nowhere
condoned." [123] He could cite the Brotherhood of Firemen and
Enginemen, which at its 1963 Convention deleted the "lily-white"
clause from one of the few remaining "lily-white" constitutions. Of
course he could also point to the 116 AFL-CIO unions that had
signed voluntary antidiscrimination agreements prepared by the
President's Committee on Equal Opportunity. He could overlook
the fact that the Plumbers International Union was not a party
to the antidiscrimination agreement, because Local 2—Meany's
home local—had refused to permit qualified Negro American and
Puerto Rican craftsmen to work on the Bronx Market.

It is doubtful that Meany took his pronouncement seriously:
that trade union discrimination against Negro Americans was now

a "bootleg product," since he pledged President Kennedy the "unstinting assistance" of the federation in "the prompt achievement of a full, enforceable civil rights program on *every front.*" He said that the federation should create a working committee to cooperate with the government in ending job discrimination "in the months just ahead in this summer of determined effort." [124] Meany was alluding to the placement of Negro Americans in the crafts, since the maximum number of workers were employed during the summer. Meany backed up his oral commitment to the President by directing the AFL-CIO local and state central bodies on June 28, 1963,

> to take active part in the formation of bi-racial committees and councils within each community, and to join vigorously with such groups where they already exist.[125]

Furthermore before a Senate labor subcommittee on July 25, 1963, Meany admitted that he had good intentions but little power to enforce his committment to the President when he stated that federal legislation was necessary "because the AFL-CIO has only limited powers, and certainly has no manpower to police all the 60,000 local unions of our affiliates." He felt that a federal agency with broad inspection powers could do the job better.[126]

Meany knew very well that even with an adequate police force the AFL-CIO did not have the jurisdiction to carry out his promise, and admitted as much when he stated that the federation "has only limited powers." What Meany refused to spell out was well known to labor leaders—many powerful locals have been able to circumvent the directives of their internationals with impunity.[127] Furthermore, since Meany had to be called in through the "back door" by Mayor Wagner and Harry Van Arsdale to settle the plumbers local problem in New York, it appears reasonable to suggest that Meany's utterances were intended for public consumption. Labor's public image became a matter of renewed interest with President Kennedy's address to the Congress. The initiative taken by the President was reflected in Mayor Wagner's politics and the efforts of the Republicans on the state level to avoid being outshined.

Thus in 1963 Mayor Wagner appointed yet another panel to study the problem of discrimination in employment. This Action Panel, which was to report on the employment situation in the construction industry, consisted of two academicians and a lawyer. Their findings appeared in the *Preliminary Report of the Mayor's Action Panel*, dated July 11, 1963.[128] Substantially, this report contained no information that the Mayor had not already received from previous investigations. The panel's findings, covering 18 trades, revealed the "racial composition of these trades [ranging] from no nonwhite to 70 percent nonwhite." [129]

By passing over some of the questionable percentages of non-whites in the craft unions cited, such as the carpenters,[130] the panel's generalizations proved misleading. (This is not intended to reflect on the integrity of the panel members.) Actually, the overall figures cited for the carpenters failed to give a breakdown of union members in the various segments under union control—construction, alteration, woodworking, and so on. These distinctions were pertinent to the issue, since the basic question was whether the Negro American could become a construction journeyman, not a semiskilled, or unskilled, worker. Hence the lumping of all union members and the dividing of the Negro American group into the total gave a distorted picture.

There were other instances where the panel's examples could lead to confusion: especially in its failure to differentiate between helpers, improvers, and apprentices.[131] The bulk of the construction unions have at least two types of membership—"A" journeyman and "B" journeyman in addition to helpers and others. What was equally deplorable was that the craft unions refused to accept what Mayor Wagner termed the reasonable recommendations of the action panel,[132] thereby asserting their indifference to the public's image of craft unions [133] and their complete variance from upper echelon union thinking.[134]

Following the unions' refusal to accept the panel's recommendations, the Mayor made two statements: He would request the City Commission on Human Rights to hold hearings on the subject; and he would cancel any contracts where unions practiced discrimination. The Mayor neglected to mention that since 1935 the law of the State of New York has legally required him to revoke such contracts. A. H. Raskin summarized the reasons for the politicians' failure to invoke the law.

> The holdbacks to enforcement [of the law] were partly the reluctance of politicians in both parties to risk the enmity of the powerful construction unions and partly the recognition that urgent public work would be held up indefinitely by locking

out the unions whose members have a virtual monopoly on skills acquired through the years of apprenticeship.[135]

Despite findings of discriminatory union practices, no city contract had been revoked as of the end of 1965.

While the Mayor's action panel was conducting its investigation, the New York Advisory Committee to the U.S. Commission on Civil Rights [136] was studying the same issue. The fact that some of the U.S. commission's figures were at variance with those found by both the Mayor's action panel and the independent researchers was stated in the preface of the commission's report:

> Unnecessary limitation was encountered as a result of the general policy of non-cooperation followed by leaders of the building trades unions. With few exceptions, union officials failed to assist the study in any way, making it difficult or impossible to obtain information that was readily available[?].

In spite of many errors of commission and/or omission, the report's general conclusions did have some merit. To cite a few examples of errors of commission: Local 2 of the United Association of Journeymen Plumbers and Steamfitters did have three Negro Americans who held "A" cards, whereas the report alleged there were none. This was not to imply that the union hiring hall (business agents) placed any of these three individuals on construction jobs. There was the correct assertion that Local 3 of the IBEW had admitted some 1,020 "new apprentices" on a nondiscriminatory basis. What the report neglected to mention was that these apprentices originally were intended to form a new division (adequate wiring), and that the program was to be for four, not five, years; that the attrition rate was about 65 per cent as contrasted with 25 to 30 per cent in the regular apprenticeship program; and that this "M" program was a one-shot deal rather than a regular program.

There were errors of omission, since the report included Local 60 of the Operating Plasterers and Cement Masons International Association but left out Local 30 of the same international. Local 60, the New York local, was treated favorably in the report; Local 30, which was omitted, happened to be an all-white local in Brooklyn. Likewise, the report stressed Local 2 of the United Association of Journeymen Plumbers and Steamfitters but omitted Local 638, an all-white local, and Local 1 in Brooklyn.

An independent group, the Building Trades Employers Association [137] went on record to say that the *Shaughnessy Report* was full of "inaccuracies" and that the association had accepted an invitation from U.S. Secretary of Labor Willard Wirtz to discuss it. Despite the fact that invitations were extended to Dr. Donald Shaughnessy and members of his committee, no one appeared to defend what the construction industry labelled "inaccuracies." [138]

Following the Mayor's suggestion, the City Commission on Human Rights held hearings on employment practices in the building construction trades on Aug. 14, 15, and 20, and Sept. 9, 1963. The officials of seven unions were heard.[139] The commission's conclusions were summed up as follows:

(1) *Pattern of Exclusion:* A definite pattern of exclusion existed in the building and construction industry, primarily due to institutionalized practices barring nonwhites from participating as journeymen and apprentices.

(2) *Apprenticeship Barriers:* A "father-son clause" was found in many apprenticeship agreements, sponsorship by one or more senior members, unadvertised apprentice openings thus limiting openings to "in group." In addition to the above, the commission found restrictive recommendations, or priority given to union members in recommending applicants to apprentice programs, and when none of the aforementioned barriers existed, colored Americans were excluded by craft unions' practice of limiting apprenticeship openings by the establishment of "ratios of journeymen."

(3) *Journeymen Barriers:* A qualified nonwhite worker to gain employment on most construction jobs, primarily union controlled, had to overcome the sponsorship barrier, current union members in good standing had to vouch for the man before he could become a union member. Although New York City contractors, usually, have the privilege of hiring workers directly, they usually hire workers directly through the union's hiring hall.[140]

There were other devices employed to discourage Negro Americans from remaining in the union. It was a common practice to send colored Americans out on short-term jobs and reserve the long-term jobs for whites. This practice existed even in the unskilled Cement and Concrete Workers Union, Local 6A.[141] It was also common in the trowel trades to send a man on a job but restrict his work to "rough work" and release him when it came to the "finish work." [142] Still another practice was to put journeymen on apprentices' jobs so that they would become discouraged and quit. The overall pattern revealed that the device employed by unions that had to live with the Negro American was to give him work that would demean him in the eyes of his fraternal brothers so that in time he would drop out of the union. Hence, a listing of unions employing a numerical classification, or of those that admitted the Negro American to their unions with nominal equal opportunity, is misleading. With the above *caveat* in mind, let us look at a representative sample of construction and building trades unions for 1963. [143]

Union	"A" Membership	Negro American "A" Membership
Local 1, Elevator Constructors	2,300	Less than 5
Local 1, Plumbers (B'klyn)	3,000	none
Local 2, Plumbers (N.Y.)	3,800	3
Local 638, Steamfitters	4,000	none
Local 3, IBEW	9,000	50–55 *
Local 28, Sheetmetal	3,300	none
Local 40, Ornamental, Bridge, etc.	1,000	none
Local 60, Plasterers (N.Y.)	2,000	300
Local 30, Plasterers (B'klyn)	600	none
Locals 1, 9, 21, 30, 34, 37, 41, Bricklayers (N.Y.), Executive Committee	8,500	550
Carpenters, N.Y. District Council	27,000	2,800 **
Local 257, Carpenters (N.Y.)	3,000	50
Local 2305, Carpenters (B'klyn)	661	35
Local 1888, Carpenters (Harlem)	285	235
Locals 14, 14-B Operating Engineers	1,600–1,750	23–50

* The business manager of Local 3 allegedly gave this figure to a high official in the New York Central Trades Council. Independent investigation revealed that there were no more than 12 Negro Americans actually employed on construction jobs.
** This figure given by one of the vice presidents of the district council appeared inflated, since the number of Negro Americans represented total membership in the district council, which controls areas other than construction work.

Union admission policies in some service trades were much more in line with equal employment opportunities. For example, there were three New York locals, 1199 and District 65, both affiliated with Retail, Wholesale, Department Store Workers Union (RWSDU), and Local 144, affiliated with the Building Service Employees International Union, that not only admitted Negro Americans to their union rolls but assisted them in upgrading to higher skills through various union manpower development programs. District 65 of the RWSDU even struck a segment of employers with whom it was under contract because they refused to permit colored Americans to work in the front of their establishments.[144] Specifically, Local 1199, Drug and Hospital Employees Union, trained some 200 nonwhites as sales clerks in retail stores throughout the metropolitan area. This program was developed in conjunction with six retail drugstore employer associations, representatives of the board of education, and the U.S. Department of Labor's Apprenticeship and Training Program.[145]

On the other hand there were those service trades locals that either had a nondiscrimination clause in their contracts or whose leadership professed to have socialist leanings, but whose practices revealed a differentiation in placement between white and black. Local 6 of the Hotel Trades Council—the latter comprising locals of five international unions—allegedly has discriminated in its employment practices. Local 6 had been picketed by the Congress of Racial Equality (CORE) and even by some of its own members because it did not press the equal-opportunity clause in its contract.[146] Local 1 of the Waiters and Dining Room Employees with its mixed membership could boast of only one Negro American in a "better house." [147] This colored American had managed to find employment only through personal acquaintance with the manager of the establishment.

Peter Brennan, president of the New York Building and Construction Trades Council, was pressured by politicians,[148] Negro American groups, liberal whites, and even a few labor leaders [149] in New York to give the façade that the building trades were relenting toward minority union admission. Thus on Aug. 9, 1963, Brennan established a six-man biracial Building Industry of New York City Referral Committee. The committee's primary function was to screen and interview Negro and Puerto Rican applicants "who claimed either to be qualified Journeymen in the Building and Construction Industry, or qualified candidates for Apprenticeship Training." [150] Following information furnished by the applicant (if qualified), the committee asked the local union to process this recommendation and "treat it in the same manner accorded any other recommended candidate and so inform the Committee of action taken." [151]

The City Commission on Human Rights interpreted the "Brennan Plan" to mean the surmounting of "a major barrier to nonwhite

entry into the construction industry, *the sponsorship requirement.*"
Thus the commission thought that local building trades unions had
agreed to regard referrals from the six-man committee as having
been acceptably sponsored.[152]

To support its contention the commission [153] cited the testimony of the official spokesman for the Building Trades Employers
Association, which consisted of about 1,000 members and was responsible for about 75 to 80 per cent of the construction work in
New York City.

> Whereas before as I stated you had to have a sponsor, this six-
> man committee now, after discussing the question with a boy
> who is interested in becoming an apprentice in one of the
> various trades, will send him to the appropriate union. So in
> effect they become the sponsors. So I would see that bottleneck
> which has been created in the past should be eliminated
> through this six-man committee.[154]

Implied support of the statement was made by a local union official when he said: "I think you will find that each and every local
union and this Building Trades Council, has pledged to President
Brennan their support." [155] However, it is dubious whether the statement was subscribed to by other members of the building industry,
since no other union representative testifying before the City Commission was willing to give "such clear and unequivocal assurances
to that effect." [156] One witness went so far as to reject, and flatly so,
the notion that the Brennan Committee be accepted as sponsors.

> But we could never consider any of these people as sponsors,
> because for instance, not to be discourteous or anything . . .
> let us say, what would a priest or minister know about qualifi-
> cations of a man to operate a three or four-yard power shovel?
> Certainly, the priest or minister wouldn't ask us to send some-
> one to him to go into this endeavor.[157]

Strangely enough, the last witness, a member of the same international union but a different local from the union representative
supporting the Brennan Committee, was not even aware of who was
serving on the screening committee and furthermore was unwilling
to accept it as a sponsor.[158]

There were other questions raised about the possible effective-

ness of the Brennan Committee, assuming that its referrals were regarded as acceptably sponsored. Since the unions take in a stated
number of apprentices each year, many unions have a lengthy waiting list that makes it virtually impossible for a person to be admitted readily into their apprenticeship program.[159] For example,
Local 40 of the ironworkers has no sponsorship requirement for applicants to its apprenticeship program. Its treasurer, Thomas Clarkson, in commenting about possible referrals from the six-man Committee, said: "We will be willing to accept applications, [and] if
we reach them will give them a chance." What Clarkson meant was
that the local took in only 20 apprentices "within a period of a year,
[thus having] applications that have been on file since 1960 . . .
and they are still waiting [August, 1963] to get into our apprenticeship program." [160]

    This situation was not unique to the ironworkers; a similar
situation existed in Local 638 of the Steamfitters' Union. The by-laws
of this local stipulate that applicants "shall be proposed by three
members. [Union officials contended that this was merely a paper
requirement.] Brennan Committee referrals would then be able to
join the union apprentice program in the year 1972, nine years
from now," unless these referrals were given preferential treatment
over some 500 candidates on the union's waiting list. If we accept
the union representative's statement at face value, the whole idea
becomes ludicrous. If the candidate had to wait nine years before
being considered eligible, he would lose his eligibility, because the
maximum age limit is 24 years and he had to be at least 18 years
of age when he filed his application.[161]

    There was some evidence that the lines of communication be-
tween Mr. Brennan and locals affiliated with the Building Trades
Council were faulty. When Chairman Stanley Lowell of the City
Commission on Human Rights questioned an elected official of the
Plumbers' Union, Local 2, he stated that he was unaware that the
Building Trades Council had adopted the Brennan proposal.
Furthermore, he was not certain that his local intended to cooperate
with the proposal.[162] The answer to Lowell's query was settled on
the national level when the Plumbers International Union an-
nounced that the plumbing industry would not abide by any quota
system "based on racial or population percentages." [163]

    On the WCBS radio program *Let's Find Out*, Brennan de-
fended the effectiveness of his proposal by contending that 204
persons had been referred to various union locals. In particular this

statement was meant to rebutt James J. McFadden's statement that to his knowledge not a single Negro or Puerto Rican had been admitted into a construction union despite summer-long efforts by civil rights groups and government officials.[164] Unfortunately, each man was referring to something different, and this lack of communication—partly emotional on the part of each individual due to personality clashes in the past—needs interpretation. There is a decided difference between a referral to a local union (and either being accepted as a bona-fide journeyman, and/or being put on a waiting list for future apprenticeship training) and actually working as an apprentice. Thus the report (*Building Industry of New York City Referral Committee*) [165] stated specifically: "The action of referral by the Committee *does not* constitute an acceptance of the applicant into a Union." There is quite a gap between referral and acceptance as a journeyman or apprentice.

In 1964 the official organ of the New York Hotel and Motel Trades Council announced: *Contract Struck First Blow Against Job Bias* [166] (the italics refer to the union's first contract signed in 1937). Twenty-five years later the same union's organ commented: "Discrimination still exists in some hotels and some departments." [167] A later issue of the house organ (still in 1964) [168] gave the impression that since "minority workers hold 40 per cent of hotel jobs," discrimination in the hotel industry was licked. The tabulation forming the basis for the percentage was based on a Book Check and Survey conducted by Local 6 of the union. What the figures neglected to disclose was that percentages can hide much, since the important item was in what "Houses" the 40 per cent of the jobs were held. After the survey the union and employers engaged in a joint venture to upgrade Negro Americans. The project failed to show much progress after two years.[169]

Local 2 of the Plumbers' International continued to defy the various civil rights agencies, the federal government, and public resentment, and its members refused to work side by side with nonunion nonwhites hired by an employer to work on the Bronx Terminal Market. While the local contended its refusal was based on the fact that the new workers were nonunion men, it failed to include the point that it was almost impossible for nonwhites to obtain union journeymen's cards.[170]

Counsel for the NLRB, acting on evidence submitted to him, namely, a union-management contract clause stating that Local 2 members must be given preference in employment, charged the union with violation of the Taft-Hartley Act (which forbids the closed shop).[171] About a year later (1965), the NLRB ruled that union plumbers could not boycott nonmembers.[172]

It was interesting to note that the first criminal prosecution of a case of discrimination in the annals of New York State was presented in 1964 by Manhattan District Attorney Frank S. Hogan.[173] He contended that although Section 700 and 701 of the Penal Law and Section 291 of the state's Executive Law had been on the books since 1941 and 1945, respectively, this was the first time the law had been invoked to prosecute with regard to discrimination in employment.

The State Commission for Human Rights also went on record when it went beyond a public hearing to initiate the case of the Attorney General of the State of New York against Union Local 28 of the Sheet Metal Workers International Association of Greater New York, *et al*.[174] The original complaint was verified in December, 1962 and filed in January, 1963. The charge was that the respondent labor union (Local 28) had discriminated against Negro Americans "in designation and approval of apprenticeship candidates for sheet metal training." The commissioners found [175]

(1) that Local 28 has engaged in and continues to commit unlawful discriminatory practices as defined in Subdivision 1(b) and 1-a of Section 296 of the Law Against Discrimination

(2) that the Joint Apprenticeship Committee has engaged in and continues to commit an unlawful discriminatory practice as defined in Subdivision 1-a of Section 296 of said law; and

(3) that the individual respondents have engaged in and continue to commit an unlawful discriminatory practice as defined in subdivision 6 of Section 296 of said Law.

Therefore the commission ordered [176]

(1) that Local Union 28 shall specify in writing the minimum qualifications;

(2) that Local Union 28 shall select apprentices on the basis of qualifications . . . on objective standards;

(3) that Standards, tests, etc., shall be duly approved by the Industrial Commissioner;

(4) that the current waiting list shall not be used in future selection;

(5) that notice in writing shall be given to the N.Y. State Employment Service, Board of Education of the City of N.Y., announcing the number to be selected on a specified date.

The case was appealed to the State Supreme Court and Justice Markowitz upheld the State Commission for Human Rights.[177] Although the union agreed to change its ways, not one nonwhite had been placed in its apprenticeship training program as of February, 1965.[178]

The year 1964 was not completely bleak. There were some unions that altered their policies toward Afro-American acceptance. One such union was Local 342, Amalgamated Meat Cutters and Butchers' Workmen, AFL-CIO. This local has two main divisions: meatcutters and other help in food stores; the meatcutters represent the skilled members of the union. (In 1963 there were about 70 Negro American meatcutters out of some 3,000 in the local.) However, the local initiated a six-week intensive training program for meatcutters at the end of 1963, and its first class graduated in 1964 included more than a representative sample of Negro Americans. There were jobs for all. At least two other classes were started in 1964, in each of which Negro Americans were represented. (Local 342's jurisdiction covered chain and independent food stores in Queens and Brooklyn.) [179]

Even though one Negro American, Michael Stewart, was accepted into the apprenticeship training program of Local 40 of the ironworkers, this should not be viewed as a breakthrough. His placement was a personal one, and was successful only because of his sponsor, Ray Corbett, president of the State Federation of Labor, and still intimately connected with the local. This is not to detract from the fact that some American Indians ply the trade in New York State, but Stewart's breaking of the iron rods encircling this local is hardly even "tokenism." [180]

Two clauses were emphasized during 1965—union security and hiring practices. The construction trades were given special dispensation with respect to *union security* by an amendment to the 1947 *Labor Management Relation Act*. A representative clause taken from the asbestos workers' contract stated: [181(1)]

The members of the Asbestos Contractors Association hereby recognize Local No. 12 as the exclusive bargaining agent for

Mechanics and Improvers who perform any of the duties as prescribed in Article XI (Jurisdiction) hereof. Such Mechanics and Improvers are in this Agreement sometimes referred to as "Employees."

In conjunction with the union security clause, each of the 18 unions had a clause requiring all employees to be, or to become, members of the union. The implementation of these clauses varied between seven and 30 days after the effective date of the agreement.[181(2, 3)] In addition, to meet the National Labor Relations Board's decision in the *Mountain Pacific Case* (a union hiring hall was judged to be an unfair labor practice until the operation of the particular hall was proven to be nondiscriminatory) each contract contained a clause similar to the one contained in the contract of the operating engineers, which read:

The *Union* shall establish, maintain and keep current an open employment list for the employment of workmen competent and physically fit to perform the duties of classifications covered by this *Agreement*. Such a list shall be established, maintained and kept current on a nondiscriminatory basis and shall not be based on or in any way affected by *Union* membership, *Union* By-Laws, Rules, Regulations, or constitutional provisions or any other aspect or obligation of *Union* membership, policies or requirements.[181(6)]

Verbal acceptance was assured by the incorporation of this clause in the contract dealing with *Hiring Practices*, but, it was questionable whether bona-fide compliance was achieved. In many instances a gap existed between the written clause and actual practice; but to prove it in terms of the laws of evidence would be difficult, since much of the evidence would have to be circumstantial. However, an attempt will be made to annotate this contention in terms of the contract provisions and to show how these provisions allow for control almost equal to that of the closed shop. The implications of the union security clause should offer some idea of the difficulties involved in proving discrimination, especially against construction unions where employment is frequently of a casual nature. Upon completion of the job, workmen seek employment on another construction site.

Union membership criteria. There was no question that each of the contracts required a union to place a nonunion man on a job, if the union maintained an employment office. However, before a nonunion man could become a member of the union—a stipulation for continued employment—there were certain qualifications imposed by the contract. Thus the boilermakers contract stated that to be qualified for registration on the boilermakers' out-of-work list a man must be able to establish proof that he had had at least four years of actual practical working experience of the boilermakers' trade in the building and construction industry, or

> [has] successfully passed a competency examination that adequately tested the degree of skill and training necessary to be a competent construction boilermaker. Any question as to what constitutes a "competency" examination shall be resolved by the Joint Referral Committee.[181(2)]

The bricklayers, in conjunction with the employers associations, agreed to a central employment bureau that would maintain a "Qualified Bricklayers' List." All union members at the time of the agreement were presumed to have met the general requirements of skill and experience for a qualified bricklayer and were to be placed on the list.

> All other persons seeking employment as Bricklayers shall be required to pass a fair and comprehensive examination as to . . . abilities and skills prior to being listed on the Qualified Bricklayers' List. Such examination shall be given by a joint union-employer testing committee consisting of an equal number of Union and Employer representatives.[181(3)]

Since most of the construction trades have similar qualifications as a prerequisite to union membership, it could be rather difficult for a nonunion man to qualify for union membership. Thus there need not be any discrimination in a nonunion man's being hired at the site, or being sent out by the union, but union membership need not necessarily follow his employment. In the case of the Bronx Terminal Market, where a few Afro-Americans and Puerto Ricans were hired as plumbers, the union plumbers walked off the job when an examination was given by the union to three of the four nonunion mechanics, all of whom failed, and thus could not be admitted to union membership. Hence there was no legal obstacle to the union men's refusal to work side by side with "nonqualified" plumbers, who could not meet the requirements of the union security clause.[181(14)]

Since the union is the best employment agency, "the employer should be able [under the Taft-Hartley Act] to make a contract with the union as an employment agency."[182] The implication is that employers in the construction trades are more dependent upon the unions for qualified mechanics than is the case in industries such as manufacturing and retailing. This would assume special cooperation between the contractor and the union. The latter depends upon its regular members to fulfill its function, many of whom are from its apprenticeship training program. Hence, some employers, working in collusion with unions to fulfill their function, have the right to fire any mechanic they deem incompetent, or to release a mechanic when the rough work has been completed.[181(9, 14)]

Although in accord with the laws of evidence it would be difficult to claim that an employer had discriminated, such practices do exist. Since construction labor is frequently of a casual nature, it would be hard to follow patterns of a particular contractor. To insure that employers will continue to be dependent in one way or another upon the union, even when the latter does not have an employment center, employers cannot seek employees from any private or governmental employment agency.

> The Employer shall be free to hire Journeymen or Apprentices from any source. However, no Journeyman or Apprentice shall seek employment through an Employment Agency, nor shall any Employer use the services of an Employment Agency in hiring Journeymen or Apprentices.[181(12)]

We have seen that members of minority groups had difficulty in gaining admission to craft union membership, either because of a refusal to accept them into a joint apprenticeship program—a main source of membership recruitment—or because Negro Americans who had learned a trade outside the domain of union sponsorship were rarely received into union membership. The above, in combination with the loopholes in the interpretation of the union security clause, revealed that despite the *Mountain Pacific Case*, colored Americans continue to remain strangers to the organized craft unions.

Most of the contracts examined contained a statement to the effect that upon change in the limitations of a closed shop imposed by the National Labor Relations Act of 1947, the contract would be subject to revision concerning union security.[181(2, 9)] One even included a provision to supersede any other union security provision once the limitations of a closed shop has been removed. It read:

> The Employer agrees to employ only members in good standing of the Union as Journeymen in all branches of the Industry covered by this Agreement.[181(4), 183]

Hiring Practices. Interpretations of various hiring practices contained in contracts referred to in this section were based on personal experience by the author while in the labor movement and the experiences of other craftsmen he interviewed in a "social way."

An examination of the contract clauses relating to hiring practices contained in the 18 contracts under survey, revealed that there were two opposites: (1) No formal hiring hall was maintained by joint agreement between union and the employer; and (2) a formal hiring hall was maintained by the union, or hiring was done through a joint referral system, usually consisting of an "equal number of Employer and Union representatives to supervise and control the operation of the job referral system." [181(2)] (3) Between these two extremes there were clauses within a single contract that permitted hiring at the site as well as through the hiring hall. To reveal how preference can be given to current union members over "outsiders" despite the *Mountain Pacific Case,* illustrative clauses will be cited and interpreted.

(A) No Formal Hiring Hall.

(1) The longshoremen's agreement reads:

> Seniority shall govern lay-offs and rehiring; that is to say the employees having the least seniority shall be the first laid off and those employees last laid off shall be the first rehired. A new member can claim seniority the first day he starts work in the shop.
>
> Upon the signing of the contract, . . . the Union shall furnish the Company with a written list of its shop stewards.[181(10)]

A superficial reading of the contract clause offers little evidence as to how it can be used to discriminate against the Negro American. One must read the last sentence of paragraph one to find a clue: a man must first be employed in a shop before the clause can be effective. However, the pipe trades have been traditionally anti-Negro American. When the latter comment is coupled with the fact that seniority is based on finding employment, and that employment in this type of situation is likely to be informal,[184] with the shop steward being apprised of the need for additional employees, the evidence becomes more apparent. If the steward does not know anyone, he may ask some of his buddies to suggest someone. This leaves little room for an "outsider" to find his way into a shop and to acquire seniority.

Management will also lean in this direction in order to keep or bring about amicable relations with the union and to maintain the "esprit de corp" necessary to facilitate unhampered work schedules. (This assumes that the Negro American would know where these shops are located and when there was need for additional employees, or that he would be acceptable as an apprentice. The standard response in most instances to a query as to why there is no Negro American in the company's employ is: none has applied.)

(2) Although there is an agreement between union and employer in the electrical industry, hiring practices are not closely related to a formal hiring hall, because all hiring can be done at the site. Thus, the contract states: "The foreman on a job shall hire all men as directed by the employer." [181(5)] One interpretation is that he is to hire all competent applicants, assuming that such applicants are aware of openings on the job and know where the job is. However, more likely—based on conversations with foremen on jobs, who have complete power to fire as well as hire employees—the foreman will hire either his cronies or those of his friends on the job.

What the clause neglected to mention was that foremen are usually members of the union. In this local there are some instances where Negro Americans who have completed the regular apprenticeship training program will find employment on the better jobs. (The term "better job" means that the employee will be brought in on the deck and will work until the job is completed.) Currently (1967) there was one Negro American foreman in the local, and he was employed at the Harlem Hospital site.

The importance of camaraderie in getting jobs, especially the better jobs, can be illustrated by an actual instance. There was a group of union "A" journeymen taking a course of instruction, and during the semester one of the journeymen came in with a cast on his leg. This meant that he was on workmen's compensation, amounting to a small fraction of his weekly earnings when you include overtime. Another member of the class, a foreman on the Queens Criminal Court House job, asked the injured man: "Why don't you report to work on my gang? We can cover up for you and you won't have to lose any time from work." A later conversation between the instructor and the foreman disclosed that the foreman has complete power to hire and fire and to cover for a man if he isn't pulling his share of the job. (Incidentally, when the bids are made on electrical contracts for heavy construction, a certain spread is allowed for "goofing-off" and the carrying of a few slow men.)

(3) Although the bricklayers maintain a central employment bureau, the said bureau's list consists of qualified bricklayers, who are subject to a "comprehensive examination as to . . . abilities and skills prior to being listed on the Qualified Bricklayers' List." [181(3)] However, there was another clause in the contract that allowed a certain amount of leeway in circumvention of the central bureau. It read:

> If the employer first obtains the consent of the Union and only with such consent the Employer may employ all Bricklayers directly without application to the Central Employment Bureau. Men so employed shall seek employment on the operation, but there shall be no restriction as to the hours of the day within which such application may be made.[181(3)]

(4) One of the operating engineers' locals removes itself completely from any possibility of being questioned as to its practices by leaving it up to its membership to find employment wherever they can. Thus:

> Any Union member, upon showing his membership card shall be permitted to seek employment on any job of any employer; where an employment office is not maintained on the job, the hiring agent of the employer shall be conveniently accessible to applicants at least once a day.[181(6)]

Among other things it should be mentioned that this type of employment situation depends upon the *buddy system* and the business agent of the local, since it would be difficult for a man to know where the job sites were and when an employer was hiring. In the past, crane and hoist operators were predominantly white union men; the same was not true for stationary engineers.

(5) The plumbers' local has a unique policy in conjunction with the Employers Association. Thus, it offers

> priority in employment opportunity to qualified and competent men based upon their length of employment in the geographical area of the Union as contrasted and compared with men who have worked mainly in other geographical areas. . . . Members of the Union may be hired as in the past without regard to prior length of service.[181(14)]

There are two things to be noted in this instance: (a) priority is given to union members who have the longest seniority in the local union and (b) work experience within the union's jurisdiction. This implies that there is no rotation system, and, since the pipe trades have a long history of nonacceptance of Negro Americans, they are thereby able to curtail colored American employment even if such workers were accepted by a local in the trade.

Although much more can be said about other construction unions and their hiring practices, the above should suffice to give some idea of the subtle ways in which the Negro American can be kept as an "outsider," except for some "tokenism," in many craft unions. These examples permit at least two implications with regard to union membership: (a) many of the construction trades have at least two categories of union membership, "A" and "B" journeymen, and only the former are qualified to perform construction work; (b) many nonunion journeymen could be placed when hiring takes place at the site if union membership were not covertly emphasized. Hiring at the site should not be confused with the union's use of a central hiring hall as the only place of placement.

(B) Formal, or Central Hiring Hall.

(1) Previously, we alluded to possible discrepancies between the written contract clause and actual practices. These discrepancies may be illustrated by the agreement of the Sheetmetal Workers Union. (To minimize the possibility of allegations that material has been taken out of context, reversion is made to the union's security clause, which implies equal opportunity in employment to nonunion men.) It reads:

> The Employer agrees to require membership in the union as a
> condition of continued employment of all employees perform-
> ing any of the work specified in Article I (Jurisdiction) of this
> agreement . . . , provided the Employer has reasonable ground
> for believing *that membership is available to such employees on
> the same terms and conditions generally applicable to other
> members* (italics added).[181(16)]

The italicized portion of the union security clause gives notice to
an employer that Negro Americans are not qualified. This allegation
is made on the basis of the local's past history and the protracted
litigation occasioned by the New York State Commission on
Human Rights' attempt to get the union to open both its membership rolls and apprenticeship program to colored Americans. It is
further reinforced by an evaluation of the hiring practices clause,
which reads:

> The Employer agrees that none but Journeymen sheet metal
> workers and registered apprentices shall be employed.
>
> The Union agrees to furnish at all times to the Employer, duly
> qualified journeymen sheet metal workers and registered ap-
> prentices in sufficient numbers as may be necessary to properly
> execute work contracted for by the Employer in manner and
> under conditions specified in this agreement.[181(16)]

The term "duly qualified journeymen" is where the union's control
over the labor supply enters the picture, since it is the union that
gives the qualifying examination and determines whether the applicant has passed. This type of control over union admission is
frequently a reserved right in most craft-union contracts. Sometimes, the evaluation is supposed to be determined by a joint-labor
management committee; in practice, the determination is usually
left to the individual local.

(2) The lathers likewise maintain that union membership shall
not be a determining factor.

> Whenever desiring to employ workmen, the Employer shall
> call upon the Union or its agent for any such workmen as the
> Employer may, from time to time, need and the Union or its
> Agent shall refer such workmen from the open employment list.

[However], the Union, in referring workmen, shall give consideration to and shall be governed by the following criteria, which shall be applied in a non-discriminatory manner, as provided for in (1) above; (a) recent employment by a particular Employer now desiring to re-employ the same workman provided he is available; (b) length of prior employment with any Employer party to this agreement; (c) competency and experience in the performance of the particular tasks involved in the job to which referral is being made.[181(9)]

On paper there is an "open employment list," but an examination of the qualifications' criteria reveals that there are many ways in which the nonunion man, and even more so the Negro American, can be sidestepped. First, since there is no rotation in placement, the preference given to those union men who had recent employment could weigh heavily in favor of longstanding union members. Secondly, the long-established employer presumably would have extensive contact with white union members, who could be shown preference without "prejudice." Thirdly, the question of competency again arises. If the nonunion man is sent out on a job, the foreman has the prerogative of placing him on any phase of the job he chooses, there is no reason why the foreman could not select an area where the nonunion man is least qualified.

The assumption here is that there is usually some relationship between the foreman and the union, and that it is the foreman's task to keep the flow of work running smoothly. Or, it could be as some contracts read: the nonunion man must pass a qualifying examination before he can be referred to a job. This raises the question of time, with a delay in giving the nonunion man the examination until there is a slack period. Should he pass the examination, it would be a Pyrrhic victory, one that has caused many Negro Americans to seek work in nonrelated trades to gain their livelihood. Of course the examination could also be so geared that the nonunion men would fail.

Finally, it would be difficult to prove that a business agent neglected to use the "open employment list" when referring men to a job. It has often been the case that the business agent sends out men who have been favorably disposed to his earlier election. This allegation has been made on many occasions against the business agents of various unions in the construction trades.[181(8, 3, 4)]

There is another gimmick that may be used. The man is sent out, but the choice of jobs to which he can be sent is left to the discretion of the business agent. The latter sends out his "buddies" to those jobs that are just started and will be of long duration, as opposed to sending out a man when the job is nearing completion. Still another way in which discriminatory practices may be manifested, especially against Negro Americans who are members of a local craft union, is to lay off the colored American when the rough work has been completed.

At least one *caveat* should be borne in mind: Where there are several locals of the same union within an area, such as carpenters, plasterers, and others, the practices of all locals are not necessarily the same. Thus, it has been found that among locals of the same international union, some have a long history of complete exclusion and others admit Negro Americans. It may be said that we have neglected the question of seniority, as implied in the preferences shown in the lathers' contract. The author would not concede that seniority as it is usually understood in industries such as manufacturing, transportation, and retailing is synonymous with that of the construction trades; differences between the two groups go beyond technicalities.

(C) Miscellaneous.

Although some contracts permit an employer to hire 50 per cent of his labor force at the job site, either through his foreman or his own employment office, there is an unwritten understanding that more often than not the employer's share of hiring will consist only of union men. An interpretation of one contract clause reveals how easily this can be done.

> Workmen shall be engaged at the shop, at the Union office, or at the job.[181(3)]

It is at the shop or at the job site that most nonunion men are excluded from full knowledge of where there are job openings. Secondly, since the union is responsible for only 50 per cent of the jobs, those seeking employment through the union—with special emphasis on nonunion men—can hope for a maximum of only one half of the jobs. It should be kept in mind that if the rotation system is used, each man at the top of the list is called into the office and given a work permit. This means that those sitting on the bench do not know where the job openings are unless the business agent or some other union official so informs them. To reiterate, this is not necessarily the case with union men. The latter may have been employed by this particular employer on previous occasions and he may ask the union for them directly or get in touch with the men by other means, thus bypassing the rotation system.[181](4)

There is another aspect not spelled out in the contracts between small contractors and the union. There are unofficial hiring halls, such as the one that existed in Brooklyn. Mechanics—carpenters, plasterers, lathers, and so on—would congregate at certain hours of the day at a particular corner, where arrangements were made between the craftsmen and an employer to start work on a particular date. This twilight zone completely neglected the nonunion man. There are also special areas where nonunion employers pick up laborers, who are usually Negro Americans who will work below the union scale.

The above examples are not intended to be all-inclusive, but merely illustrative. There are many other ways in which circumvention can and does take place, but their mention would run far beyond the intent of this study. What is meant is that the law, as good as it is, can be and has been circumvented (even as many people find loopholes in the income tax laws and are not subject to criminal action). Thus the law, in the opinion of the author, can only fill a very small gap in the existing situation.

In summary, some restrictive practices employed by unions were:

(1) *Full restriction caused by union practice:*
   (a) exclusion by way of constitutional provisions;
   (b) exclusion by way of tacit consent and/or ritual;
   (c) exclusion because of employers' bias (airline pilots, navigators, etc.);
   (d) exclusion from apprenticeship training programs;
   (e) exclusion from the union hiring hall of an employer who decides to include Negro Americans in his work force;
   (f) exclusion from many trade unions of the Negro American, thus barring him from qualifying for a license, which he could use to operate as an independent contractor.

(2) *Partial restriction caused by union practice:*
   (a) partial exclusion through segregated and/or auxiliary locals;
   (b) partial restriction of occupational mobility through segregated and/or auxiliary locals;
   (c) partial restriction of full work weeks by denial of union hiring hall;

(d) partial restriction based on "tokenism" in the union's apprenticeship program.

(3) *Discriminatory union retrenchment:*
  (a) refusal to accept a journeyman's transfer card where locals were members of the same international;
  (b) refusal to apply the same seniority rules to all members in upgrading;
  (c) refusal to offer equal occupational mobility to all members seeking employment, especially in the crafts where the business agent has control over placement;
  (d) refusal to offer equal opportunity to Negro Americans, even where the union constitution barred discrimination on the job or in upgrading;
  (e) refusal to carry out the suggestions of the union's fair employment practices committee on equal opportunity findings.

(4) *Miscellaneous:*
  (a) collusion between union and employer in order to maintain "lily-white" shops;
  (b) confinement of "A" mechanic union member to the "hole" (basement of construction site), bending pipe, threading pipe full time, and so on; jobs usually assigned to helpers or apprentices.

CHAPTER 7

The New York Afro-American's Battle for Political Rights, 1777–1865

Another arc in the circle of discrimination is political status, which can and does affect the Negro's socioeconomic status. Thus, to be consistent the white man had to include various restrictions on the Negro's political and civil rights.

The American Revolution, which was fought in part to equalize political representation, failed to change pre-Revolutionary public attitudes toward the Negro's political and civil status in society. This was in accord with the "outsider status" imposed upon the Negro by white society and carried out by both the federal and state governments. Although the federal constitution fails to mention the question of race or color, "in interpreting it, American lawgivers arrive at the conclusion, that the United States are the property of whites, and all persons with a tinge of dark color in their countenance, though born free, are not citizens." In short, "there seems to be a fixed notion throughout the whole of the states, whether slave or free, that the colored is by nature a subordinate race; and that [under] no circumstances, can [the Negro] be considered equal to the white." [1]

Specifically, Congress carried out the mandate of the people when it excluded the Negro from "certain federal rights and privileges and sanctioned a number of territorial and state restrictions." For example, "in 1790, Congress limited naturalization to white aliens; in 1792, it organized the militia and restricted enrollment to able-bodied white male citizens; in 1810, it excluded Negroes from carrying the United States mails." [2]

When Congress failed to legislate directly, it accomplished its end by indirection; by not legislating in certain areas. Thus, an act of Congress barred the Negro from the militia, but no legislation was passed circumscribing the Negro's later acceptance into the Army, the Navy, and the Marines. Thus, the armed forces excluded the Negro until necessity made it expedient to accept him, as was the case during the naval war with France and again in the War of 1812.[3]

On the state level the Negro's political position in society was merely a reflection of what the Congress had enacted, or had failed to legislate, on the national plane. Thus, although the free Negro was known as "free," in none of the New England States was he as free as the white man. However, he was part of the community. Some Negroes did exercise political rights, but always in a restricted manner; in the Northern states special property qualifications demarcated Negro suffrage from that of the whites.[4] It should be noted that there was not a single Northern slaveholding state that permitted unlimited manumission; or one that permitted Negroes to testify in litigation. These rules were rigidly enforced after the Revolution.[5]

From the American Revolution through the Civil War, the Negroes' reaction to unequal suffrage was one of aggressiveness. This aggressive attitude is contrary to the commonly held belief that Negroes are apathetic toward their political and civil status in American society,[6] as can be seen in their struggle to make democracy work during the period from 1777 to 1865.

SUFFRAGE UNDER NEW YORK STATE'S 1777 CONSTITUTION TO 1826

Like the framers of the federal Constitution, those who drew up New York State's first constitution, adopted on April 20, 1777,[7] specifically omitted any reference to race, creed, or previous condition of servitude as a bar to suffrage. However, the constitution did state that the right to vote at elections for the state Assembly was granted to "every male inhabitant of full age" who met the residence and property requirements. These were: (1) the ownership of a £20 freehold, or (2) the leasing of a tenement at 40 shillings.[8] The voting requirements for state Senator, however, were different; here the property requirement was £100.[9]

By 1785 most New Yorkers were opposed to the continuation of Negro suffrage. This was true despite the introduction in that year of a bill entitled "An Act for the Gradual Abolition of Slavery Within this State," which received a two thirds senate vote and a majority vote in the Assembly.[10] The title of the bill is misleading, since its contents actually favored curtailment of Negro suffrage. The Council of Revision vetoed the bill because (1) it contained a clause that prohibited Negroes from exercising their franchise, and (2) it was contrary to the principles of the revolution, since it "supposes that those may rightfully be charged with the burdens of government, who have no representative share in imposing them." In this instance, the black man's suffrage was preserved because of the council's veto.[11]

In 1799, John Jay signed an act while his Federalist party was in power, revealing its liberal attitude toward Negroes. This act provided for the gradual abolition of slavery—the freeing of males at age 28 and females at age 25. The close association of many free Negroes with their Federalist employers and the passage of the act gave rise to the allegation that Negroes were under the domination of the Federalists.

We do not know whether the alignment of Negroes with the Federalists was coincidental; but we do know that the Federalists won the election of 1800 by the vote of a single Negro ward.[12] We also know that John Jay and Alexander Hamilton helped to organize the Manumission Society in 1785, which had strong leanings toward abolition. Furthermore, L. Litwack contends: "As early as 1777, Jay had felt that revolutionary consistency required the abolition of Negro bondage." [13] However, Litwack's contention is questioned by D. S. Alexander, who maintains that even though "the closing days of Jay's public life included an act of gradual abolition of domestic slavery, it cannot be called an important feature of his administration." Jay is entitled to "little credit for bringing it about," since he failed "to recommend emancipation in his messages [but merely] emphasizes the suggestion that he was governed by the fear of its influence upon his future political career." [14] To emphasize his point, Alexander raises the question as to why Jay resigned his presidency of the Abolition Society "at the moment of his aroused ambition immediately preceding his nomination for governor in 1799." William Jay, the son of John Jay, tried to rationalize his father's position by claiming that the "people of the State did not favor abolition; yet the reform apparently needed only the vigorous assistance of the Governor, for in 1798 a measure similar to the Act of 1799 failed in the Assembly only by the casting vote of the Chairman in the Committee of the Whole." [15]

The opposing political party, the Democratic-Republicans, accepted the allegation of an alignment between the Negroes and the Federalists and sought to minimize the Negroes' effect as a political force.[16] The Democratic-Republican opposition gained momentum, and they were able to restrict black suffrage. Thus in 1809, polling inspectors of the Democratic-Republican party, assuming that all Negroes were born in slavery, refused to permit Negroes to take the prescribed oath that they were born free.[17] A special act "to prevent frauds and for other purposes" was passed by the state legislature in 1811. It dealt specifically with Negroes and stated that "whenever any person of color, or black person shall present himself to vote at any election of this state, he shall produce to the inspectors, or persons conducting such an election, a certificate of freedom under the hand and seal of one of the clerks of the counties of this state, or under the hand of a clerk of any town within this state" [New York].[18]

To obtain such a certificate, a Negro or person of color had to appear before a judge of the Supreme Court, where the proof of freedom could be obtained in writing. The cost of this certificate would involve the services of a lawyer, plus twenty-five cents to the court and a shilling to the county clerk for filing the certificate in his office. Finally, the man of color had to take an oath that he was the person whose name was listed on the certificate.[19]

Again the council came to the defense of Negroes. On April 5, 1811, its objections were sufficient to override the act. Chancellor Lansing gave the following reasons for rejection: Given the fact that according to the act "persons of color" must produce certificates of freedom at all elections; he found "that the description of 'persons of color' was too indefinite and might be made to include all gradations and/or mixtures between the African and the white man. . . . [Furthermore] the act established the principle that all blackmen and men of color are presumed to be slaves until they prove that they are free." [20] However, the opponents of Negro suffrage were to have their victory three years later.

In 1813 it was alleged that the votes of some 300 free Negroes in New York City again decided the election and swept the Federalists into power, thus determining the character of the state legislature.[21] Some delegates at the 1821 Convention contended that this Negro vote was responsible for passage of a new and more stringent law in 1814.[22] This law, which was limited to New York City, was very similar to the ill-fated 1811 law, since both required that a certificate of freedom had to be recorded in the office of the registrar and that a copy of the record had to be presented at each election before a free Negro could vote.

The effectiveness of the new law can be gauged by the number of Negroes who actually voted in the spring election of 1821—163, as compared to the 300 in the 1813 election.[23] Its effectiveness is heightened when we note the composition of the Negro population in 1810 and in 1820. In 1810 [24] there were 9,823 Negroes in the city, 1,686 of whom [25] were slaves, as compared with 10,886 Negroes in 1820,[26] 518 of whom [27] were slaves. In other words there was an increase of some 2,000 free Negroes between 1810 and 1820; yet the number of Negroes voting in 1820 was almost 50 per cent less than in 1810.

Again, in 1815 [28] new amendments were made to the law, applicable in all of the state except New York City and New York County (Manhattan), where the law had taken effect a year earlier. The amendments stated that free Negroes in New York City were exempted from the law if they had obtained certificates prior to passage of the 1815 act. However, those persons of color affected had to register five days prior to the election, and they had to deliver their affidavits to the mayor for inspection. Opponents of Negro suffrage had finally achieved their goal.[29]

Negroes, firm believers in the revival of causes, felt that success was within their grasp when on March 13, 1821, the New York state legislature passed an act to revise the state constitution. To insure the success of their cause, a colored people's convention was held in New York City and a "Memorial" was drafted and sent to the legislature. Basically, the plea requested the legislators to forbid the passage of any laws that would interfere with Negro political and civil rights. Anti-Negro sentiment however was strong enough to pigeonhole the memorial.[30] One Republican delegate summed up the political resentment toward the Negro when he stated "that the political character of the national government was changed [in the 1800 election] by the vote of a single Negro ward in the City of New York." [31] The curbing of Federalist power meant the restriction of Negro suffrage. One of the new restrictive provisions in the new constitution was that Negroes, in order to be eligible to vote, had to own $250 worth of real property.[32]

Some 60 persons of color did own the requisite amount of real property, but only 16 actually voted. These 16 represented 12,575 colored residents in the City of New York in 1825.[33]

When all property qualifications for whites were abolished in 1826, Negroes were still subject to special property requirements, also in 1826, the residence requirement for whites was reduced to one year, but Negroes had to meet a three-year residence requirement in addition to the property requirement in order to vote.[34]

In addition to petitioning state legislatures, some Negroes sought other avenues of redress. One of these was the proverbial back-to-Africa movement. The American Colonization Society succeeded in purchasing the Montserado Territory in West Africa in December, 1821. A group of American Negroes settled on Cape Montserado in 1822, with J. Ashmun as one of their leaders. The colony was plagued with fever and barely managed to survive the first few years. In addition to fever, the colonists were attacked by surrounding tribes but managed to come to terms with them in time.[35] Later this settlement was to form the state of Liberia, with its capital of Monrovia, named after President James Monroe. Most American Negroes refused to join the society or leave the United States for Africa, possibly because, as we read repeatedly, members of the Colonization Society "know little of the colored population of this city [New York], except that segment that has come into contact with the law." [36]

THE NEGRO MOBILIZES HIS FORCES, 1827–1840

The legal abolition of slavery in 1827 saw the Negro in New York mobilize his own forces and secure the cooperation of some whites in his bid for equality. This period saw the emergence of Negro leaders in a divided Negro world. However, despite the dissention within Negro ranks, an organized Negro convention movement did arise.[37]

The Phoenix Society of New York, founded in 1833,[38] was the first organization completely devoted to the task of equalizing the Negroes' political and civil rights with those of whites. In 1834 the Fourth Annual Convention for the Improvement of the Free Colored people in the City of New York,[39] a well-established organization, appointed a special committee to study the laws of the State of New York with special reference to inequities based on color. The committee's findings were incorporated in a series of proposals and sent to the state legislature for action. In essence, the proposals requested and urged an end to Negro second-class citizenship.

By 1835 many Negroes realized that their ineffectiveness lay in their lack of political strength. They therefore decided to utilize the press to pressure the politicians into giving them what they wanted. The Negroes' lack of political power can be gleaned from an examination of two counties in New York City. In Kings County (Brooklyn) there were some 1,977 Negroes, but only 38 could vote. It was similar in Queens County (Queens), where some 2,813 Negroes resided and only 10 voted.[40] In 1837 there were some 44,000 Negro residents in the State of New York but only a very small fraction of this number could vote.[41] Negroes finally recognized their need for an alliance with other political groups in order to strengthen their political power.

The new Negro strategy consisted of bombarding the politicians with petitions and of currying public favor. Toward this end numerous Negro newspapers were established. A few of the better-known ones were *The Liberator*, the New York *Observer*, and the *Colored American*. There were many others that never got off the ground.

Petitions were the favorite method employed by Negroes to alert the public to their plight: they mentioned their needs continuously in the newspapers. On March 4, 1837, the colored citizens of New York State sent three petitions to Albany. One sought repeal of all laws authorizing out-of-state slaveowners to bring their chattel (slaves) into the state for the permissible nine-month period. (It was not until May 1, 1841,[42] that this was accomplished.) A second sought trial by jury for Negroes.[43] A third sought equal suffrage rights without regard to race, creed, or previous condition of servitude.[44] Again and again the petitions that were sent to Albany met the same fate as the 1821 Memorial—tabling or pigeonholing. The lack of action on the petitions caused some Negroes to become disgruntled, and they decided to align themselves with interracial groups to bolster their cause. Thus, in 1837 many Negroes joined hands with members of the New York Anti-Slavery Society and drafted 39 resolutions relating to civil rights and liberties.[45]

Many Negro organizations supported these demands, and they never lacked in numbers. Both the abundance of organizations and members offered a reservoir from which Negro leadership sprang. In 1838 several new organizations were formed. One was the Political Improvement Association of New York City under the aegis of

Charles L. Reason, an accomplished poet and journalist. This organization held its first meeting on Oct. 11, 1838.

An executive committee was appointed, and one of its functions was to appoint ward committees. The committees in turn were to distribute petitions for signature. When a sufficient number of names were collected, the lists were to be sent to both local and national politicians: the objective was to force the politicians to note the strength of Negroes in combination with whites and to have the politicians introduce legislation to giving the Negro equal citizenship with whites. The group held its second meeting on Oct. 24, 1838, to evaluate its effectiveness as an organization in promoting the Negro's cause.[46]

Many young colored persons joined their elders by forming organizations to push for equal suffrage. One such organization was the Political Association of New York City, formed in 1838. This organization started as an independent group. Later it became affiliated with the Political Improvement Association of New York City. To help insure success throughout the state, similar youth organizations were established in many cities. The objective was first to gain public sentiment for the cause and then turn this sentiment into pressure on the politicians.[47]

Over and over again the Negroes' experience with politicians made them aware of their precarious position in the fight for equal suffrage. They recognized that the politicians would respond only to organized voting pressure, and they lacked this kind of prod. Their predicament became more pronounced when they realized that the state constitution specifically differentiated between white and colored suffrage requirements. Negro leaders felt that the only way to resolve this problem was for Negroes to increase their real property holdings to the minimum legal requirement, and thus possibly sway the politicians toward giving them equal suffrage; the three-year residence requirement was considered of little significance. Toward this end the editors of the *Colored American* agreed to underwrite the acquisition of real property. They pledged to supply up to one half of the purchase price for anyone who would put up the other half.[48] But taxes were based on real, rather than on personal, property, and many Negroes who had the cash were loath to put their money into real estate.[49]

Even though the petition movement was fraught with weaknesses, it continued to be a leading factor in the Negroes' efforts to gain equal suffrage. Some Negroes also utilized the direct approach. The Colored Freeholders of the City and County of New York was one such group. At a meeting held on Oct. 29, 1838, members of this group resolved to vote only for political candidates whose platform would include the elimination of "all distinctions in the constitutional rights of the Citizens of the State." [50] Toward this end they interviewed the candidates of all parties in the 1840 election. Support was given only to those who agreed to plead the Negroes' cause.[51]

Negro leaders, as individuals and in cooperation with organized groups, pushed their special interests through politics. They emphasized again and again the importance of the ballot as *the* means of eliminating the Negroes' "second-class citizenship." Negro leaders active during the late 1830's and throughout the 1840's included Charles Reason, Samuel Ward (a runaway slave), and the Rev. H. Garnett. While Mr. Reason was mentioned earlier in connection with the Political Improvement Association of New York City, it was not noted that he often expressed in poetry the deplorable condition of the Negro. A few lines taken from his poem, "The Spirit of Liberty Call to the Franchise," illustrated the political aspirations of many Negroes.

> Come! rouse ye brothers, rouse nor let the voice
> That shouting, calls you onward to rejoice,
> Be heard in vain! but with ennobled souls,
> Let all whom now an unjust law controls,
> Press on in strength of mind, in purpose bent
> To live by right; to smell the free tones sent
> A glorious promise for the captive's fate.
> Then up! and vow no more to sleep, till freed
> From partial bondage to a life indeed.[52]

Samuel R. Ward was a strong supporter of the Liberty party, which stood for universal suffrage, without regard to race, creed, or previous condition of servitude. This organization lasted for about a decade (1840–1851).[53] Reverend Henry Garnett, publisher of the *Clarion* [54] during the years 1839–1840, also did much to apprise the Negro of the importance of the ballot.

NEGROES STRESS THE BALLOT 1840–1850

The 1840's revealed the Negroes' increased stress on the importance of the ballot and their willingness to ally themselves with white "liberals." In 1841 the Freedmen's State Central Committee held a convention at which it was decided that a more consistent course of action was needed. This meant increased ballot power and a greater effort toward moral suasion of white "liberals." The convention closed on the note that each colored elector had a duty to perform—to vote on May 11, 1841.[55]

A new act was passed on April 4, 1842, affecting the colored man. This time each Negro elector had to swear that he was 21 years of age and that he had been a citizen of the State for one year and a resident of the county for four months prior to an election. In addition to the age requirement, the colored man had to possess $250 in real property. If he refused to take the oath, assuming that he owned $250 in real property, he was automatically disqualified from voting.[56]

In unison, Negroes raised their voices to protest the new law. They rallied behind the Liberty party, which promised them relief. The Colored State Convention's delegates backed the party to a man at its 1842 Convention. Reverend Garnett addressed the convention and informed the group that the Liberty party was its only salvation. There were powerful white political figures who also favored the Negroes' cause. One was William Seward, governor of New York State from 1838 to 1842. Again and again, Seward addressed himself to the question of equal suffrage. On Jan. 5, 1843, he sent a letter to the colored citizens of New York, thanking them for their support.[57] On Jan. 10, 1843, he reiterated his feelings on the subject: "I should not deny them any right on account of the hue they wear, or of the land in which they or their ancestors were born." [58] In 1843 Garnett addressed the National Convention of of Colored Citizens of Buffalo and urged them to give their unqualified support to the Liberty party.[59]

Failure to achieve a goal usually gives rise to dissention; thus in mid-1843 we find discontent manifesting itself within the Negro group. One group of dissidents, spearheaded by the National Convention of Colored Citizens, opposed the petitioning campaign. William Davis, a delegate to the convention thought that more effective means were available to the Negro to push his cause.[60] He stressed self-reliance rather than dependence upon white folk: Negroes should "seek a way to secure their own equal rights." [61]

Despite the differences in strategy suggested, petitions remained the main source of protest by Negroes seeking to obtain equal suffrage. A statewide organization, the Fifth Annual Convention of Colored Citizens of the State of New York, met on Sept.

18, 1844, in the City of Schenectady. This group reasserted its belief in the use of the petition as a major vehicle of change and set up a special agency to facilitate the presentation of appeals to the state legislature.[62]

In 1845 some Negroes again had misgivings as to the effectiveness of the petition program, because political power and change is related to the number of votes a group can muster. The group's misgivings were based, in part on the fact that only 1,000 colored persons voted.[63] One opponent of the petition program, Wendel Phillips, a white man, advocated revolution as the solution. He was chairman of the business committee section of the Anti-Slavery Society. His alternative was presented to the society's members at a meeting held on May 6, 1845, in New York City.[64] Revolution, it was claimed was the only solution, since there was "no hope of political regeneration, except in a revolution that would shake the very elements of society as they were in the fifteenth century, [a revolution that] would lay the political institutions of the land in ruins." [65] New political institutions, in turn, would pave the way for equal political and civil rights for all persons regardless of color, race, or previous condition of servitude.

Despite the Negro's standstill in the area of equal suffrage, radical solutions failed to sway him from his peaceful methods. His constant pressure on the politicians began to show some success in 1845. In that year the state legislature presented to the voters a special act for referendum—the abolition of special voting qualifications for the Negro. However, the voters rejected the proposed amendment.[66]

White rejection of the Negro in the area of civil rights caused him to to hold out little hope for change when New York State held its 1846 Constitutional Convention. As at previous conventions, some equal suffrage advocates were present. One, Andrew Young,[67] offered a resolution that the special property qualifications be abolished. Immediately after his presentation, the Committee on Elective Franchise modified the resolution by dividing it into two sections: the first offered every white qualified citizen the right to vote for all officers on the state; the second offered the same privileges to the Negro. Each section was to be voted upon separately. Past experience repeated itself; the Negro continued to have unequal suffrage.

Most of the equality arguments enunciated at the 1846 Convention were repeats of those voiced at the 1821 Convention. Once more it was suggested that the word "white" be deleted from the first section of the law and made applicable to all citizens regardless of color.[68] Other equal-righters requested that the convention delegates reestablish the voting requirements for blacks found in the 1777 Constitution.[69]

Like their counterparts, opponents of the extension of equal suffrage reiterated the objections heard at previous conventions. "The Negro was created inferior," and "the history of the world has shown him [the Negro] incapable of free government." [70] The debate commenced on June 13, 1845, and continued through Oct. 1, 1846, except for a short recess. When it came to a vote, it was decided that two separate sections would be presented to the voters; 63 were for two sections and 37 for one section.[71]

Although accustomed to failure, proponents of equal suffrage refused to admit defeat. This time they sought to modify the real-property qualification by reducing the $250 figure to $100. Once more white liberals suffered a setback, but they did manage to convince some delegates to switch their vote. This time the vote was 50 to 42, a much narrower margin than on the previous issue.

Finally, the equal suffrage amendment was placed before the voters on Oct. 9, 1846.[72] Subordinate rights for Negroes were again upheld by the voters; 224,336 voted against liberalization of Negro suffrage [73] and 85,406 voted in favor of the amendment.[74]

Defeat meant a renewal of efforts to increase the Negroes' political power. These efforts concentrated on increasing the number of colored landowners. In an effort to enlarge the number of eligible Negro voters, a white liberal, Gerrit Smith, donated a huge tract of land to be distributed among Negroes.[75] Negro leaders like Ward [76] and Garnett also kept both the colored and white public sensitive to the issue both during and after the 1846 election. In 1847 Garnett summoned the National Convention of Colored People to Troy, New York. At Garnett's behest the delegates adopted a resolution stressing the growing impatience of Negroes with their "second-class citizenship." It was also agreed that more conventions should be held, and that more newspaper articles should be published to sensitize the public to the Negroes' cause.[77]

OLD REMEDIES AND NEW APPROACHES, 1850–1865

The next 15 years (1850–1865) saw the organized colored movement stress greater need for direct political action. Again, the old panacea of colonization was raised. Also during this period there was a favorable change in attitude by politicians toward the suffrage issue.

In 1851 the colored residents of New York City called a mass meeting to advance their cause. At this meeting it was resolved that (1) when voting, Negroes should consider the political parties' previous action toward their welfare, and (2) when new schemes were being considered, they should first be submitted to the special committee for clearing.[78]

Another theme of this meeting was introduced by J. J. Simons, an influential member of New York City's colored society, like William Davis in the 1840's, he revived the idea that Negroes should develop their own resources. Thus, the first meeting ended on a note of self-reliance.[79]

A second meeting was held on Oct. 3, 1851,[80] at which the chairman outlined the special committee's recommendations—on proposals previously submitted to it for clearance. The major theme that emerged was emigration to a foreign land. A country in Africa was to be chosen, then an agent was to be sent to make the necessary arrangements. These arrangements were to include the guarantee of equal socioeconomic and political status with the indigenous population of the country.[81] (No mention was made of the previous colony set up by the Colonization Society in Liberia.)

If self-reliance meant emigration to a foreign land, this was not what Simons had in mind. To him, emigration meant defeat. After the chairman had completed his report, Simons took the floor and reviewed the emigration question as it had developed over the past 25 years. He pointed out its failure to lure Negroes abroad. Such a failure, he said, indicated that Negroes preferred life in the United States. Still, many Negroes continued to embrace the idea of emigration. For example, R. H. Van Dyne, who followed Simons to the platform, introduced several resolutions related to emigration. With respect to the unequal treatment of Negroes, Van Dyne [82] resolved: "We, the free colored people of the City of New York . . . have, for a series of years suffered from unjust and cruel prejudice and degradation to which they have consigned us; . . . we do, after due consideration, deem it indispensibly necessary to our future well-being, that some immediate and decisive action on our part be suggested and wisely entered into." His second resolution made the direction in which Van Dyne was heading obvious—emigration—since he called for the organization and propagation of a group to be called "United African Republic Emigration Society." [83] Since, logically, such an organization had to be implemented to fulfill its purpose, the third resolution included the necessary functions to activate the new society.

In other parts of the state other Negroes were also leaning toward emigration. On July 6, 1853, the National Colored Convention met at Rochester, New York, and the delegates were addressed by Frederick Douglass on the question of foreign colonization. Like Simons, Douglass implied that emigration was no solution to the problem of unequal suffrage: "We ask that an unrestricted right to suffrage, which is essential to the dignity of the white man, be extended to the free colored man also." [84]

On Jan. 13, 1857, the state Senate reopened the question of the special property qualifications required of Negroes to vote. One Senate resolution dealt with the deletion of the word "white" from Article 2 of the constitution. The law required that any such proposed change must be published at least three months prior to the next election.[85] Both the Assembly and the Senate passed the resolution.[86] However, it was not published within the required three-month period previous to the next election. This made it technically impossible for the voters to act upon it. One explanation for this oversight was given by Gov. John A. King in his annual message to the legislature: "In the hurry of business, the amendment to the Constitution relating to Negro suffrage was inadvertently sent to the Executive Chamber, among other bills. . . . [It was] laid aside." Governor King suggested that the legislature reenact this amendment.[87]

By the end of the 1850's equal suffrage for Negroes had become a perennial issue. In 1859, the Hon. Charles S. Spencer of New York City argued in the legislature that "neither the color of one's skin nor African descent should be a basis for unequal citizenship." [88] The state Assembly adopted a resolution abolishing the special property qualifications required of Negroes to vote. This resolution was likewise required to be published three months prior to an election.[89] A rider to the bill would have extended suffrage to all females by deleting the word "male" from the election laws.[90]

In May 1860 the Free Suffrage Convention held its meeting in New York City, a further indication of the Negroes' sustained interest in the suffrage question. The convention chairman made public two resolutions formerly adopted by the group: The first stated that the colored people of the state based their claim to the elective franchise on the principles of human freedom and equality as set forth in the Declaration of Independence.[91] The second, proclaimed that, "as descendants of the revolutionary dead, as citizens of the

Empire State, as citizens of the United States, we appeal to every voter in the State to give us practical recognition of the principle upon which this government professes to be based, by voting at the November election to strike out from the State's Constitution that anti-Republican qualification clause which now disgraces it." [92]

On April 10, 1860, an act was again read to perfect an amendment to the State Constitution: an act to abolish the property qualifications in force against Negroes. This time the amendment was unanimously adopted and then referred to the judiciary committee for final drafting.[93] On April 13, 1860, both houses approved the bill; [94] the amendment was defeated by a majority of 140,429.[95] However, the relative decrease in the majority since the 1846 election was a form of victory for the Negro.

Rejection by the voters did not deter the Negroes from pressing the issue during the 1860's. February 27, 1861, saw the Negroes presenting a new petition to the state Assembly, demanding equal suffrage, and yet another on Jan. 6, 1864.[96] Negroes recognized that the legislature was only an initiating body, and that they had convinced this august body of the righteousness of their cause. Why could they not do the same with the voters?

So while the state legislature was discussing the issue, Negroes now concentrated on persuading the voters. One group headed by E. C. Sprague and William Wilkerson, with some 1,000 helpers, went out gathering signatures on Jan. 23, 1865. The petitions were then turned over to the state Assembly, requesting another public confrontation on the issue.[97] Reverend Garnett continued to keep the issue alive before the public. He made an impressive and impassioned speech before the National Convention of Colored Men on Oct. 4, 1865, at Syracuse, New York. However, despite Negro activity and the assistance of certain white groups, the public failed to grant equal suffrage to the Negro until the Fifteenth Amendment to the Federal Constitution was passed in 1870.

SUMMARY

Despite the institutionalization of black "outsider status" from Colonial times, New York State's first constitution, adopted on April 20, 1777, made no specific reference to race, creed, or previous condition of servitude as a basis for suffrage. However, by 1809 Negro suffrage was well within the orbit of a pariah class, a status in accord with the social and economic restriction of the Negro's equal opportunity in society. Restrictions became more stringent after the Negro was freed by an act of the state legislature in 1827. Abolition of slavery saw the beginnings of the Negro's reaction against his moral subjugation. To attain his ends on the political front, the Negro continuously petitioned the state legislature to right a wrong. Passage of the years saw the Negro win over the politicians but not the public before passage of the Fifteenth Amendment.

It was heartening to the Negro to note that the legislature could be prevailed upon to present an amendment to the public, even though it was constantly defeated by the voters. On the other hand the willingness of the politicians to present the amendment over and over again to the public may have been predicated on the fact that the public would reject it. This would be one way in which the legislators could shift the wrath of the Negroes from themselves to the public.

These setbacks failed to deter the Negro from pressing the issue, and such radical solutions as revolution or emigration never affected the grass root Negro population. In 1870 passage of the Fifteenth Amendment to the Federal Constitution saw the Negro attain, at least nominally, equal suffrage rights in New York State.

The New York Afro-American's Struggle for Political Rights and the Emergence of Political Recognition, 1865–1900

Although in the summer of 1967 many Afro-Americans had achieved an absolutely higher economic status in relation to their past condition, thcy continued to resort to violence to demonstrate their desire for economic, social, and political equality in American society. They also used political leverage in seeking to achieve this goal. In the chapter covering the period 1777–1865, it was seen that many New York Afro-Americans had refused to view with dispassion, or even with equanimity, their changed political status following the end of the American Revolution. Under New York State's 1777 Constitution, freed black Americans had held equal suffrage rights with whites, but shortly thereafter they discovered that most of these voting rights were being whittled down, a process begun by the Democratic-Republicans.[1]

New York Afro-Americans, individually and in concert, reacted to the watering down of their political rights by consistently petitioning the New York State Legislature to restore the rights they had held under the 1777 Constitution. However, the dominant group's stereotype of the colored American prevailed, and petition after petition failed to convince the legislators, at first, and later the white voters that they should restore equal political status to Afro-Americans in New York.

Although after the Civil War there was a peripheral upsurge in national awareness of the discrepancy in voting rights between

black and white, the colored American had to wait until passage of
the 15th Amendment to the Federal Constitution (1870) before the
New York State Legislature and the voters conceded to Afro-Americans a franchise similar to that enjoyed by the foreign born. As early
as 1826 all property qualifications had been abolished for whites
and white residence requirements had been reduced to one year.
However, Afro-Americans were excluded from this change. In addition to special property requirements, they had to meet a three-year
residence requirement in order to vote.

We shall deal at this point with some aspects of the post-
bellum period in American history, which brought a temporary renewal of national interest in the freedman's suffrage question. Our
primary emphasis will be on New York's colored Americans.

After New York's Afro-Americans finally obtained equal suffrage rights (citizenship and voting rights), many soon discovered
that they were still without such equal rights as nonsegregation in
public accommodations, schools, cemeteries, churches, housing, hospitals, and union membership. Many black Americans discovered
that politicians were able to curtail newly won political rights
through various political subterfuges, thereby reducing the effects of
political equality.

UNEQUAL POLITICAL RIGHTS PERSIST, 1865–1870

The termination of the internecine conflict revealed the existence
of a polarity within the Republic organization with respect to Afro-
American suffrage. At one extreme were the Radical Republicans,
and at the other, President Andrew Johnson. Ostensibly, both
sought to resolve the issue of Afro-American suffrage. The Radical
Republicans were led by such men as Thaddeus Stevens and Charles
Sumner. Stevens was the "unquestioned leader of the House of
Representatives from July 4, 1861, when it was assembled at the
call of Lincoln, until his death," in 1868. He was also chairman of
the Reconstruction Committee.[2] Sumner was a senator from Massachusetts.

The Radical Republicans contended that colored American
suffrage should be used as one basis for congressional representation
in Washington, D.C. These Republicans feared that the new freedmen would be deprived of their citizenship and voting rights after
the Civil War. They also suspected that the Southern states would
use freed colored Americans—now counted as whole men instead of

three fifths of a man on the basis of representation—thus increasing Southern representation by about one fourth in Congress [3] without extending the vote to the freedmen. To forestall this possibility—the use of the total male population as the basis for apportionment of United States Congressmen—the Radicals sought to restrict Congressional representation to the number of voters actually registered. This political move was intended to sway support in favor of universal manhood suffrage.[4] The anticipation of political manipulation was realized in the *Elkins* v. *Wilkins* case,[5] which stated:

> Slavery having been abolished, and the persons formerly held as slaves made citizens, this clause fixing the apportionment of representatives has abrogated so much of . . . [Art. I., par. 2, Clause 3] of the original Constitution [which] counted only three-fifths of such persons [slaves, as to alter the number used in apportionment of the House of Representatives].[6]

Although Andrew Johnson came from a state (Tennessee) that had joined the rebellion, he displayed unusual loyalty to the Union during the internecine conflict. This loyalty won him the nomination for the vice presidency. When Johnson took office on April 15, 1865, the Radical Republicans thought that they would now see the punishment of their former enemies, since Johnson had stated: "I hold treason is a crime and must be punished. Treason must be made infamous and traitors must be impoverished." [7]

The Radicals soon discovered, however, that they had misunderstood Johnson's views on politics, since his vision of treason and traitors was restricted only to those he termed responsible for secession, or members of the official and higher classes. It did not extend to the states nor to the masses of people of the seceded states.[8] The Radicals' realization that Johnson's plan was not to punish the Southern states led them to label the program "gradualism" and pro-Southern. In addition to pointing out that Johnson's program was favorable to the restoration of Southern states rights, they also pointed to his veto of the 1866 Civil Rights Act and his advocacy of leaving the Afro-American suffrage issue to the future action of the states, and other actions.[9]

Johnson's plan of reconstruction was contained in two papers and may be summarized as follows: (1) Repeal of secession, or the granting of amnesty to all the rebellious states, and (2) a presidential order, originally applicable only to North Carolina but later applied by successive orders to all the rebellious states,[10] based on the Constitutional clause that provided that the United States should guarantee to each state a republican form of government. The order provided for the appointment of a provisional governor of North Carolina, who was to prescribe the rules for "convening a convention." The delegates to the convention were to be chosen from the loyal people of the state, and were to amend the state constitution and adopt a republican form of government. The loyal people included only those granted amnesty, and *these were restricted to qualified voters in accord with the laws in force at the time of the secession.*

The irony of Johnson's plan was that he imposed Reconstruction upon white secessionists, and at the same time put them in control of its implementation. (This enabled them to reestablish the Civil War hierarchy, since they remained in the majority. It may be recalled that Afro-American freedmen were denied the vote before the war started, and thus by proclamation were excluded from the establishing of the new government under the Johnson plan.) This Southern majority was given the power to establish a new state constitution and, more importantly, to set the conditions of suffrage and other fundamental rights.

The new legislatures arising from Johnson's plan speedily proceeded to enact laws aimed expressly at curtailing the rights and privileges of the Afro-American. These enactments in turn produced a rift between the President and the Congress.[11] Concretely speaking, Mississippi passed laws requiring its officers to report to probate courts all free Afro-Americans under the age of 18, whose parents were without means to support them or who refused to do so. The court was to make the decision in each case and determine whether or not the youngster was to be apprenticed. Furthermore, in choosing the master for the new apprentice the court was to give preference to the apprentice's former owner.

New laws little different from the old "runaway-slave laws" were enacted to insure that the new apprentice was tied to his old master as he had been when he was a slave, and severe penalties were provided for the "apprentice" who ran away. The same legislature provided for blacks over 18 years of age. It determined that all free blacks found with no lawful employment or business were to be viewed as vagrants and subject to a heavy fine. If the "vagrant" was unable to pay the fine, he was "hired out," again preferably to his old master, for a term sufficient to produce the amount of the fine.[12] Laws similar to those passed in Mississippi were enacted in South Carolina, Alabama, and Florida, and elsewhere.[13] At a time when poverty was so prevalent among both blacks and whites, very few could prove judicially that they had the means to support themselves, so how could they establish that they could support their offspring!

Since the Republicans gained control over both houses of Congress in the 1866 election, it appeared that the extreme Radicals would hold the upper hand in the legislative branch of the national government. This view seemed even more plausible when Congress overrode the Presidential veto of the 1866 Civil Rights Act,[14] and, to forestall the Southerners' finding possible loopholes in the act, passed the 14th Amendment, which was ratified by the states in 1868.[15]

Emphasis on the Radical Republican program should not be taken to mean that there was no dissention within the party. Indicative of difference of opinion was the resolution passed at New York's 1865 Republican State Convention, held at Syracuse, to recognize the jurisdiction of the states in local affairs. However, there was party unanimity in the principle that the spirit of equal and impartial justice should be exercised in order to raise and perpetuate the full rights of citizenship to all people.[16] Thus, in accord with party principle, convention delegates recognized that New York State had been remiss with regard to granting equal suffrage to its own Afro-American population.[17]

Still, such Congressional action as did take place—passage of the 1866 Civil Rights Act, and the 14th Amendment—was intended as a challenge to the Southern whites' position on the equal suffrage. Many New York Afro-Americans recognized Congress' intent when they memorialized the Congress to table New York's Sen. James G. Blaine's proposal,[18] which was to be incorporated as section 2 of the 14th Amendment. It read:

> Representatives shall be apportioned among the several States according to their respective numbers, counting the whole number of persons in each State, excluding Indians not taxed. But when the right to vote at any election for the choice of electors for President and Vice-President of the United States, Representatives in Congress, and Executive and Judicial Officers of a State, or members of the legislature thereof, is denied to any of the male citizens of the United States, or in any way abridged, except for participation in rebellion, or other crime,

the basis of representation therein shall be reduced in the proportion which the number of such male citizens shall bear to
the whole number of male citizens 21 years of age in such State.

Ostensibly, Congress had the power to force states to extend
the right of suffrage to all citizens of the United States, unless the
state was willing to forego apportionment based on the whole
number. The U.S. Supreme Court's interpretation of this section
proved favorable to states rights. Thus, in the matter of a reduction
in state representation, the Supreme Court denied a petition to
curtail the State of Virginia from sending its quota of representatives in spite of its violation of Section 2 of the 14th Amendment.
The court reasoned as follows:

> Questions relating to the apportionment of representatives
> among the several States are political in their nature, and re-
> side exclusively within the determination of Congress.[19]

Utilizing the Supreme Court's decision, a U.S. district court was
obliged to dismiss an action for damages against Virginia's Secretary
of State for his refusal to certify an Afro-American plaintiff as a
candidate for the office of congressman-at-large, inasmuch as the
plaintiff's case rested on the theory that the apportionment act
passed by Congress and the Redistribution Act of Virginia, by
failing to take into account the disenfranchisement of 60 per cent
of the state's voters occasioned by the poll tax, were both invalid,
and that Virginia, according to Section 2 of the 14th Amendment,
was entitled to only four instead of nine congressmen elected at-
large.[20] Thus the plaintiff sought to force the State of Virginia either
to lose five of its congressmen for its failure to comply with the 14th
Amendment or to permit black as well as white citizens to run for
elected office and thus be entitled to its full quota based on the
total male population. The court's opinion read:

> It is well known that the elective franchise has been limited
> or denied to citizens in various states of the Union in past years,
> but no serious attempts have been made by Congress to enforce
> the mandate of the second section of the 14th Amendment,
> and it is noteworthy that there are no instances in which the
> Courts have attempted to revise the apportionment of Repre-
> sentatives by Congress.[21]

New York State, like the states below the Mason-Dixon Line, had its own method of disenfranchisement—special property qualifications. The 14th Amendment did confer citizenship of the Afro-American as a citizen of the United States, but not in the state in which he resided.

This statement can best be illustrated by offering in testimony Section 1 of the 14th Amendment and the U.S. Supreme Court's interpretation of implied Congressional intent. It reads:

> All persons born or naturalized in the United States, and subject to the jurisdiction thereof, *are citizens of the United States, and the State wherein they reside.*[22]

However, in the *Slaughter-House Cases,*[23] the Supreme Court offered the interpretation that

> with the ratification of the 14th Amendment a distinction between citizenship of the United States and citizenship of a State was clearly recognized and established, *not only may a man be a citizen of the United States without being a citizen of a State, but an important element is necessary to convert the former into the latter.* He must reside within the State to make him a citizen of it, but it is only necessary that he should be born or naturalized in the United States to be a citizen of the Union. [Therefore], *there is a citizenship of a State, which are* [sic] *distinct from each other, and which depend upon different characteristics of circumstances in the individual.*

To a great extent the foundation for the above opinion was established in 1857, notably in the *Dred Scott Case.*[24] In that case, Chief Justice Taney of the U.S. Supreme Court ruled that United States citizenship was enjoyed by two classes of individuals:

> (1) white persons born in the United States as descendants of persons, who were at the time of the adoption of constitution recognized as citizens in the several states and [who] became also citizens of this new political body, [the United States of America, and (2) those who, having been born] outside the dominions of the United States, [had migrated thereto and been naturalized therein].

Furthermore, Taney conceded that the states had the authority to confer state citizenship upon anyone in their territory, but could not make the recipient of such status a citizen of the United States. According to Chief Justice Taney, however, the Afro-American was ineligible to attain United States citizenship either from a state or by virtue of birth in the United States, even as a freedman descended from an Afro-American who resided as a freedman in one of the states at the date of ratification of the original constitution. In other words, the Constitution of the United States did not envisage the possibility of colored American citizenship.[25] However, the 14th Amendment rectified this deficiency by granting the Afro-American national citizenship.

Since the Congress had no intention of reducing a state's representation because it denied citizenship to the Afro-American, the ground work for denial of voting rights was laid. Ultimately the 14th Amendment did give each state the right, with some qualifications, to confer the vote on its citizens, as interpreted in the *McPherson* v. *Blacker* case.[26]

> The right to vote intended to be protected refers to the *right to vote as established by the laws and constitution of the State,* subject however to the limitation that the Constitution, in art. I, sec. 2, adopts as qualifications for voting members of Congress, these qualifications established by the States voting for the most numerous branch of their legislature.

Previously, we have noted that the qualifications were abandoned for all practical purposes by the states without Congressional enforcement. Thus the political promises made to the black American continued to be unfulfilled. On the question of Congressional intent, Horace Greeley [27] held qualms similar to those of the Afro-American when he alleged that the Congress of the United States purposely deferred the suffrage issue to the states because it feared adverse Northern reaction to federal enactment of legislation making it mandatory for United States citizenship to be synonymous with state citizenship. (It is recognized that there are vital constitutional issues involved between state sovereignty and federal jurisdiction.)

New York forced the suffrage question on the Southern states and on millions of incompetent ex-slaves, but denied the same to a few thousand Afro-Americans who were capable of exercising the right intelligently.

In his annual message to the state legislature in 1865, Governor

Fenton expressed his opinion concerning black suffrage in the South. He stressed the duty of each state to throw its whole weight and influence firmly on the side of the fundamental requirement and associated himself with all persons in a patriotic determination for "unity and the Constitution." [28] Thus, while there were many sincere believers in universal manhood suffrage, the power structure continued to ignore the issue. For example, in 1865 the New York State Republican platform ignored the suffrage issue; [29] the New York *Tribune* categorized many Northern politicians as those

> who desire the Right of Suffrage for the Blacks in the South [but are] opposed [to] the extension of the same right to the Blacks in the North.[30]

On the suffrage question, Leslie H. Fishel, Jr.,[31] affirmed the zeal of many Afro-Americans for the cause when he stated that race leaders sought relief in universal manhood suffrage from 1865 until ratification of the 15th Amendment in 1870. Understandably, both before and after the Civil War and in New York no less than elsewhere, political suffrage was espoused mainly by Afro-American politicians, intellectuals, and professionals, and at Afro-American conventions, in newspapers, and at local meetings. The audiences were primarily Afro-American with a sprinkling of white sympathizers. These audiences, aside from a hard core, were ever-changing in composition. Perhaps it was this lack of mass support that caused New York Afro-American petitions to the delegates of various state constitutional conventions for universal manhood suffrage to fail.

There were "soul-brothers" outside the Afro-American community, and among these were some outstanding politicians, and newspaper and magazine editors. One white soul brother, Wendell Phillips, addressed the Anti-Slavery Society at Cooper Union Institute in May, 1865. He suggested that the Constitution of the United States be amended to read:

> No State shall make any distinction in civil rights among the people born on her soil, of parents permanently resident, on account of race, color, or descent.[32]

Editorials in various newspapers sympathized with Phillips' suggestion. In essence they contended that the Afro-American was no longer a slave. He had acquired title to the rights of manhood and was entitled to these rights not only because he was native to the soil but also because there were thousands of his brethren throughout the country fully qualified by training and experience to exercise these rights.[33] Notwithstanding such instances of individual white support, the voters of the State of New York continued to deny the Afro-American the right of equal suffrage with naturalized immigrants.

Prior to and after the Civil War, various Afro-American leaders traveled throughout New York and New England to enlist public support for the cause of universal manhood suffrage. One of the most notable was Frederick Douglass, a self-educated runaway slave, who was publisher of *Northern Star* (later, *Douglass' Weekly*), was implicated in John Brown's raid on Harpers Ferry, served as minister to Haiti during President Grant's administration, and was a staunch Republican politician. On April 17, 1865, in the City of Boston, Douglass gave a speech before the Massachusetts Anti-Slavery Society, a predominantly white organization, wherein he emphasized that "taxation can only go with representation," and since the Afro-American paid his taxes, and fought for his country—then, "he knew enough to vote on good American Principles." [34] In conclusion, Douglass mentioned that only three times in American history was the Afro-American considered a citizen, each time during a war period—1775, 1812, and 1865—at all other times he was considered an alien.[35]

On June 2, 1865, Douglass spoke again on the future of the colored man before a mixed audience in New York City. This time he attacked New York State's politicians because they had refused permission to Afro-Americans to march in the Lincoln funeral procession.[36] Douglass pointed out that "slavery had been abolished forever—now we have no North, no South, no East, no West in American politics, but [we do have] one nation of all and for all." [37]

Another vocal Afro-American leader was the Rev. Henry H. Garnett, who obtained his primary education in New York City's African Free School and took his advanced education in theology at Oneida Institute. After graduating from Oneida, he was licensed to preach the gospel, and held the pastorate at Shiloh Presbyterian Church in New York City for almost a half century. In an address entitled "The Restoration of the Rebel States and the Claims of the Black Man" before a group at Cooper Union Institute in New York, he enunciated three points worth repeating: (1) The Afro-American was liberated by the Civil War; and he, as an American citizen, was entitled to vote. (2) The Afro-American was as intelligent as the immigrant who came to this country, usually ignorant of our culture and our history; on these grounds alone the Afro-American was as qualified as the white immigrant to the franchise. (3) The Afro-American was entitled to full suffrage because the future stability of the republic depended upon the extension of universal manhood suffrage to all citizens.[38]

Supplementing the efforts of individual Afro-Americans, was the concerted Afro-American action, which manifested itself in numerous conventions and memorials throughout the state. On Nov. 9, 1865, one such convention was held in Poughkeepsie,[39] at which the representatives agreed to finance a delegation to seek an audience with President Andrew Johnson. Among those included to represent the colored man were George T. Downing and Frederick Douglass. They were granted an audience on Feb. 6, 1866.[40] Downing, after paying his respects to the President, stated that the purpose of the delegation's visit was to obtain equality before the law in all states.[41] Douglass embellished the delegation's case by presenting arguments similar to those he had stressed at the Massachusetts Anti-Slavery Society's Convention the previous year.[42]

President Johnson listened sympathetically, but responded in the negative.[43] To placate the delegation, Johnson said that he had always been a friend of the colored population but that he could not adopt a policy that would end in a contest between the races. He answered the query on universal manhood suffrage by saying: "Suppose by some touch of magic, you could say to everyone, you shall vote tomorrow, how much would that ameliorate their condition at this time?" [44] He further pointed out that both he and the Afro-Americans were anxious to accomplish the same ends, "but that they proposed to do so by following different roads." [45]

In New York State there were some white politicians who did plead the Afro-American cause. One member of this group was Senator O'Donnell, who in 1866 reintroduced resolutions previously pigeonholed by his colleagues.[46] O'Donnell could even claim a degree of success for his program, since both houses of the state legislature adopted several of his resolutions. However, resolutions are not laws, and, like their predecessors, these measures followed the old pattern— tabled into extinction.[47]

Despite these setbacks, the black American continued to have faith in the democratic process; he believed that the dominant group would in time rectify the existing inequality by granting suffrage to all persons regardless of color. Many Afro-Americans displayed this faith at meeting after meeting in an effort to pressure the establishment into taking positive action. To wit: On June 6, 1866,[48] some New York colored Americans met to discuss the proverbial question: How can Afro-Americans obtain equal franchise qualifications? Numerous suggestions were offered by the audience; a distillation of these suggestions revealed at least one consensus: every American citizen had the right to vote by virtue of his national citizenship. Since citizenship gave a person the right to vote, then it was inherent in the basic principles of the Constitution of the United States, and any denial of this basic right was contrary to the Bill of Rights (the first ten amendments to the Federal Constitution). If this contention was denied, it was an appropriate issue for the Supreme Court of the United States to decide. To insure wide spread propagation of the issue, a Council of Fifteen was elected, and it was agreed to raise funds for the initiation of legal proceedings, if necessary, to carry the matter until the judicial process was exhausted.

There were more radical groups who felt that direct political action was the answer, and that legal proceedings would prove nugatory. To substantiate their position, they offered historical references. In 1866 this group held a convention in Syracuse, New York, and attempted to reconstruct the Union party of 1862.[49] The new party platform advocated support of a Congressional plan that would exclude any and all Southern states from the Union until Congress and the state legislatures extended universal manhood suffrage to all Afro-Americans.

The Union party had come into existence one year after the Civil War had started. It arose because of the reappearance of a party of opposition to the federal administration calling itself the Democratic party. That there was need for a new party that could unite the war Democrats and Republicans was amply demonstrated by the state and congressional elections of 1862.[50] Thurlow Weed, a Republican, therefore summoned a convention at Syracuse in 1862 at which time the Union party was organized and officially named.[51] The party's primary purpose was to maintain the integrity of the Union at all costs. It was well described by the convention's temporary chairman.

I see before me not only primitive Republicans and primitive Abolitionists, but I see also primitive Democrats and Primitive Whigs . . . primitive Americans. . . . As a Union Party I

will follow you . . . to the gates of death; but as an Abolition
Party, as a Whig Party, as a Democratic Party, as an American
Party, I will not follow you one foot.[52]

The party's two cardinal aims—destruction of the Confederacy and
passage of the 13th Amendment (abolition of slavery)—were achieved
after the 1864 Convention. However, the Afro-American suffrage
question was not fully developed as a part of the radical movement
until after 1866.[53]

On Oct. 23, 1866, a third approach to the attainment of universal manhood suffrage was enunciated at still another colored
convention held in Albany, New York. This body was credited with
being "on the whole, the most sensible body of its kind which had
yet met." Speeches made at this convention and at various places
throughout the state were temperate and "intelligent," and the
group's moderate treatment of public issues exemplified the "con-
servative politics of the State of New York" on the suffrage question.[54]

A fourth variation on the theme of attaining universal manhood
suffrage was the suggestion that Afro-Americans merge with other
minority groups. On Nov. 19, 1866,[55] in New York City such a convention was called: to press for equal privileges for all in the eyes of
the law. The convention's roster included such names as Mrs. Elizabeth Cady Stanton, Mrs. Susan B. Anthony, and Frederick Douglass.
Many persons in the audience were startled to learn from John
Bright that only three eighths of the country's adults could vote
and that five eighths of all adults, including women and Afro-Americans, were denied this right. Elizabeth Stanton stated that "as we
are now agitating the question of suffrage for the Colored Man, we
should do so for the women." Another delegate, Mrs. Elizabeth
Jones, presented a resolution to the effect that the right to suffrage
was the only possible security one can have, and that the denial of
this right to the Afro-American was only a consequence of slavery.[56]

Douglass pleaded for the right of women to vote and for a
coalition between Afro-Americans and women members of the
American Equal Rights Association. He requested that the women
take the colored American by the hand to elevate him. He thought
that these highly articulate women could exert some pressure on
the delegates to New York State's 1867 Convention.[57] In addressing
the American Equal Rights Convention, Pillsbury, a white advocate
of equal suffrage, paraphrased Thomas Jefferson and echoed Douglass

when he contended that all who fight and pay taxes have the right
to suffrage. Pillsbury played down the importance of the women
equal-righters when he stated that equal suffrage was more important to colored Americans than to women.[58]

Even when the New York Afro-American held the special property qualifications for voting, he frequently discovered that some
politicians had devised ways of stripping him of his potential political power. To wit: the law 1866 New York law,[59] which stated that
the name of no person (theoretically this applied to all potential
voters) should be placed on the register unless that person appeared
personally before the Board of Registrars during a registration period
as prescribed by the law. (This law covered the cities of New York
and Brooklyn where the bulk of New York State's black population
resided. The City of Brooklyn was incorporated into New York City
in 1890.) Prior to the passage of this law it had been common practice to copy the previous year's list.

The legality of the law was challenged on Nov. 22, 1866, in New
York's Supreme Court. The issue was whether or not members of
the board, when registering voters, should determine solely on the
basis of skin color whether a voter was an Octoroon, Quadroon,
Mustee, or African.[60] To be eligible to vote under the 1866 law,
Africans had to hold prior ownership of a $250 freehold; residence
requirements were the same for all citizens.

A product of a mixed alliance (miscegenation), James Darnall
decided to contest the constitutionality of the law by obtaining a
court order to show cause why the Board of Inspectors of Registry
and of Elections of the Second District of the 18th Ward of New
York should not place his name on the register. When the board
failed to comply with the court's order, the state's Supreme Court
issued a temporary Writ of Mandamus.[61] During the legal proceedings, attorney Gilbert, representing the plaintiff, informed the
court that his client was as white as any member of the bar then
practicing before the court. The defense counsel objected and
countered that Darnall was denied his right to register because he
was an African.

In an effort to clarify the issue, the presiding justice posited
the question: "What criteria should be used to determine when a
man is an African?" Plaintiff's attorney suggested that this question
be left to a jury to decide.[62] The case was adjourned until Nov. 26,
1866, and when it was reopened, the board's counsel submitted two
additional statements as to why the plaintiff's plea should be
denied: (1) Darnall had failed to present himself as an African, and

(2) Darnall, being an African, had not owned a freehold of $250 since Nov. 6, 1865; hence he was ineligible to be placed on the registry.[63] The court never rendered a decision in this case.

The suffrage status of the black man in most Northern States was summarized as follows:

> Neither in this state [New York], nor in Pennsylvania, nor in Ohio, nor in Indiana, nor in Illinois has Negro suffrage been generally presented as an article of party faith. On the contrary, in each of these States, the Constitutional Amendment [13th Amendment] has been approved as an official embodiment of terms presented by the victorious North to the defeated South.[64]

The New York Afro-American who had been granted equal suffrage by New York State's 1777 Constitution and had lost it in 1821, now placed his faith in the 1867 Constitutional Convention. (The 1846 revised State Constitution made it mandatory that every 20 years there be a constitutional revision. This placed the next constitutional convention on June 4, 1867.) Even though the state constitution had been amended in 1845, 1857, 1859, and again in 1860, the Afro-American's petitions for equal suffrage during these years had been bypassed.[65] By 1867 colored Americans felt that the post-Civil War climate was ripe for the eradication of the $250 freehold requirement for the black man.

Amid the proceedings and debates of the 1867 Convention, another petition was prepared by Dr. W. H. Johnson, chairman of the State Central Committee of Colored Citizens. This petition, pleading for equal manhood suffrage, was submitted to the convention's Committee on the Right of Suffrage, which was chaired by Horace Greeley.[66] On June 28, 1867, Greeley submitted the committee's recommendation to the full convention: that all discrimination based on color should be eliminated since all races are governed by the same state laws. The recommendation included a suggestion that these views be incorporated into the revised state constitution.[67]

Even though the Republican delegates at the convention were committed to the franchise issue, and even though they held a majority of 14, the committee's recommendation led to a protracted debate.[68] The Democrats opposed Afro-American suffrage, and they sought to have the question submitted to the voters on a separate referendum. Although the Republicans recognized the Democrats' strategy, aiming at ultimate defeat of the suffrage issue if submitted on a separate referendum, and stood for the question's submission with the total constitution, the debate stymied them. In the end the Radical Republicans managed to push the revised constitution, including the Afro-American franchise question, at least through the state Assembly, but the state Senate refused to accept the franchise as part of a total package.[69] This impasse resulted in a recess from Sept. 24, 1867 until Nov. 12, 1867, taking the franchise issue out of that year's election. Republican failure to incorporate the Afro-American issue on the ballot of the November, 1867 election proved a favorable political issue for the Democrats.[70]

Finally, on Feb. 27, 1868, both parties reached a compromise on the question of how universal manhood suffrage should be presented to the voters. They agreed to submit the question to a referendum, which was in fact merely a resubmission of Sec. I, Art. II, of the 1846 Constitution.[71] The referendum requested the voters to decide whether the $250 freehold should be eliminated as a requirement for Afro-American suffrage.[72] In the November, 1869 election, the voters refused to remove the freehold clause from the constitution. This denial of equal suffrage rights to the Afro-American was an expression of prejudice, a prejudice that revealed the "second-class" status of New York's colored population.

Deeprooted "racism" was exemplified in New York State's 1869 election. Citizens showed their displeasure with the Republicans by rejecting the newly revised constitution and putting the Democratic slate into office.[73] On taking office, the Democrats proceeded to rescind their predecessors' approval of the 15th Amendment.[74] It was only in 1870, after three fourths of the states had ratified the 15th Amendment, that New York State's colored population was assured of obtaining the franchise on an equal basis with whites.[75]

RESTORATION OF EQUAL SUFFRAGE

The State Committee on Federal Relations opened debate on the 15th Amendment in the state legislature by recommending its ratification on March 17, 1870. The Democrats continued to question on principle the giving up of a state right—to control the elective franchise. However, the resolution was adopted, along party lines, on April 14, 1870.[76] Still it took a state constitutional commission in 1873 to transmit an amendment to Section 1, Article 2, of the constitution erasing the property qualification.[77] The revised constitution was passed during the general election of Nov. 3, 1874.[78]

While the 14th Amendment had offered the Afro-American national citizenship, it had failed to bestow upon him *state citizenship* and the right to vote. Section 1 of the 15th Amendment sought to rectify this inequity. It reads:

> The right of citizens of the United States to vote shall not be denied or abridged by the United States, or by any State on account of race, color, or previous condition of servitude, [and Sec. 2, like that of the 14th Amendment, gave] the Congress the power to enforce this article by appropriate legislation.

However, the U.S. Supreme Court, in its initial appraisal of the 15th Amendment, was inclined to emphasize only the negative aspects. Thus,

> the 15th Amendment did not confer the right . . . [to vote] upon anyone, [it did merely] invest the citizens of the United States with a new constitutional right which is . . . exemption from discrimination in the exercise of the elective franchise on account of race, color, or previous condition of servitude.[79]

On April 27, 1870, the New York State Legislature passed an act amending the law relating to elections that repealed the property oath for colored voters; it also provided for a uniformity of oaths and abrogated the registry law requiring a special form of oath for Afro-American voters. Furthermore, the law provided that all existing laws and parts thereof that directed registrars and inspectors of elections to require colored voters to take the oath were to be abolished. The interrogation of Afro-American citizens or their witnesses was to be done away with, and it was made unlawful to administer any oath to Afro-Americans that was not required of other citizens. To enforce the intent of the law, it was stated that any inspector who failed to comply with the new law would be guilty of a misdemeanor, punishable by a fine of $500 and/or six months imprisonment. Although this act was to take effect immediately,[80] it was not a constitutional amendment, since it had not been voted on.

Afro-American reaction to the 15th Amendment ran the gamut from elation to skepticism. On the national level, Frederick Douglass, a staunch Republican, for political reasons eulogized his party, alleging that the Republicans instigated the enactment of the amendment: "It was in such humane acts that the glory and grandeur of the Grand Party lays." [81] In retrospect, an Afro-American political scientist described the 15th Amendment as a shift in the constitution from the state's right document it had been prior to the *Dred Scott Decision* to one of a new charter of liberty with the shift of power to the federal government.[82]

At the other extreme was the cautious reception given it by W. H. Johnson, a leader in New York's struggle for equal suffrage. His skepticism was revealed when he requested a legal opinion from the State attorney general.[83] (For a number of years, Dr. Johnson had been identified with the Republican party; he left it after experiencing some difficulty with Republican leaders over passage of the 1866 Civil Rights Act. Although he aligned himself with the Democrats for a while, he did not hesitate to criticize both parties.[84])

On April 9, 1870, Dr. Johnson wrote to Attorney General Peckham requesting legal clarification of the following:

(1) Is the 15th Amendment ratified?
(2) Does it confer the franchise upon colored Citizens?
(3) Is it the right of colored Citizens of this city [New York] to be registered with a view to voting on next Tuesday?

The attorney general's office was prompt in responding in the affirmative on all questions; its chief concluded his letter with the comment that inspectors who failed to comply were subject to a fine and/or imprisonment.[85]

During the early 1870's some political change was effected in the municipal scene. The change was initiated by the New York *Times'*[86] disclosures of Boss Tweed's nefarious manipulation of municipal finances. The *Times'* disclosures were complemented by Thomas Nast's cartoons in *Harper's Weekly*.[87] With the city on the verge of bankruptcy, a mass meeting was held at Cooper Institute on Sept. 4, 1871, resulting in the appointment of a Committee of 70. This Committee aided in the passage of a new charter for New York in 1873.

Although the new charter was a compromise between the recommendations of the committee and Republican politicians, it did offer a semblance of equal rights and representation for all. Now, minority voters could enjoy increased representation in the unicameral common council. Three aldermen were to be selected annually from each of the municipality's five Senate districts. Each voter was restricted to voting for only two candidates, and six additional aldermen were to be elected at-large, with each voter restricted to choosing four.[88] Its purpose accomplished, the Committee of 70 went out of existence on October 23, 1873.[89]

THE EMERGENCE OF POLITICAL RECOGNITION

Those Afro-Americans who had the vote—before 1870 and after—tried to pit one party against the other in an attempt to gain political benefits from both. During the post-bellum period, John A. Nail, a leading citizen of his community, organized a colored American Democratic club in New York. (This club had a continuous existence from its initiation in 1868 until well into the 1940's.) [90] Also there was the previously mentioned instance of W. H. Johnson, who left the Republican party alleging that the party had neglected the Afro-American in politics, and temporarily pledged allegiance to the Democratic party in the late 1860's. Following ratification of the 15th Amendment, political recognition became more widespread with the increase of Afro-American eligible voters. Thus, at the Republican State Convention held in Troy, New York, on May 8–9, 1872, rival factions agreed to send a colored delegate-at-large to the National Republican Convention in Philadelphia.[91]

The convention chose Frederick Douglass as its delegate-at-large and instructed him to deliver a certified statement of the state delegate's votes for the Republican nominee.[92] Douglass continued to embrace its ideology with great emotional intensity, saying: "I would rather be with the Republican Party in defeat, than with the Democratic Party in victory." [93]

The majority of the North's Afro-Americans continued their loyalty to the Republican party, but many of their disillusioned fellows defected to the Democratic party.[94] Thus, we had Dr. Johnson, who felt that some Republican leaders had let the Afro-American down by not supporting the 1866 Civil Rights Act, and others like George T. Downing, who felt that the party did not accord the colored American sufficient patronage. Peter Clark agreed with Downing.[95] James C. Matthews, a very able lawyer, whose legal suit against the City of New York opened the white schools to Afro-Americans, cast his first ballot for General Ulysses S. Grant and remained a strong supporter of the Republican party until 1872.

Judge Hamilton ascribed Matthews' shift from the Republican to the Democratic party when he stated: "In keeping with the ideas . . . which drove so many of the best men from the Republican Party in 1872, he [Matthews] joined the liberal movement in that year, and attended the Liberal National Convention as a delegate." [96] However, although they were aware of the Afro-American's new political power through equal suffrage, colored American leaders were unable to unite black voters into a force capable of extracting the full benefits from the politicians. If the franchise had been more generally exercised, its effect would have been very noticeable. [97]

Ever on the alert for their own benefit, the politicians managed to circumvent the principle of minority representation incorporated in the revised city charter [98] by the use of the gerrymander. [99] On June 8, 1874, [100] an act to amend the already amended Sec. I of Art. II of the City Charter—referred to earlier in relation to elections in the City and County of New York—was passed. This act contained a provision for the redistricting of the city and the county and for a change either in the number of, or the boundaries of, any election district. On June 12, 1874, the City of Brooklyn passed a similar act. Under these acts, Brooklyn and New York were to be redistricted, and election inspectors were empowered to challenge any person listed as a qualified voter until he had taken an oath that he was a bona fide voter in that district. Challenges proved plentiful in both cities.

Believing that the Afro-American was wedded to the Republican party, the Democrats pressed for passage of the districting act. Their belief was based on colored voting patterns and on the strong statements made by such Afro-American leaders as Douglass. He said, for example: "The Republican Party is the ship, all else the sea." [101] on Sept. 17, 1876, the Colored Republican Committee of New York informed the colored voters that they enjoyed the rights of American citizens under the Constitution only because of the Republican party, which stood for "free schools, free speech, hard money and universal suffrage." [102]

On the other hand, the Republicans did not object too strenuously to the new amendment, since they felt assured of the colored vote and thought that redistricting might even gain them some white votes. The loss of power in any given district would mean a reduced need to pass out political patronage to the Afro-American, and it could be used to bolster the white segment of the party.

In the process the emergence of political power in both a positive and a negative sense was revealed. On the positive side, the Afro-American did obtain equal suffrage rights, but his failure to unite behind his own leaders meant that he could not extract as much from the social structure as would be the case under a united banner. Certainly, Afro-Americans, by pitting one party against another and shifting allegiance from Republican to Democratic and often back to Republican, did so with a view toward extracting political patronage, sometimes with success. But these tactics often favored their opponents' chances to curtail the real impact on elections by gerrymander.

EQUAL VOTING RIGHTS BUT UNEQUAL STATUS

Using the experience gained during the post-bellum period, the Afro-American decided that his best strategy to obtain status equal with his achievement of full suffrage was to attack the Republican party from within while continuing to play off one party against the other. These tactics were used to reveal the pragmatic intentions of both parties toward the black American and gain him additional political patronage.

Many Afro-Americans consistently voted the Republican ticket. However, it was felt by some that the party had failed to carry out its pledges. One articulate observer said in a letter to the editor of the New York *Times:*

> Politically, I am a Republican. My first vote was cast for Fremont and my last for Hayes; socially, I am a "Colored American Citizen." Why talk of obliterating the color line in politics while the cause of it remains intact! To enable the Negro to occupy the status which the Constitution accords him, the Negro needs the aid and protection of wise laws, humanely administered through the influence of a public conscience—of that rare power which is the product of rising intelligence. There is only one resource left to the Negro, and that is to abandon the [Republican] party, that betrayed him, then to go to the Democratic Party. Finally, the Negro question is not one of politics, but one of human rights, of organic law, and the preservation of the spirit, as well as the form of republican government.[103]

To some extent the letter exposed the fact that most of the Republican platforms—those adopted between 1877 and 1885,[104]

which endorsed equal civil rights, theoretically a concomitant of
equal suffrage—were meant to hold the Afro-American loyal to the
party rather than to be put into practice. Even Douglass, a loyal
party man and one who had gained much personally from the
party, had some harsh things to say about the politicians' failure to
extend civil rights beyond equal suffrage.

> Out of the depths of slavery has come this color line. It is broad
> enough and black enough to explain all the maligning influences
> which assailed the newly emancipated millions today. . . . In
> one breath they tell us that the Negro is weak in intellect, and
> so destitute of manhood, that he is but the echo of [the] de-
> signing white man. . . . On the other hand, the whites vir-
> tually tell the Negro that he is so clear in his moral perceptions,
> so firm in his purpose, so steadfast in his convictions, that he
> cannot be persuaded by arguments, or intimidated by threats,
> and that nothing could restrain him from voting for the man
> and measures that he approved.[105]

In reviewing the political status of his brethren during the
1870's, an Afro-American newspaper editor suggested that the only
way the colored man could establish his rights was by using his
vote wisely, and that the black leaders take over the power in their
own districts from white wardheelers.

> Here in New York where the white wardheelers have con-
> trolled our vote ever since the war, what have we to show for
> it? These white heelers have made millions of dollars and a
> widespread notoriety which we cannot call fame, but what
> have the colored voters gained? The same is true of Boston,
> Providence. . . . Not one blackman in New York State enjoys
> the respect and confidence of the Republican politicians, or
> can they approach one of these sharpers on terms anything like
> an equal footing. *And this may apply to the colored leaders*
> *throughout the country in their relations to the National Re-*
> *publican Party.*[106]

However, despite various allegations made against the Republican
party's leadership by responsible Afro-Americans, as we have said,
the majority of registered colored Americans remained loyal to the
party on the national level.[107]

The repeated charges made by colored spokesmen did have some effect on the Republican State Committee that met in New York on March 4, 1884. The delegates declared that equal civil rights should be maintained, that the franchise should be respected, and that each voter should have a free ballot that would be counted honestly. At the 1885 Republican State Convention it was reiterated that it was unlawful to deny equal civil rights to colored Americans.[108]

Aware of the constantly voiced discontent, the Republicans, used a form of "tokenism" as a political expedient. Thus Afro-Americans like Douglass, W. H. Johnson, and others were accorded honors considered exceptional to men of color. Doctor Johnson was elected state committeeman-at-large and reelected in 1888. These black symbols proved politically remunerative, since they did sway some 25,000 registered black Republicans to vote the party ticket about 90 per cent of the time.[109]

Despite such tokenism, however, there was further evidence of dissatisfaction with the Republican party during the 1880's. For example, Downing made a complete break with the party in 1883 after he had talked with some leading Northern Democrats who convinced him that their party both believed and practiced racial justice. In part, Downing's political moves were based on a philosphy of competition between the parties that would give greater political recognition to the Afro-American. Downing thought that if more than one party was concerned, each would cherish the hope that it could obtain part of the Afro-American vote by concessions.[110] Timothy Thomas Fortune, a staunch Republican and a leader in the Afro-American community, advocated a political philosophy similar to Downing's. Fortune told his audience that their activity should be based on the motto: "Race First, and then Party." [111]

This philosophy began to have its impact on both political parties as early as 1884, when Grover Cleveland won New York State's electoral vote by only 1,109 ballots, foreshadowing the potential importance of Afro-American voting power in the state.[112] In 1886, President Cleveland paid off his political debt to the colored voters when he appointed James C. Matthews, an Albany Democrat, to the post of Recorder of Deeds.[113] The fees connected with this office were so sizable that the New York *Times* carried an article entitled "Matthews' Great Bonanza." It contrasted Matthews' salary with that of the managing director of the Democratic party. The article added that the combined salaries of the President's cabinet officers and his private secretary were less than what Matthews were earning in office. (Shortly afterward Matthews was recalled from his post).[114]

Following Cleveland's narrow electoral margin in New York State in the 1888 election, the Democratic party in New York made a concerted effort to win over the Afro-American vote. Its success may be gathered from the fact that the Democratic candidate for governor carried the state by 19,000 votes and that some 30,000 Afro-Americans voted for him.[115]

In 1889 the Chapin Democratic Club was established to create a sentiment among politicians that would make the suffrage of the colored citizens more forceful and effective. It also gave expression to the fact that Afro-American voters were anxious to line up with any agency that would promise assistance in their struggle for simple justice and a fair representation in public service.

Two Afro-American politicians controlled the Chapin Club and made their presence felt. They were Matthews and McCants Stewart. On Oct. 27, 1891, Stewart addressed the club's members and prophesied that "the time would come when it would no longer be necessary for Afro-Americans to hold special political meetings." Stewart further stated that the political skies were clearing and that Afro-Americans were growing thoughtful in political discussion, but that *they were dividing their forces in political action*. Finally he stressed the point that some Afro-Americans were against the division of the vote; these were the colored Republicans who clung to that party because it had emancipated and enfranchised them. Stewart contended that this was only a partial truth. It should be remembered "in political discussion . . . that in the Grand Army of the Republic, Democrats, as well as Republicans, fought side by side." [116]

To sway those Afro-Americans unconvinced of the "liberality" of the Democratic party, Stewart claimed that over 40 colored persons were employed in the public service with an average annual salary of $10,000.[117] C. H. Lansing, Jr., president of the club, buttressed Stewart's claims when he stated: "If, as I insist, the Democratic Party has been [a] cooperating and a contributing force to bring about this desirable condition, I am sure that with me you will applaud its liberality, and agree that it deserves the consideration of continued support." [118]

Afro-Americans in New York continued to form organizations to improve their welfare and attain full American citizenship. One such organization, the National Relief Association, had as its main purpose a crusade to secure the rights and privileges of colored Americans. It claimed that it had formed chapters in nearly every sizable city in the country and had enlisted the cooperation of nearly every prominent colored man. A call for a national convention to be held in Washington, D.C., brought its scheduling for Feb. 3, 1890.[119] The purpose of the convention was to take remedial action, especially in the Southern sections of the country where the political and civil rights of the Afro-American citizens were being denied, contrary to the Constitution of the United States.[120]

The political power held but not fully exercised by the Afro-American was noted in the New York *Tribune*, which contended that colored citizens could realize enfranchisement by their own efforts if only they were organized and directed wisely. The article was in part an attack on the poor leadership that existed in black politics. It was further argued that colored citizens should gather themselves peaceably in those states, counties, or towns where they could be assured protection of these rights and to leave those places where they were not protected. Wherever they decided to reside, they could, with assured protection and the aid of a powerful organization, purchase property and become respected members of the community. The power of their vote in those areas where they settled would soon make their influence felt.[121]

During the 1894 State Constitutional Convention, neither party could use the suffrage issue as a political tool, since both had already accepted in principle the suffrage right of the Afro-American in the middle 1870's. In order to gain the colored American's vote, therefore, each party stressed the amount of political patronage it had dispensed to the colored community. As is typical of politicians, each party claimed the complete allegiance of the Afro-American voter. It may be stated categorically that the majority of the Afro-American leaders still favored the Republican party at election time. However, the bulk of the colored voters did not always follow their leaders.[122] Still, Republican black committees followed the standard line, eulogizing their party at the expense of the Democrats.[123] The policy of extracting political patronage continued with the pitting of one party against the other. Thus Jacob Sims, editor of the New York *Echo* (a colored newspaper), who helped to organize the Afro-American Republican League in 1895, had his price for loyalty. Sims pressured the Republican leaders in New York to give more state and municipal jobs to the colored. Like his predecessors in both parties, he argued that the Afro-American vote warranted such action.[124]

Once more in 1898 the Democrats felt optimistic; they thought that they would capture a sizable portion of New York's Afro-American votes. Again they miscalculated. This time Tammany Hall's hopes were shattered in part by the strong personality of their opponent's gubernatorial candidate—Theodore Roosevelt. Many Afro-American soldiers had served under his command in the Spanish-American War, and many had distinguished themselves as "Rough-Riders" in capturing San Juan Hill. Colored folk were indebted to Roosevelt because he was instrumental in getting the Civil Service Commission to place persons in jobs through criteria based on qualifications rather than on color. In his speeches, Roosevelt praised the Afro-Americans' achievement on the battlefield and promised them he would aim at equal opportunity in government service. In fact, Roosevelt's attitude as well as the agitation by many Southern Democrats against the black man helped to win over the Afro-American clergy.[125]

Ever optimistic, the Democrats thought they had the city's Afro-American vote in the palm of their hand in 1900, but they had overlooked the New York race riot earlier that year. The Democrats who were in local political control were held responsible by leading Afro-Americans and some white newspapers for the police brutality exercised during the riot. One newspaper went so far as to allege that many dark Democrats were fleeing the party.[126]

CONCLUSIONS

It should be recognized that the Afro-Americans had won definite advantages in the 1870–1900 period: freedom, education, and organization. However, they failed to capitalize fully on their political position. Moreover, it should be realized that these advantages were limited when compared with the progress made by the whites. The New York Afro-American did reside in a state where the two-party system offered him a vote, and certainly a greater power potential than in the South; yet he failed to maximize his advantage. To achieve the latter would have required united action to break his ties—materially, ideologically, positively, and negatively—with the Republican party. However, this united action never materialized because of "token patronage," corruption, and political promises continually renewed in campaign speeches but rarely delivered in practice.

Of course there were other basic reasons for the Afro-Americans' failure to acquire power in the existing political structure. They were outnumbered. They lacked the experience and resources to support a strong organization of their own. They had a press that was subsidized by one party or the other—and the subsidies were curtailed or stopped between election years, making for little or no continuity in an Afro-American press.

Most vital was the factor of racism: usually, New York State's laws proved ineffectual; the politicians neglected to grant the Afro-American full political and civil rights. Thus, Afro-Americans were never fully accepted on a par with other men, only as "second-class citizens." When they acknowledged their "second-class status," they rationalized by using race as the basis, but this rationalization came as an afterthought, since the color line had previously been drawn by whites. Such programs as they did try to develop were based on a moral appeal. The turn of the 20th century did see a mild breakthrough, however, as some Afro-American politicians gained occasional perquisites from both parties, given in order to hold, or to gain, their allegiance.[127]

Afro-Americans in New York: A Circle of Discrimination, 1625–1965

Previously, by utilizing history, we have sought to establish the formation of, and the institutionalization of, a circle of discrimination. We shall now employ a longitudinal approach, although not strictly a chronologically historical one, in an effort to implement the theoretical framework outlined in our introduction. It may be recalled that this framework had the following salient features: (1) Afro-American subordination to the white man, (2) his social subordination, reflected in limited economic or employment opportunities, (3) his restricted social mobility, even when he was able to upgrade his economic status, and (4) his noncompetitive employment status because of social discrimination. It should be remembered that the above are subject to *inverse causation*, that is, starting with the economic rather than social subordination, but the end results would be the same.

THE FORMATION OF NEW YORK'S CIRCLE OF DISCRIMINATION

Afro-American subordination. It is of secondary importance to our thesis whether or not Afro-American subordination preceded or antedated the introduction of slavery into New Amsterdam; what is primary was the white man's denial of an independent social status to the Afro-American. This denial became part of our folkways.

Later it was institutionalized and was to form the basis of the circle of discrimination.

Of course, under Dutch rule some Afro-Americans could look forward to manumission, but emancipation carried with it a "mark of distinction," and restricted economic and social status. To wit: the 11 Afro-Americans manumitted by the Dutch were unable to fulfill their role of pater even in a manner accorded to indentured servants. Thus, they could not impart even a semblance of middle class values to their offspring, since they had no continuous control over them. (It may be recalled that children born and yet to be born were legally subject to involuntary servitude.)

What hope the Afro-American had for future manumission, possible acculturation, and accommodation in white society was curtailed when the English took over New Netherland. They made it next to impossible legally to manumit slaves, institutionalized social distance between blacks and whites, and laid the groundwork for institutionalization of the circle of discrimination. This was substantiated by the various legal codes passed by the common councils of New York; codes that restricted manumission, assemblage, and freedom of movement and established a wall between the freed black American and white society. It was was further evidenced by a society in which social status was linked to land holding and agriculture,[1] and landholding was denied to Afro-Americans. This might have left education as an avenue of upgrading status, but educational outlets were either closed or highly restricted.[2]

Furthermore, the English, in order to ensure the almost complete walling in of the Afro-American, refused to permit black conversion to Christianity. Perhaps one of the most vivid illustrations of white racism was the instruction to Justices of the Peace "to kill, destroy . . . any Negro who threatened the stability of the colony." Thus, English Colonial society extended little hope for the Afro-American to acculturate and forced him to develop his own sub-society.

Social subordination, limiting employment opportunities. What seemed to be a liberal Dutch policy toward Afro-Americans—manumission—was actually a matter of expediency. The granting to slaves of company-owned land and even the transfer of land ownership to the 11 manumitted half-slaves in 1644 was in line with the company's profit-oriented economic policy. Dutch expediency was beneficial to most Afro-Americans, since they could look forward to manumission. At least the exceptional Afro-American could hope for some recognition from Dutch society, as exemplified in the instance of one named Francisco, an Afro-American, who was granted a patent in Boswyck, and managed to amass sufficient sums of money to become a large landowner. Another Afro-American named "Antoon, the Negro" found escape through the Dutch armed forces.[3]

The Dutch policy of manumission and economic expediency can be explained by the monopoly held by the Dutch West India Company and its lack of concern with colonization. The inhabitants of New Netherland expressed their dependent status as "a long and bitter struggle with successive directors for some measure of home rule," which was long in forthcoming.[4] New Amsterdam did attain municipal status in 1653, when local government was turned over to the Burgomasters and Schepens. However, the lack of either an indigenous and/or imported population forced the Dutch to rely heavily on Afro-Americans as their main source of labor.[5]

To minimize the loss of slaves (runaways, joining the Indians, and the like, the Dutch tried to wed the Afro-American to the land by promising him possible manumission and land ownership. In turn, the latter formed a stable labor source for the company, permitting it to exploit the New World's resources. Secondly, colonization schemes having failed, the small number of freed Afro-Americans made for little competition between white and black man.

Although the Dutch and English both subscribed to some of the broad tenets of mercantilism,[6] the Afro-American's status regressed under English rule. Unlike the Dutch, the English did foster colonial economic development (notwithstanding such restrictive enactments as the Molasses, Townshend, and Grenville acts).[7] This was manifested in New York's economic and population growth. In 1660, four years prior to the English takeover, New Netherland had a total population of 1,800. By 1680, after some 16 years under English rule, the total population had risen to some 2,400, showing an increase of about 75 per cent.[8] It was the proportional change favoring white as against black during this period that brought on the need for the displacement of blacks from employment. This was manifested in the pressures applied by whites to local governments and the passage of various black codes. These codes included the limiting of Afro-Americans in the trades and a denial of their ownership of private property. Thus it was under English rule that the circle of discrimination had its beginnings, and it was to become institutionalized after the American Revolution.

Restricted social mobility, even when the Afro-American was able to upgrade his economic status. Historically, a change in the economic status of an individual has led to an upgrading in the social status either of the original amasser or his progeny.[9] For example, during the Colonial period one John Lamb, whose father Anthony Lamb was sentenced to death for a crime committed in England, was able to join the social elite. When the elder Lamb's sentence was commuted because of his age, he was banished to Virginia. Here, the younger Lamb started his economic and social career by learning his father's trade of instrument maker; later turning his talents to selling wine and sugar. He married a girl out of his class, and became a member of the upper class. "Special significance attaches to this story since it so well demonstrates that a man's parents proved no bar to gentility, even for an artisan, provided he had other qualifications." [10]

Seymour Lipset and Rheinhold Bendix contend that in an industrial society there are two basic reasons why social mobility exists: "Changes in demands for performance, and changes in the supplies of talent." [11] This has taken place in American class society since the American Revolution, especially in the North. However, when these two reasons did work for the Afro-American, it was only in isolated instances. This blocked social mobility has been chiefly responsible for the formation of a parallel black social society.

Social discrimination and economic status. To repeat, the denial of independent social status to the Afro-American limited his ability to realize his future aspirational social status. (Future aspirational attainment or realization may be linked with a class society and has served as an incentive to many white immigrants.) Taking the example we explored in the previous paragraph from the point of view of the father's history, we learn that "in 1724 a youthful mathematical-instrument maker named Anthony Lamb was standing in the gallows of Tyburn awaiting execution as the accomplice of the notorious Jack Sheppard." Because of his youth and the fact that it was his first offense, his sentence was commuted and he was banished to Virginia for seven years. Following his sojourn in Virginia, Lamb migrated to Philadelphia and started a technical school. Later in life, Lamb moved to New York, married, and became accepted as a respectable citizen in the business community." [12] Physical mobility, even in our open class system, failed to solve the Afro-American's problem because of his visibility. When he was a slave his occupational mobility depended upon his inborn traits, and these were maximized to enhance the social and economic status of his owner. When he was free, his visibility restricted his occupational entry into the trades. Another factor proscribing his social and economic upgrading was that he was a heathen. One foreign visitor to the American colonies described the Afro-American's social and economic status as follows:

> I visited a coal-pit: the majority of the mining laborers [were] slaves, . . . but a considerable number of white hands [were] also employed, and they [occupied] all the responsible posts.[13]

The relationship between the social and economic is further established when we return to our earlier example of the carmen's strike. In this instance the city council issued an order that all able-bodied persons could seek such employment without a license, but Afro-Americans were excluded.

Before we turn to the *Institutionalized Circle of Discrimination,* the relationship between social status and land ownership in an agricultural economy should be mentioned. Land ownership was a primary source of income and status. Since the 1712 law curtailed any accumulation of land by Afro-Americans other than that previously acquired under Dutch rule by manumitted slaves, the English laws circumscribed the black New Yorker's present and future social status.

In summarizing the Colonial period it may be noted that both the Dutch and English contributed to the formation of the Afro-American matriarchal family.[14] Under slavery there was complete dependence upon the mother for psychological sustenance. The Negro's economic maintenance was left to the slaveowner, who cared for him like any other chattel. Once manumitted, the father could not establish and maintain a "father image," since under Dutch rule his children were subject to company slavery and under English rule he had difficulty in maintaining a family financially. The embodiment of the matriarchal family in slavery had been extended to include the legal system.

> Thus the law could permit no aspect of the Slave's conjugal state to have an independent legal existence [no independent social status] outside the power of the man who owned him: The relation of master and slave [was] wholly incompatible with even the qualified relation of husband and wife, as it [was] supposed to exist among slaves.[15]

AN INSTITUTIONALIZED CIRCLE OF DISCRIMINATION

Social subordination: The American Revolution, with its consequent political changes, failed to affect the Afro-American's second-class status. In the early 1800's one organized group described the colored American's status by saying that

> any attempt to improve the Negro's [status] would defy public sentiment, threaten, if not destroy the very fabric of American society, and inevitably produce commotion, effervescence, collision and bloodshed. [Furthermore], if no conceivable amount, or type of legislation [could] successfully temper white prejudice, neither could Negro education and economic independence.[16]

After the passage of the 1863 Conscription Act,[17] white racism reached a feverish pitch, as manifested in the week-long riots. During these riots colored men, women, and children were brutally attacked in the streets.[18] Once the draft riots subsided, "a more kindly spirit toward colored people began to manifest itself in New York in the weeks and months" that followed. However, this changed attitude proved evanescent.[19] During this same period organized labor allegedly accepted the prevailing social prejudice and used it to "restrict competition so as to safeguard job monopoly." [20] This allegation has some substantiation in the history of the American labor movement.[21]

During the middle 1860's there were at least 32 national unions whose records showed that Afro-Americans were refused membership because of their color.[22] Continuation of Afro-American social subordination by craft unions was illustrated by an early 20th-century editorial in the *Electrical World* (official organ of the International Brotherhood of Electrical Workers of America, IBEW). The editorial stated: "We do not want the Negro in the International Brotherhood of Electrical Workers." [23] Again in 1936, when Local 3 of the IBEW struck the Standard Electrical Equipment Company, the local refused to accept striking Afro-Americans when the dispute was settled. Following a contract containing a closed-shop clause, the Urban League of Greater New York charged the union with discrimination against Afro-American electrical workers, some of whom had been employed by the company for periods from two to ten years. What heightened the Afro-American belief in his social subordination was the fact that the colored strikers had been requested to join the picket line by the union's organizer.[24] (It is the usual practice to accept all strikers into the union when the strike is settled to the satisfaction of the union.)

The 1940's revealed a continued practice of social subordination by businesses and craft unions. This was illustrated in a statement made during the height of World War II by the secretary-treasurer of the Seafarers' International Union (SIU).

> Mr. Hawk stated that [neither] the President [Franklin Delano Roosevelt] nor anyone else is going to tell men with whom they are going to live and to a seaman a ship is his home.[25]

It was little different in industry or on the railroads. In 1945, Miss Thelma Williams was assigned by the U.S. Employment Service as a file clerk with the reservation bureau of the Pennsylvania Railroad. Following her interview, she was politely but firmly informed that the company did not hire Afro-Americans for white-collar positions.[26] In the 1960's the same pattern persisted in organizations such as General Motors Corporation.[27]

To generalize the situation in New York we have assumed a normal distribution curve with respect to native intelligence for both white and black. Based on this assumption it was found that social differences were partly responsible for New York City's occupational distribution. Thus in 1960, in terms of the total population, the proportion of whites in financially rewarding positions was notably higher than that of nonwhites. There were some 26.1 per cent whites employed in professional and technical posts compared to only 10 per cent of nonwhites so employed. A similar disproportion was found to exist in other occupations, including clericals, factory operatives, and kindred workers; service workers; and even those in the unskilled trades. To single out two categories, service and laboring, the Afro-American proportion was at least twice that of the whites.[28]

A similar statistical contour was prevalent among the black female population. The proportion of white females in professional classifications was much greater than the corresponding proportion for nonwhite. Whereas white females constituted some 18 per cent of the professional and technical workers, nonwhites numbered only 10 per cent. Social subordination is further highlighted when, in the critical area of clerical employment, the proportion of white to non-white is examined. The 1960 Census revealed that white females accounted for at least 44 per cent of the total in this category, whereas nonwhites accounted for less than 19 per cent.[29]

In 1965 social subordination was still practiced by the business community and many craft unions. To cite but one example, a young Afro-American "with a modest amount of experience and skill as a clerk-typist" was referred to a Wall Street bank to fill a vacancy. He was rejected as "socially unacceptable." When the agency's interviewer was asked why, he made the following comment:

> Listen, I get my fees by putting people to work and I don't care what color they are as long as I get my money. But if you offend a client you lose an account. This guy was well qualified, young, personable. I didn't know the bank. The day after I sent him over my boss got a call from the bank's personnel manager and he said: "What's the idea of sending me a Number Two?" [30]

At this juncture it may be helpful to recapitulate and elaborate on some of the sociological effects upon the Afro-American: (1) His legal emancipation in New York failed to erase the white man's association of the Afro-American with his former slave status, thus helping to institutionalize his subordinate social status; and (2) his subordinate social status helped to prescribe the colored American's modus vivendi. (This low status was deepened by the preference given to immigrants in employment and in social mobility.) In combination, segregation in housing and *de facto* segregation in primary and secondary schools, among other factors, aided in creating a disorganized Afro-American community; a community that was "weak in its control . . . [making it] easy for its institutions to disintegrate and [its] behavior not to be controlled by conventional standards." [31] The disorganized community found it difficult to acquire and to hold on to middle-class values. Thus, those "non-acceptable" social standards that were adopted by the Afro-American contributed to a huge percentage of psychologically broken homes and made for the absence of spiritual and ethical values in those homes.[32] When compared with white homes in similar financial circumstances, these broken Afro-American homes revealed a relatively higher rate of families headed only by a mother and with neglected children.

A few statistics may help to give this contention sharper focus. In the August, 1959 report of New York City's Department of Welfare it was shown that colored Americans constituted at least 31 per cent of all persons on home relief. In addition to those on home relief, at least 58 per cent were labeled as being in the category of needing Aid to Dependent Children (ADC).[33] The department's 1962 study of ADC families revealed that at least 36 per cent had only illegitimate children, whereas some 20 per cent had both legitimate and illegitimate children.[34]

Again in 1964 the agency's report analyzed the impact on its rolls of fatherless homes resulting from desertion, divorce, or illegitimacy. Thus, of the 2,511 cases accepted by mid-1964, at least 66⅔ per cent of the families had no father at home. Converting this percentage into numbers, we have the following breakdown: (1) from common law marriage, there were 802 families added to the agency's rolls, (2) from desertion, 857 families, and (3) from legal divorce and/or legal separation, 175 families.[35]

S. and E. Glueck believe that children of families without a father are predisposed to delinquency, because the lack of a male parent tends, "either by affecting their character, or by leaving them inadequately supervised, or both," to make them less susceptible to normal controls.[36] Other investigators, such as Shaw, Cloward, and Ohlin, lean in the same direction or state that culturally and economically deprived children will display greater tendencies toward delinquency and crime.[37] In other words, these children "learn to accept delinquent patterns as the natural way of behaving," [38] in order to compensate for their circumscribed social, economic, and cultural milieu.

In 1968, Dr. Blumstein, executive secretary of President Lyndon B. Johnson's crime commission and an official of the Institute of Defense Analysis, lent credence to this thesis when he contended that the urban Afro-American boy, age 10, will have a 90 per cent chance of being arrested for a nontraffic violation in his lifetime; whereas all urban boys, age 10, would have a 60 per cent chance of arrest for the same violation.[39]

Social subordination, with its attendant economic repercussions, was influential in aggravating the Afro-American male's failure to achieve social approbation in accord with middle-class standards and values. Hence it assisted in the growth of maternal families by having the female assume the father image. To wit: In 1963 the U.S. Department of Health, Education and Welfare disclosed that the number of colored American females with bachelor's and/or master's degrees greatly exceeded that of males. Since highly "educated Negro women outnumber Negro men with comparable education, Afro-American women frequently marry below their educational and social level." Many of these colored females were able to earn more than their spouses—a condition found in many areas of Afro-American employment—and it often created a state of insecurity, jealousy, and antagonism on the part of the husband toward the other members of the family. The deflation of the male ego, or his failure to achieve a "normal pattern" within the family circle, added to the rate of desertion and divorce. This further increased the number of matriarchal Afro-American families, dependent and neglected children, and potential delinquents.[40]

There is some evidence that the matriarchal family with dependent and neglected children tends to be self-perpetuating.[41] New York State's Moreland Commission on Welfare reinforced this contention when it stated that "dependency can be a continuing situation for generations." In New York, 26.9 per cent of the welfare recipients were children of parents who themselves had been on public assistance.[42]

Blocked economic opportunities. Since we have alluded to the impact of social subordination on blocked economic opportunities, it may be well to examine some of the economic effects and reveal the interrelationship between these two factors.

Max Weber has defined economic opportunity as

> the way in which the disposition over material property was distributed among the plurality of the people, *meeting competitively* in the market for the purpose of exchange. [This] in itself created specific life chances.[43]

Thus it was within the control of the employer to help create a competitive market. But the employer, frequently in combination with the public, decided to use formal and informal controls to block the Afro-American's economic or specific life chances. (It was the employers' refusal to hire Negro Americans or, if they did hire, to restrict them to deadend jobs, that was condoned by the public.) These discriminatory practices, which were tantamount to blocking job entry, occupational mobility, and income, were related to the white man's stereotype of the Afro-American and his feeling that white people generally must hold a higher economic status than the average colored American. There are at least two manifestations to support this contention. (1) The Afro-American's degree of job entry depended upon the phase of the business cycle in operation at any time; best during prosperity and with great likelihood of displacement during depressions.[44] (2) The Afro-American's rate of unemployment historically has been about twice that of whites. In combination, these two items help to illustrate why the Afro-American's income and life's chances have been relatively lower than those of his white counterpart.

By and large, education did not give the Afro-American equal economic opportunity and equal earnings with his equivalently educated white counterpart. During the 1930's a Temple University professor, while waiting for his train, talked with some Afro-American waiters in Pennsylvania Railroad Station. He was shocked to learn that many of them held a doctorate in philosophy from recognized universities, but could not find academic employment.[45] (Admittedly this is an extreme case and one that existed during the Great Depression, but in degree it was little different from what many Afro-Americans found to be the case during the 19th century.) A 1963 study covering New York State again disclosed that many educated Afro-Americans were discriminated against in employment, even as their skilled and semi-skilled brethren. This study found that Afro-Americans with education comparable to whites and employed on similar jobs were paid much less for the same work.[46]

There were many instances where the Afro-American found himself in a noncompeting group.[47] In May, 1965 a national survey of manufacturing and business organizations revealed that a "considerable gap" existed between paper policies favorable to Afro-American employment and everyday practice. An Industrial Relations Counselors study reported that

> Negroes, generally, [were] still being hired for the lower paying, low status jobs. [The report exonerated employers by alleging that] well-qualified Negroes [were] in short supply today . . . and will continue to be in short supply for some years to come.[48]

Although the report was issued in mid-1965, it may be of some interest to see what "well-qualified Negroes" with educational backgrounds comparable to whites were earning in New York City. The 1960 Census revealed that some 4 per cent of New York City's Afro-American population had earned a college degree. (Of the total population about 10 per cent had attended college and approximately 25 per cent had earned a high school diploma.) Equating formal education for white and black in the $10,000 per annum bracket, the whites constituted 29 per cent of those earning $10,000, whereas the blacks comprised only about 7 per cent. When we drop to $7,000–$10,000 per annum, white college graduates constituted at least 52 per cent of this group as compared with about 21 per cent nonwhite. Dissimilarities in earning power with equal educational background are heightened when it is noticed that nonwhite college graduates had at least double the proportion of their total in the $3,000–$5,000 category.

Nonwhite educated females found their situation similar to that of their male counterpart. Thus, in 1959, in the $10,000 per annum category and over, white female graduates constituted some 7 per cent of the total, whereas the nonwhite females accounted for less than 1 per cent. The ratio was more favorable in the $7,000–$9,999 salary bracket. In this category white females held a little more than 15 per cent of these positions, whereas nonwhite females held somewhat less than 7 per cent.[49]

Although the Industrial Relations Counselors' report painted a dark picture, it did end on an optimistic note, based on Title VII of the Civil Rights Act of 1964, which went into effect one month after the counselors' report was issued (July, 1965).

The optimism expressed by the counselors was not shared by attorneys for the U.S. Department of Justice entrusted to enforce the mandate of Congress. Department attorneys were far from sanguine about the new law's ability to change the existing social order. They based their off-the-record comments on the following: (1) The complexity of the law is rarely fully understood or appreciated by journalists and laymen. (2) The Department of Justice does not have a sufficiently qualified staff to handle any huge number of cases. (3) The law lacks sufficient precision to establish the success of the act with any degree of certainty. (4) Under law, the individual can start an action; but it is expensive and time-consuming. The judicial process is so protracted, that by the time the case is resolved, the plaintiff can only hope for a Pyrrhic victory. To sum up, Richard Berg, a Justice Department attorney,

who [was] deputy general counsel of the commission, stated that Title VII was "in rather terrible shape" by the time it emerged from two filibusters.

Berg felt so pessimistic about the legal success of the 1964 act that he hoped that the mere existence of Title VII would prove salutory. "The average businessman doesn't like to violate a law once it's on the books." [50]

Now we turn to a more detailed analysis of blocked economic opportunity and employers' hiring practices. These practices were subsumed under three headings: (1) full restriction in employment, (2) discriminatory employment retrenchment, and (3) partial restriction in employment.

What was particularly devastating about these artificial restrictions was that they plagued the Afro-American during his entire working life span, commencing with the adolescent colored American seeking his first job. Although the social and economic aspects of this process is our main concern, we do recognize that the psychological complements the other factors with an equally vicious pattern of subjective relations. Usually it begins with disappointment and leads to frustration-aggression and an almost all-consuming hatred of the "White Cat."

Employment mobility is relevant to economic and social status and will be dealt with on three levels: (1) initial entrance into the job market without previous occupational experience, (2) job mobility—the ease with which an individual can change jobs within the same occupation with previously acquired job experience, and (3) upgrading on the job following demonstrated ability and/or seniority. That many Afro-Americans had difficulty, based on color, in obtaining their first job has been illustrated in previous chapters (as in the case of Miss Bell, the instance of the clerk-typist denied employment in a Wall Street bank, and others.) It was this failure to obtain employment that precluded the possibility of acquiring experience for job mobility and possible upgrading. These restrictions placed a ceiling on the individual's economic security and status essential in any attempt to break out of the circle of discrimination.

Where the Afro-American was able to circumvent *full restriction in employment,* his economic mobility was frequently modified by the use of *discriminatory employment retrenchment.* Thus, in

Occupations and Industries [where] the Negro had made his greatest employment advances he [was] . . . the last hired. . . . Under seniority rules he was more likely to be laid off than the average worker in these occupations and industries.[51]

> After 1950 the situation changed. Gains for the average Negro
> worker stopped [between 1950–1962]. The Negro's relative
> economic status, in fact, declined slightly. The postwar reces-
> sion hit the Negro worker especially hard. In the 1958 down-
> turn, for instance, two Negroes lost [their jobs] for every white
> worker laid off.[52]

Historically, the overall situation as late as 1965 was relatively
little different from the past, since "any business contraction hit
[the Afro-American] because he was so often working in an ex-
pendable job and had low seniority in his union." [53] This historical
picture (extending for some 300 years) helps to explain why the
Afro-American remains at the bottom of the economic ladder. His
job mobility has been restricted because (1) the released Afro-American has to face the "usual aversions" to being rehired even when he
has the qualifications for the job, and (2) he is usually refused upgrading. In combination, this means that he has little opportunity
to acquire additional skill and thus be upgraded.

The above conditions are confirmed when we examine the
Afro-American's relative income status over a period of years as
compared with the white worker. The U.S. Department of Labor
conducted a number of income-employment studies from the
1930's [54] through the 1960's [55] that were supplemented by various
New York State Commission reports.[56] On the whole, the data
indicated that the Afro-American's relative economic status in the
United States and in New York City was consistently below that of
comparable white groups.[57] In part this status may be linked to
employers' restrictive hiring policies.

The U.S. Department of Labor's Bureau of Labor Statistics
conducted a special income study of New York City in 1963. It
revealed that the predominantly black Bedford-Stuyvesant area in
Brooklyn had an unemployment rate of 17.3 per cent as compared
to the citywide rate of 5 per cent. Perhaps even more important than
the disproportionate unemployment rates was the relative differences
in the median per capita income between the city as a whole and
Bedford-Stuyvesant. New York City's median per capita income was
$6,091 (average for the United States as a whole), as compared with
$3,672 for Bedford-Stuyvesant residents.[58] Likewise, for the United
States as a whole, the 1940–1960 period revealed that the black American was unable to raise his *relative economic status*. However, between 1951 and 1962, in terms of absolute dollars, the Afro-American's average yearly earnings did increase from $2,060 to $3,032. This

increase was attributed to a sizable increase in urbanization of colored Americans rather than to an upgrading in occupations. Despite this rise in absolute dollars, Dr. Herman P. Miller's study revealed that the relative rise in income was far below that of whites.

Valid, but only superficially, was the contention of the U.S. Department of Labor that more education meant *greater absolute earnings* for the Afro-American.[59] It is superficially valid because it deals only with one side of the coin. Economically speaking, it would be more accurate *to measure the relative rate of return on educational investment rather than the absolute return.* Thus by 1963, Afro-Americans with education comparable to that of whites still failed to realize a return relatively equal to that of whites.[60] Although this is not intended to detract from educational opportunities offered to the colored American, it does reveal that social discrimination is a factor in the Afro-American's income being proportionately lower than that of whites comparably qualified by education for employment.

The tangle in the Afro-American's income-employment cycle is further articulated when his economic security and standard of living are examined. Economic security consists of two parts: job security and occupational status. Although economic security is related to continuous employment, the latter is not the sole factor in economic security. The full equation consists of job security, occupational mobility, and status. Usually there is a link between a man's occupational status and his economic security. Hence a man with high occupational status has greater job mobility, which allows for a more constant yearly income. However, we have seen that the Afro-American has a special blend of "blocked mobility" or social subordination (sponsorship-rejection by coworkers, management, and union business agents) that frequently relegates him to the bottom of the ladder. It is obvious that this would affect his social status and aid in any rationalization of the status quo.[61]

Having dealt with employers' practices in hiring, we still have to show how craft unions have added a link to the circle of discrimination, with some mention of their rationalization for accepting the colored American's social subordination as a basis for their artificial economic restrictions. Thus we may start with the question: Is there a reason for the craft unions' acceptance of, and persistence in practicing, black social subordination? Unions have rationalized their attitudes on the basis of self-preservation rather than malice, and this attitude is consistent with a craft union philosophy founded on the premise that the demand for skilled

labor is limited and that our economic system is inherently un-
stable.[62] To help themselves maintain self-preservation, unions have
resorted to such controls over employment as the union shop, apprenticeship ratios to skilled mechanics, control over hours and
wages, and other measures. This means that strong craft unions can
be "natural outlets" for vested interests, since restriction of membership in combination with the union shop offers more than mere
job security. Thus, during the busy season limited union membership provides premium rates via overtime; during the slack season
it means the spreading of the work over fewer hands.

Like employers, the unions use a tripartite set of categories to
restrict Afro-American employment: (1) full restriction, or complete
exclusion from union membership through such devices as the
Caucasian clause, tacit consent, ritual, and so on; (2) full acceptance
of Afro-Americans into the union, or pseudo-equality, as was the
case in the Seafarers' International Union; and (3) partial restriction
of Afro-American membership, or the assignment of the colored
American to auxiliary and/or segregated unions with separate
seniority clauses and other devices.

The first category—full restriction—bars most Afro-Americans
from acquiring occupational status or mobility in a trade under the
jurisdiction of the union. To acquire occupational status ("A"
journeyman), a satisfactory apprenticeship must be passed. This
serves as a three-way prong to curtail the Afro-American's acquiring
occupational status in most craft unions: (1) denial of union membership a requisite for completing an approved apprenticeship program, which leads to a full mechanic's rating; (2) dependency upon
the union's hiring hall for employment; and (3) partial control of
the licensing board. Thus the union can restrict the Afro-American's
occupational status and mobility by the denial of union membership.

Partial occupational status was confined to those unions that
extended subordinate membership to Afro-Americans. Thus their
membership was restricted to special locals, many of which were
established in accordance with the international's constitution: this
was the case with the International Brotherhood of Blacksmiths,
Drop Forgers and Helpers. There were instances where colored
Americans mingled with white union members, but upgrading was
next to impossible: as with the Seafarers and the International Ladies
Garment Workers Union.

Whether Afro-American occupational mobility is better under
auxiliary unions as compared with exclusionary unions is contest-

able, since both bar him from possible upgrading to skilled status. It is true that unions with auxiliaries do offer him some occupational status; a status that is usually related to separate seniority clauses so that his layoffs do not affect the white craftsman.

As we have seen, another device was used by the Seafarers Union, which maintained separate hiring halls until 1944, even though there was no such provision in its constitution. Although this practice was eliminated under pressure from a state agency, there are affidavits on file with the Negro American Labor Committee alleging the continued restriction of colored Americans in job placement. Until 1944 this union confined blacks to two occupations—stewards and firemen. Moreover, the stewards were confined to all-colored galleys and the firemen, to coal-burning vessels.

Unions offering equal occupational status often failed to grant the Afro-American equal job mobility with white members. To wit: all members of the car washers union held equal membership, but white union officials consistently showed preference in placement to whites. Another example of a union nominally having no separate class membership was the Motion Picture Projectionists Union, Local 306. Although this union had a mixed membership, colored projectionists were confined to Harlem theaters.

Since economic status depends upon income, and income is recompense for skill, there is a relationship between occupational mobility and economic security. The circle becomes obvious in those instances where the Afro-American was denied occupational status through union exclusionist policies,[63] which forced him to accept menial jobs paying the least in dollars and with limited horizontal employment mobility. The general increase in the total working population brought greater competition for unskilled jobs.

A decrease in the Afro-American's relative economic status was further intensified because many exclusionist unions were successful in obtaining wage increases for their members at the expense of the unskilled. This in turn tended to spread the differential between the two groups, especially where the increases were at the expense of the unorganized.

However, where he had partial occupational status, the Afro-American found his lot somewhat improved over his unorganized brother. In these instances the union would get some gains for him in terms of wages, hours, and other working conditions. But it should be kept in mind that where the same percentage applied to diverse wage bases, the gains proved favorable to the higher base. To wit: a menial helper gets a wage of $25 a week and the master mechanic gets $75. A ten per cent increase across the board would give the black helper $2.50, whereas the mechanic would receive $7.50. This amounts to a one-to-three ratio in favor of the master mechanic, and has changed the existing differential in favor of the mechanic. Thus, both relatively and absolutely, the master craftsman has benefited.

Justifiably, it may be stated that this illustration is arithmetically correct, but it does not exclude other possibilities. It can be argued that the unskilled will get a higher percentage increase than the skilled; let us assume 10 and 5 per cent, respectively. Ten per cent of $25 would yield $2.50 but a 5 per cent raise for the mechanic would yield $3.25. Again, the mechanic's raise is absolutely higher than the helper's and would leave the original differential between the two workers. Only if the helper's percentage increase continued to rise and that of the mechanic remained constant or decreased could the helper gain absolutely, but rarely relatively. To wit: only if the helper were to get a 15 per cent raise and the mechanic a 5 per cent increase would the former gain absolutely. Another solution would be to give straight dollar increases, with the helper getting a $10 increase and the mechanic, a $5 increase. This would change the differentials between the two occupations. However, past labor history reveals that such a change would be only temporary.

Finally, equal occupational status often produced two adverse effects on the Afro-American's income status. Although carpenters' and longshoremen's contracts call for equal wages for the same type of work, the colored American usually wound up with lower yearly earnings, because the carpenters' union confined the Afro-American to an auxiliary local, whose territory was limited to Harlem, where there was little or no new construction. This meant fewer days per year to work, and it is simple arithmetic to say that less hours worked multiplied by a constant rate will give you lower earnings than would obtain with more hours worked multiplied by a constant rate. We have purposely omitted the question of overtime at premium rates.

Longshoring put the black man in a similar bind. It was common to have at least three shape-ups per day. However, the shape-up is related to a man's being part of a regular gang assigned to a given pier. Most Afro-Americans were casuals, that is they had no assigned pier and had to depend upon an overflow of work to be assigned. Again, although the motion picture projectionists have no differentiation in membership classification, they confined their

Afro-American members to the Harlem area. Unfortunately, the rate of pay in movie houses depends upon "the class of the house, the seating capacity and the paying ability of the clientele." [64] This meant that Afro-American operators could work as many hours as did white projectionists in midtown Manhattan, but their salary would be less.

Economic, or job, security is part of occupational and economic mobility and status. These depend upon upgrading and are linked to union affiliation and seniority. In denying Afro-Americans membership, exclusionist unions force them to accept menial jobs with low pay and easy replacement. Since advancing age makes the colored American an easy prey for replacement by younger men at lower pay, it brings on the insecurity that is caused by low or transient earnings in contrast to the security of union craftsmen, whose skill and wages increase with their years of service.[65]

All is not black for the Afro-American. There are unions that accept him, and acceptance, even if not on an equal basis, does bring some job security. However, the failure to be upgraded does adversely affect the Afro-American. There have been instances where "bumping" was based on job classification and seniority was ignored. In such instances an Afro-American with long standing in a company could be "bumped" by a junior man with a higher job classification.

Thus far we have tried to develop the institutionalization of a circle of discrimination, with initial emphasis on the sociological effects leading to the economic aspects of the problem. Now, we should revert to our earlier assertion that the same end result can arise by *inverse causation,* that is, starting with the economic aspects.

THE CIRCLE REEXAMINED

The low income status of the Afro-American family forced the mother to become a supplementary breadwinner. This created social problems linked to low income and family structure. Male job instability leading to low income was a factor in the increase of desertion and illegitimacy. During the 1950–1960 decade, this was manifested in an increase in Afro-American matriarchal families, which jumped from 16.7 to 18.8 per cent, adding to the number of neglected and delinquent children.[66] This was partly manifested in the high percentage of black school dropouts between the ages of 17–19. The male dropouts had an unemployment rate in excess of

19 per cent, and the females, a rate of 15 per cent. Both had an unemployment rate far in excess of unemployed white dropouts.
Furthermore, white school dropouts did find employment at a
much faster rate than did blacks.[67]

Although we recognize that there are sources of instability
other than unemployment that affect high, as well as low, income
groups, and the employed as well as the unemployed in American
life, one would not expect to find unemployment per se to be the
major correlate of delinquency. However the combination of family
structure as a function of income and unemployment does lend
credence to our thesis. One student reasons:

> If it is true . . . that family structure is a function of income,
> then changes in income not only will operate directly upon
> delinquency rates but indirectly through family structure, as
> well. . . . A 10 percent rise in incomes may be expected to
> reduce delinquency rates between 15 and 25 percent when the
> income change occurs in a very delinquent area and is of the
> type, i.e., especially increased earning power, that will reduce
> the number of broken families as well.[68]

This same student found that there is much to be said about the
relation between unemployment and juvenile delinquency. Thus,

> an examination of delinquency rates and other variables by
> age and through time suggests that the effect of unemployment
> on juvenile delinquency is positive and significant. [Further-
> more], the fact that school drop-out rates, unemployment rates,
> and delinquency rates all reach a peak at age 17 may imply
> that the high unemployment rate which youths encounter upon
> entering the labor market is at least partly responsible for the
> observed age distribution of arrests.[69]

Another student tried to provide an empirical relationship between unemployment and juvenile delinquency. He concluded that
a cross-sectional analysis suggests that a 1 per cent reduction in the
rate of unemployment would lead to a diminution in delinquency
rates of from one fourth to one sixth of 1 per cent.[70]

Some students of juvenile delinquency allege that there is more
than an ephemeral relationship between it and unemployment. One

study of federal prisons revealed that many inmates had experienced frequent unemployment.[71] In 1962 a study of New York State's prison inmates revealed that some 95 per cent of them were school dropouts.[72] Both studies showed that prisoners in all types of institutions had previously been concentrated in low-skilled occupations, characterized by low wages and high rates of unemployment, certainly to a much greater extent than that for the labor force as a whole.[73] These economic conditions aggravated the social pathology of the Afro-American. Since welfare institutions "refused" to open their doors to most Afro-American neglected and/or delinquent children, there was little chance of their being rehabilitated. In New York City, colored children found delinquent were frequently sent to penal institutions because private welfare agencies shunned them.[74]

The above pattern—low income, school dropouts, disproportionate martriarchal families, and desertions—form a self-generating circle. The offspring of these families form new families who repeat the pattern—low economic and social status with a predisposition toward above average desertions, growth of matriarchal families, high relief loads, and unemployment. These affect the family structure, by encouraging Afro-American youth "to learn and to accept delinquent patterns of behavior as the natural way of behaving." [75]

Although the fact that many young people turn toward crime is a matter of grave social concern, our primary concern is that many of them do so because there are so few legitimate outlets for their making a living. Those who are employed earn wages far below federal government estimates of "subsistence." In such industries as hospitals, department stores, and cardboard manufacture, average gross weekly wages are about $70.

In conclusion, we may say that the relative status of the Afro-American is little different from that held by the "old immigration" during its period of accommodation in the 19th century. Namely, expanding immigration saw a disproportionate share of paupers among the foreign born. In 1835 there were 4,786 native-born, and 5,303 foreign-born, paupers in New York City's almshouses. By 1837 the city was spending $279,999 annually for the support of its poor, and of this sum 60 per cent went to sustain the foreign born. The situation became worse with the years. By 1860 about 86 per cent of New York's paupers were of foreign birth.[76]

Two authorities associate poverty with crime and illustrate their contention by stating:

Closely associated with the growth of poverty in eastern cities was the increase in crime. By 1840 the leaders in New York and elsewhere were concerned about the appearance of crime and immorality. Particularly noted were the gangs of youthful criminals who made war on each other and terrorized neighborhoods. New York boasted of its Bowery Boys, Plug-Uglies, Highbinders, Swipers, Dead Rabbits, etc.[77]

The stereotype of the foreign born and crime that is today applied to the Afro-American was associated with the immigrant as the crime rate in the cities rose. For example, in 1828, A. Pintard wrote to his daughter: "As long as we are overwhelmed with Irish immigrants so long will the evil abound." Police arrested immigrants in poor areas for inconsequential crimes that were often ignored elsewhere. A further similarity exists between the old Irish immigration and the current Afro-American. Life's desperation and the ready availability of alcohol contributed to a high rate of serious crime among immigrants and particularly among the Irish. For example, in 1849 crime had reached such huge proportions that the chief of police in New York City saw fit to devote his entire annual report to the subject of *juvenile crime*. Later years found that the largest number of people arrested were immigrants. Thus in 1859, New York reported that over 55 per cent of persons arrested were Irish, compared with 23 per cent of native stock. Another example was the period covering 1850–1858, when New York recorded that about 87 per cent of those committed to the city prison were foreign born. The situation failed to get better with the years, since in 1860, when only one half of New York City's population was foreign born, they constituted over 18 per cent of those convicted.[78]

One more similarity should be mentioned; the appointment of commissions. In 1857 the New York State Legislature appointed a special committee to investigate the housing situation. It reported:

Had the evils which now appall us been prevented . . . by wise and simple laws, the city would now exhibit more gratifying bills of health, more general comfort and prosperity, and less, far less, expenditure for the support of pauperism and crime.[79]

The "hot summers" and riots are also reminiscent of what earlier reformers had to say after the Civil War; the mobs that precipitated riots "were gathered in overcrowded and neglected quarters of the city."

All of this is meant to illustrate that in previous periods of American history, white immigrants reacted in a manner similar to that of the Afro-Americans today: overcrowding and low income brought riots and crime. However, the passage of time permitted accommodation and elimination of these conditions for the immigrants, whereas, some 300 years after the Afro-American's introduction to New York, many of these sordid conditions persist for him.

CHAPTER 10

Some Afro-American Reactions
to a Circle of Discrimination

Historically, some Afro-Americans revealed their dissatisfaction with their socioeconomic status by attempting to break the circle of discrimination. Like most minority groups, they sought to blend into white society by utilizing economic, social, and political devices similar to those employed by other ethnic groups. These devices included education, benevolent societies, and employment clearinghouses. However, these measures altered the Afro-American's status very little.

New York Afro-American reaction to discriminaion first manifested itself during the English Colonial period when slaves at varying times instigated a series of insurrections. Following the Revolution, black freedmen, with the aid of missionary societies, established primary schools for colored children, and after 1800 public grants were obtained to operate the schools. Afro-Americans were the first beneficiaries of tuition-free grammar schools, and many colored Americans seeking to elevate themselves took advantage of this offer.

In his history of the African Free School,[1] C. W. Andrews asserted that the school's standards were at least equal to, if not higher than, those prevailing in white private schools. However, Afro-American youngsters soon discovered that education was not a panacea in overcoming racial prejudice and discrimination. Even white liberals, including abolitionists who eulogized the benefits of education, refused to employ educated Afro-Americans in any responsible position.[2]

His failure to capitalize on the imputed benefits of higher

221

education saw the Afro-American's anticipatory aspirations drop to an acceptance of manual labor. Like many immigrants, the colored American felt that he had to climb the economic ladder step by step before he could advantageously utilize higher education. Thus, in New York City, a manual labor school was established in the 1830's to bridge the gap.[3] Although education failed to bring the economic and social recognition sought by the Afro-American, he still stressed its value. For example, in 1851 the New York *Tribune*[4] reported on a Afro-American convention in New York where the main topic was the interrelationship between the mechanical arts and higher education. In 1852 educated colored Americans made an effort to capitalize on their educational investment by seeking employment in commercial houses owned by members of the executive committee of the American and Foreign Anti-Slavery Society. They were employed, but only as menials.[5]

Frederick Douglass, a self-made man and one of the few who gained partial acceptance by white society, advocated mutual self-help, with special emphasis on trade schools. He felt that such schools were necessary for the Afro-American before he could find "salvation" in attending liberal arts colleges.[6] Dr. James McCune Smith's statement on the effectiveness of mutual self-help within the black community showed the futility of this approach.

> City life shuts us off from general mechanical employment; . . . and colored bosses have either too little capital, or too little enterprise, to bring up and employ apprentices and journeymen. . . . The enormous combination of capital which is slowly invading every calling in the city, from washing and ironing, . . . must tend more and more to grind the face of the poor in the cities, and render [Afro-Americans] more and more the slaves of lower wages and higher rents.[7]

There were colored Americans who refused to heed Douglass' advice and tried to bypass manual training by seeking direct advancement through higher education—in the law, medicine, and teaching. Except for teaching, the law and medicine, both personal enterprises, depended upon the individual. Still, some 40 years after slavery was legally abolished in New York State (1867), the New York *World* said of such personal enterprise: There were two Afro-American attorneys acting on behalf of the city's Negroes and "no colored lawyer [had] as yet practiced before the bar of New York."[8]

Those who had completed their studies in medicine found the environment hostile and professional advancement barred, because New York hospitals refused to admit them to residency and/or staff. Failure to affiliate with a hospital meant a retardation of skills normally developed by experimentation in the hospitals. Until 1890, New York and Brooklyn had only 16 colored physicians. A hostile environment caused the group to toy with the idea of establishing its own clinic as one way of overcoming the lack of hospital affiliation.[9] As for colored American teachers, since most Afro-American grammar school students were confined to specific areas, such teachers were assigned to all-black schools. One school even had a colored principal—Charles Reason.[10]

Many Afro-Americans attained financial success without formal education, notably in such fields as catering, vaudeville, and tailoring. Unfortunately, these success patterns were rarely transmitted to the next generation. Afro-American restaurateurs date back to the American Revolution (Fraunces Tavern) and in later years there was Thomas Downing's restaurant near Wall Street.[11] Jennings, the black tailor who had a gift with the needle, had his custom tailoring establishment on Nassau and Chatham streets.[12] An unusual case was that of Madame Walker, who ingeniously capitalized on the vanity of her ethnic stock by developing the first hair-straightening process.[13]

The enterprise of another Afro-American, Philip A. Payton, Jr., was used to take advantage of his ethnic stock's housing needs. He gouged his own people and made and lost a fortune. Payton started his career as a janitor in a white realty office, soon gave up janitoring and advertised himself as a specialist in the management of colored tenements. Thus, without ready capital he convinced white realty owners to let him manage their property. His success permitted him to found the Afro-American Realty Company, which specialized in acquiring Harlem property leases owned by whites. After acquiring the property he boosted rentals in excess of what whites were paying for similar accommodations.[14] Other Afro-Americans reinforced the white man's stereotype of the black man through their roles in vaudeville and minstrel shows. In every case, the Afro-American played the role the white man associated with him. Since these efforts required little formal schooling, the noneducated had a better chance in personal enterprise than those who had followed the path of education.

In an effort to gain more steady employment and in the hope of raising his economic status, the Afro-American established employment offices. Founded in 1808 and chartered in 1810 was the

New York African Society for Mutual Relief.[15] Its main purpose
was to place both skilled and unskilled black workers in jobs; sub-
sidiarily, to serve sick and infirm members of the community. To
place its members in jobs, the society requested them to report job
openings to the central office for referrals. Once notified, the society
would try to match its employment register with job offerings. (This
is little different from the National Urban League's Skilled Bank,
which is supposed to be on a nationwide scale.)

Another organization, the American League of Colored Laborers, was established in 1850 for a dual purpose: to find employment for Afro-Americans by utilizing its members as a grapevine
and to upgrade the skills of black youth. The organization suggested
that each colored mechanic become an entrepreneur and take a
black youth under his wing. Aware of Dr. McCune Smith's *caveat*—
lack of capital—the league suggested that the program include
financial assistance to any colored mechanic wishing to start a
business.[16]

In 1870 the New York City Colored Mission added to its
functions that of an employment agency.[17] Although it was to
serve both settled and newly arrived Afro-Americans, its register
revealed a heavy preponderance in the area of domestic service. It
operated as an employment agency until 1875. The agency's files
revealed: that it was relatively effective in placing colored Americans
in jobs (in 1872 the agency had some 600 applications on file and
placed some 470 persons); they also showed that the Afro-American
was not lazy, since the agency had at various times as many as 1,200
applications on file for employment.[18] By 1890 the mission had been
transformed into social service agency. During the Panic of 1893 it
reported that many colored Americans had "no fire, no food, . . .
and [many] were found actually dying of want." [19]

The Afro-American refused to accept setbacks with indifference. He tried again to help himself through the Afro-American
League, formed in 1890. This organization was to have a bureau
of industrial education; it was to stimulate black business potential
and to assist the colored American in learning trades, since trained
artisans, farmers, and laborers were more valuable than "educated
lawyers, agitators and loafers throughout the country." [20]

When the Afro-American felt that one type of special organization failed to meet his needs, he rarely gave up, but rather
tried anew. Thus in 1897 the White Rose Industrial Association
was formed with the primary purpose of protecting domestics from

exploitation. Its agents met colored girls coming to New York and assisted them by "escorting [these] women to their places of employment, or to the White Rose Home." This was done because many colored girls were lured North under false pretenses and frequently forced into prostitution.[21] At least one other social service agency deserves mention—the National Urban League established in 1911 under white-colored American auspices. Although it started as an employment agency, and still claims this function, it is primarily a social service agency.

Thus for the period 1777–1920 the Afro-American tried to follow in the footsteps of the old and new immigrants by establishing his own employment agencies and benevolent societies. These organizations were primarily uplift societies since they ministered to the poor and paid unemployment benefits, death benefits, and other such items.[22] Many societies required that the recipients' children be sent to school or they would otherwise forfeit their benefits.[23]

The 1920–1965 period revealed a shift in emphasis. Now the Afro-American felt that economic (boycott) and political pressures could alleviate his condition. Thus in 1925 a group of Harlemites pressured the white power structure to open white-collar jobs to the Afro-American. After about two years of agitation, some "tokenism" was gained.[24]

In 1933 the Afro-American resorted to the boycott and colored American chauvinism toward Harlem merchants. These movements were led by the Rev. John H. Johnson, rector of St. Martin's Protestant Episcopal Church, and Fred R. Moore, then editor of the New York *Age*, a Negro weekly. When the white merchants failed to respond to pleas, the boycott was extended to all of Harlem. To publicize the boycott, such chauvinistic slogans as, "Don't buy where you can't work" and "Lily-White," were painted on signs that were carried through the business districts of Harlem. To assist those who didn't care to read, or couldn't read, the pickets chanted their slogans up and down 125th Street. Many white employers relaxed their "lily-white" hiring practices, at least temporarily, as a result of the boycott.[25]

Although the 1940's saw a continuation of collective pressure on white employers to hire Afro-Americans for white-collar jobs, there was increased pressure on the federal government to enact a fair employment practices act. Thus the Urban League of Greater New York in conjunction with some of its white backers was able to prevail upon such organizations as Johns Manville Company, Alexander's Department Store in the Bronx, and others to mitigate some of their "lily-white" personnel policies.[26] A. Philip Randolph and Walter White, then secretary of the National Association for the Advancement of Colored People (NAACP), organized the "March on Washington." [27] Since the march never materialized, because President Franklin D. Roosevelt issued his Executive Order No. 8803—later amended by Executive Order No. 9346—which created the Fair Employment Practice Act, Randolph and White pronounced their political tactic a success.[28]

In 1943 the "City-Wide Citizens' Committee on Harlem," an interracial group, exerted pressure on some local department stores, unions, and city officials to intercede on behalf of the colored American.[29] This intercession again offered some immediate gain; however, it was not sustained.

In 1948, New York City's Mayor William O'Dwyer created the Consumer Arbitration Board to alleviate the Afro-American employment situation. The New York *Times* alleged that the Mayor was reacting to black political pressure rather than from any belief in the principle of black equality.[30]

In 1945 the Urban Housing Management Association, an affiliate of the National Urban League, persuaded white bankers that it would be more profitable to turn over the management of their property in the black belt to the association. Once the association took over, it tried to open to Afro-Americans jobs formerly restricted to white craftsmen.

When the first buildings were taken over, only 25 percent of the repairs and redecorating was done by Negroes. [Now, 1946] 70 percent of the work goes to local [Afro-American] Mechanics.[31]

The 1935 riot in Harlem, an indication of the Afro-American's failure to accept accommodation in white society, forced the mayor of New York City to appoint a special commission. The commission's report stated that the riot was a reaction to discrimination in employment.

It is idle to deny that the situation in Harlem remains serious and will continue to do so not only until the depression has passed. . . . The blame belongs to society, [one] that tolerates . . . unemployment . . . discrimination in industry and public utilities against colored people.[32]

The 1938 New York State Temporary Commission Report entitled "On the Condition of the Urban Colored Population," emphasized once more the Afro-American's failure to accommodate and reiterated the long-held claim that the cause of the 1935 riot was economic restrictions in employment. The commission emphasized this point by saying:

> most of the problems confronting the colored population arise primarily out of an inadequate income. . . . It is also true that no successful attack on these secondary problems [social] may be made until the basic handicap of inadequate income is removed.[33]

The period from 1950 to 1965 was marked by the Afro-American's attempt to utilize his historical experience in an effort to get society to acknowledge him as a full-fledged member of society. During this period the Afro-American utilized existing legal measures, pressured the politicians, and tried to appeal to the moral and social conscience of society to help him break out of the circle of discrimination. For example, in July, 1955 the Urban League of Greater New York tested the effectiveness of the President's Committee on Government Contracts by requesting the commission to invoke its contractual clause with the country's airlines to bar discrimination in employment. The league was informed that there were legal technicalities, hence the government could not initiate action unilaterally. Even after the league initiated action there was no change in airline policy toward Afro-American employment.[34]

The state commission was more successful in 1957, when it managed to get Mohawk Airlines to hire its first colored stewardess.

> The event is noteworthy because it [was] the first time, despite many applications, that a Negro has been accepted for such a post by a scheduled United States carrier.
>
> A virtual ban has been maintained by the scheduled lines against employment of Negroes in air-crew positions.[35]

In 1958, Trans-World Airlines was the first transcontinental airline to hire an Afro-American hostess.

> As a result of the airline's pledge, the Commissioner [Charles Abrams] has postponed a public hearing on a charge by Miss

Dorothy Franklin of Astoria, Queens, that the T.W.A. had refused to hire her as a stewardess solely because she was a Negro. The hearings had been scheduled for tomorrow [Feb. 11, 1958].[36]

Whitney M. Young, Jr., the newly appointed executive director of the National Urban League, declared in 1962 that it was now time to close the "gap left open by 300 years of deprivation." His suggestion amounted to discrimination in reverse—that favoritism should be accorded to Afro-Americans in hiring.[37] Many Afro-American and white intellectuals reacted negatively, expressing their belief that this was an acknowledgment of a handout and was in line with the preachments of "white racism."

In 1942 a new group called the Congress of Racial Equality (CORE), headed by James Farmer, a former employee of the NAACP, felt that social pressure in the form of picketing public places would be effective in breaking down discrimination. One case that was unique because of the parties involved, occurred early in April, 1963, when a picket line was thrown around the Waldorf-Astoria Hotel shortly before the U.S. Department of Labor announced that it was to hold its 50th anniversary dinner there on April 18. The interposition of the City Commission on Human Rights and behind the scenes counseling of Department of Labor officials helped to mediate the matter.

On paper, management agreed, with qualifications, to hire some 40 to 55 Afro-Americans over a two-year period. This number was to be distributed as follows: 20 banquet waiters, 20 a-la-carte waiters, two waitresses, 10 bus boys, and two barmen. The bartender category was left open indefinitely.[38] Some of the hotel's qualifications included the question of who was to assist in recruitment of personnel, and the possibility of conflict with the union's contract in hiring.

In part, the public's new awareness of conditions in the hotel industry plus previous union-management preachments helped to bring on a promise that in the future closed job categories would be opened to the Afro-American. However, there was little concrete evidence to support any bona fide change in hiring practices in the better class hotels and restaurants as of the end of 1965.[39]

Early in 1963 various companies began to public announcements that they were trying to wipe out discriminatory hiring practices. The press and magazines also began to carry stories about companies that were hiring Afro-Americans. There were even some individuals who subscribed to this "tokenism" as the result of Afro-American group pressure and governmental intervention.[40] However, as we have seen from the results of studies made after previous announcements of this nature by many companies, there is a strong suggestion of mere lip service.

Other companies refused to be pressured into changing their hiring policies, even for public consumption. Indicative of the attitude of this group of companies was the statement made by some personnel men. "NO one, but no one, is going to tell us how to run our business." A stronger statement was made by officials of Montgomery Ward's Oakland, Calif., branch, who sent a letter to both the store's customers and employees suggesting that CORE was trying

> to force Montgomery Ward to actively discriminate against white and nonwhite applicants for employment, other than Negro, in order to conform to certain objectives of CORE leaders.[41]

In their effort to change existing hiring practices, Afro-Americans have picketed department stores, hotels, and other service industries. By mid-1963 they had placed pickets outside industrial plants. Thus, on Aug. 8, 1963, a group of Afro-American United Auto Workers (UAW) members picketed the headquarters of General Motors Corporation with placards carrying such slogans as "Don't Make Us Boycott, Mr. Donner" (Donner was chairman of G.M.'s board of directors). Another sign read: "Better Jobs Our Goal." [42]

Since the Truman administration, the federal government has stated unequivocally, that it would enforce equal job opportunity on all federally financed projects. Loopholes were invariably found, and the late President Kennedy attempted to plug these loopholes when he issued Executive Order No. 11114, effective July 22, 1963, dealing with various details on compliance procedures. Still, at the end of 1964, allegations were being made that many federal projects were staffed with "lily-white" labor.[43]

Hiring practices on state projects were little different, despite Gov. Nelson Rockefeller's numerous public utterances, and by the end of 1965 the employment situation had not improved.[44] To wit: in 1963, the Legal Defense and Educational Fund, separately incorporated but linked with the NAACP, filed a case against a num-

ber of unions and government officials. The case amounted to a
stay of payment involving some $10 million on contracts involving
city and state projects because of discrimination in employment. On
a technicality, the court threw the case out. The judge contended
that the plaintiff had failed to include the names of the contractors
hired to do the projects in addition to those of the craft unions
and certain government officials involved.[45]

Between 1963 and 1965 various civil rights groups sought to
have both city and state government cancel contracts on the
grounds that discriminatory hiring practices were in opposition to
Section 220-E of New York State's labor law, enacted in 1935. During this period neither the governor nor the mayor cancelled a
single contract, even when it was established that contractors were
discriminating in employment. It may be mentioned that the 1935
law has been amended over the years, but it has had little practical
effect in changing hiring policies of contractors vis-à-vis Afro-Americans.[46]

In previous chapters we have noted some craft union policies
toward membership admission, auxiliary unions, preference in employment, and other practices. It might be well at this point to
give some idea of the Afro-American's reaction to these discriminatory practices.

When the Afro-American found that organized labor refused
to offer him equal membership in the labor movement, he resorted
to strikebreaking. Thus, he helped the Morgan shipping line to
break a longshoremen's strike in 1855.[47] Less than ten years later, in
1862, the Ward Line used the same tactic—Afro-American strikebreakers. The Ward Line found it expedient to repeat the experience
in 1895, and it was copied by the Mallory Line in 1899.[48] After the
1889 waterfront strike Italian longshoremen accepted Afro-Americans into their locals, but only with subordinate status.[49]

In 1867, during the National Labor Union's second convention, at least one labor leader, William Cathers, recognized that the
Afro-American would refuse to accept segregated and auxiliary
unions. Cathers contended that the colored American would "combine of themselves and by themselves without the assistance of
white workers." [50] His prophecy materialized that same year, when
the Afro-Americans formed the Colored National Labor Union. As
a counterpart of the National Labor Union, it was active until the
early 1870's, when it changed its focus to politics and faded away.

Afro-American professionals, like white professionals, usually
shunned unions and preferred to call their organizations *associations*.

In this tradition, a group of colored nurses formed the National Association of Colored Graduate Nurses in 1909 with its base in New York City. This organization catered to the needs of the colored nursing profession until 1958, when the American Nurses Association opened its doors to nonwhite membership.[51]

A. Philip Randolph started his career in the field of organized labor in 1917. Prior to his active participation, his only experience in the field of organized labor had been that of porter with the Consolidated Edison Company.[52] Also in 1917 he assumed the editorship of the *Messenger*, a socialist magazine, combining his duties of editor and labor organizer. In New York City he tried to organize elevator operators, starters, and porters. His first attempt at organizing the black worker was a failure, even though the American Federation of Labor (AFL) had granted him a federal labor union charter. However, mindful of this ethnic group's past, he tried again to organize shipyard workers in the tidewater district of Virginia. Again he failed, but his faith in unionization as the colored American's economic salvation was enunciated in the following:

> The Negro should organize himself, because with organization he will be better able to break down the barriers and prejudices of white workers against him than he will without it.[53]

Randolph launched the first black international union to become part of the AFL in 1925. Although he had never worked as a pullman porter, he formed with Milton Webster and Ashley Totten, both pullman porters, a series of federal locals, each with a separate charter issued by the AFL. In 1936 Randolph realized his dream when the first international charter was "awarded to an all-Negro union in the [50] years of the AFL's history." [54] Thereafter, as an official delegate from his union at almost every AFL convention, Randolph took the floor to try to persuade organized labor to open its doors to all Afro-Americans.[55]

Randolph was not alone in his response to the needs of unorganized black labor. There were other individuals and groups, some who preceded Randolph. Thus in 1920, two New York City groups organized the Brotherhood of Dining Car Employees and the National Brotherhood of Dining Car Employees.[56] Another organization, called the United Association of Colored Motion Picture Operators, was formed in the early 1920's.[57] These groups were but a few instances of the Afro-American's attempt to force organized

labor to accept him into the fold as an equal: through dual unionism.

In 1924, Frank Crosswaith helped to form the Trade Union
Committee for Organizing Negro Workers, modeled after the Hebrew Union Trades. During its formation the future trade union
committee met at the Civil Club and held a second session at
Arlington Hall. It resolved that white and black must unite under
one banner so

> that never again must organized labor lose another strike in New
> York City through the activities of unorganized Negro work-
> ers [employed to break strikes in the 1920's].[58]

Once formed, the committee claimed a dual purpose: to organize Negro workers and to secure justice for blacks inside the
fold of organized labor. To achieve its goals it sought "to educate
both Negro and White workers toward a realization of their common
interest." [59] (This philosophy was little different from that espoused
in the 1860's by Powderly, Gompers, and others.)

New Deal legislation brought a revival of Afro-American labor
activity in the form of the National Negro Congress (not to be
confused with the American Negro Labor Congress, a communist-
dominated organization). In his keynote address to the National
Negro Congress, Randolph stressed the need for unity in the Afro-
American community in order to guide the colored American worker
in taking advantage of New Deal legislation.[60] Another indication of
revived interest in unionization was the birth of the Greater New
York Coordinating Committee for Equal Opportunities, which was
extremely active in picketing the New York 1939 World's Fair. The
committee also pressed the City Commission on Human Rights to
publicize the discriminatory practices of craft unions.[61]

There were some Afro-Americans who alleged that President
Franklin D. Roosevelt was "coerced into" issuing his executive order
creating the short-lived Fair Employment Practices Committee in
order to ward off Randolph's 1941 march on Washington. In the
middle 1940's there were such Afro-Americans as Peter Ottley, who
managed to obtain a charter for Local 144 from the Building Service
Employees International Union with original jurisdiction over hotels
and residence clubs. The local's jurisdiction has since been extended to cover hospitals and nursing homes and is in competition
with Local 1199, headed by Leon Davis and Moe Foner and also

affiliated with the AFL-CIO. Peter Ottley has been successful in upgrading many Afro-Americans within his own union and apply-ing pressure on sister locals to train Afro-Americans for elective positions. Ottley started his labor career as a bellhop in one of the smaller midtown hotels.[62]

The year 1963 witnessed a new upsurge of collective action by various colored groups, some formerly dormant and others newly organized. All had one aim in common: equal opportunity in em-ployment for the Afro-American. A few of the better-known or-ganizations active on the New York scene are the Negro American Labor Committee, started by A. Philip Randolph and now headed by Cleveland Robinson, secretary-treasurer of District 65 of the Retail, Wholesale, Department Store Workers International Union; CORE, formerly headed by James Farmer, who was also a former employee of the NAACP; the Urban League, headed by Whitney Young, a former professor of social work; and the NAACP, headed by Roy Wilkins. It was these four organizations plus the Southern Christian Leadership Conference (SCLC), headed by the late Martin Luther King, that spearheaded the Christian Leadership Conference's first meeting at Arden House. A group of Afro-American scholars as-sembled at this conference to discuss the colored American's situa-tion both at home and in Africa. The most recent mass drive was the second "March on Washington" on Aug. 28, 1963. There are those who contend that this "March" was responsible for the enact-ment of the 1964 Civil Rights Act, which included Title VII relat-ing to fair employment. Title VII went into effect in July, 1965.

In juxtaposition with the Afro-American's desire to become in-tegrated on such different levels of society as employment, housing, and public accommodations is his still blocked social and economic mobility in most spheres of life. In response to those who contend that the Afro-American is happy with his lot, or those who contend that the Afro-American must set up his own state—Garveyism, a type of black nationalism, the Back to Africa Movement—Kenneth Clark, like his predecessor Frederick Douglass, says:

> There is no point of talk, regardless of how poetic it may be, about whether the Negro wants to be integrated with America. He has no choice. He is involved, inextricably so, with America as he knows it. And the sensible Negro is a man who takes pride in his involvement and accepts it as a mandate to work for the change that is written in the way of things.[63]

Even those who preach the "separation of the races" as do the Black Muslims, actually are seeking a type of integration in the form of equal recognition between the colored and the whites.

In 1965, Cleveland Robinson,[64] president of the Negro American Labor Committee, entered into an agreement with Locals 3 and 46 of the International Brotherhood of Teamsters, and the Brewers Board of Trade "at the behest of the City's Commission on Human Rights."[65] This agreement altered the former seniority rules in the brewery industry. Hitherto, a man had to put in 150 consecutive days in the employ of one brewery to be placed on the seniority list. Under the new agreement, seniority takes effect after a man has put in 15 days in the entire industry within one calendar year. This has favorably affected the Afro-American who makes brewery deliveries.[66] Thus the Afro-American persists in his efforts to find equal opportunity in employment through his own organizations or in conjunction with private and governmental organizations.

Epilog

Despite the enactment of various government civil rights acts from 1866 through 1964 and private civil rights activity such as *Plans for Progress* and the *National Alliance for Business*, the Afro-American's position in the economy of the nation and New York City has not improved significantly between 1965 and 1968.

In 1967 national nonwhite unemployment remained at least double the jobless rate of white workers in spite of the improved job situation for Afro-American men and women throughout the postwar period. For example, in the first eight months of 1967, the ratio of the unemployment rate of Afro-American adult males to that of white males was 2.1 to 1, the same as that in 1965 and 1966. The unemployment rate for Afro-American women has remained about twice the rate for white women since 1964.[1] Teenagers fared much worse because unemployment for Afro-American youngsters was 26.9 per cent, a rate consistent with the 1964–1966 rates, but a rise by about 8 per cent since 1956.[2]

Miss Susan Holland summarized the nonwhite employment situation as follows:

> The national averages show that Negro jobless rates are twice as high as those for whites and that, despite the strong economic expansion of the last few years, Negroes have been unsuccessful in closing the gap.[3]

The intensity of discrimination in employment suffered by the colored American may be witnessed in other ways. One such way was that "the employment situation of white workers in *poverty areas* was better than that of Negro workers in *nonpoverty areas*." Statistically, the unemployment rate for white workers in poverty areas was 6 per cent, as compared to a 7.2 per cent unemployment rate for Afro-Americans in nonpoverty areas. In addition, white workers in poverty areas were more likely than Afro-Americans in nonpoverty areas to have white-collar or skilled jobs.

Thus white workers in poor neighborhoods—though their employment situation was much worse than that of whites in nonpoverty areas—had a comparative advantage over Afro-Americans in both poverty and nonpoverty areas.[4]

Again in May, 1968 the Bureau of Labor Statistics continued to report that "nonwhites had higher unemployment rates than whites in all areas surveyed, and for some 20 Standard Metropolitan Statistical Area's (SMSA), the combined nonwhite rate (7.5 per cent) was more than double the white rate (3.3 per cent)." This study revealed also that nonwhite teenagers had a jobless rate of at least three times the rate for white teenagers.[5]

In New York City the nonwhite unemployment rate was about 5 per cent in 1967. It was among the lowest of the 20 SMSA's surveyed. This was reflected in the city's nonwhite-to-white unemployment rate (1½ to 1). Paul O. Flaim ascribed this discrepancy, lower ratio between white and nonwhite employment, to possible statistical skewness rather than to an improvement in employment opportunities. He contended that with the recent influx of persons of Spanish descent, mostly Puerto Ricans, the latter were more likely to have a high unemployment rate and they would tend to raise the white rate vis-à-vis the nonwhites. Implied in Flaim's analysis was that the city's nonwhite rate of unemployment was closer to the national average of 2 to 1.[6] There is additional evidence to support Flaim's contention when we set apart slum areas from the rest of the population in terms of unemployment.

Unemployment and Subemployment Rates and Metropolitan Area Rates for Three Slum Areas in New York City, November, 1966 [7]

New York Slum Area	Unemployment Rate	Subemployment Rate [8]	N.Y. Metropolitan Area
Harlem	8.1	29	
East Harlem	9.0	33	4.6
Bedford-Stuyvesant	6.2	28	

Another index of discrimination in employment would be occupational mobility. The period between January, 1965 and January, 1966 was covered by a survey that revealed color was evident in occupational distribution of those changing occupations. Thus there was an increase in the proportion of white men in higher-paying white-color classifications and an increase in the proportion of Afro-Americans holding blue-collar jobs "and they largely at the lowest level, as laborers." (These findings substantiated the conclusions of other recent studies: [9] that many Afro-American occupational changes were aimless and involuntary.) Thus

in intraplant occupational changes, a few Negroes move upward in the skill-grouping occupations; and when Negroes do move to higher paid occupations, they tend to enter in the least skilled categories at the lowest earnings levels, particularly Negro men 25 to 34 years old, when the propensity to change occupations is high.[10]

This bears out our earlier thesis that Afro-Americans do not, as a rule, displace whites; rather they get jobs vacated by whites who have moved upward.

The Equal Employment Opportunity Commission (EEOC) prefaced its January, 1968 hearings in New York with the following: "Of the 4,249 reporting units, 27 per cent reported not a single Negro in any job. Forty-three per cent had no Negro employees at the white collar level." [11] In all five industries analyzed (wholesale, retail, finance, insurance, telephone-telegraph, and broadcasting), "Negroes are heavily concentrated in clerical jobs and, with the exception of retail trade, are poorly represented in managerial, professional and sales positions." [12] Where Afro-Americans were able to get white-collar status, frequently they were paid less than their white counterparts in the same occupational categories. For example,

New York's nonwhite families in which the chief wage earner was employed in a managerial capacity had an average income in 1959 that was only 55 per cent of that of all families in the same occupational group. The comparison came to 63 per cent in families headed by sales workers and 71 per cent in those headed by professional and technical workers. Among families headed by clerical workers, nonwhites came closest to the average income for all families headed by such workers, but even here there was a discrepancy of 18 per cent.[13]

To summarize, the OEEC's report through 1967 revealed that some 70 out of New York City's 100 major corporations showed nonwhite employment to be minuscule.[14]

Counterattacking the argument that the small extent to which so many private employers use people from minority groups was due to the lack of qualified workers, the Commission presented figures revealing that well over 61,000 Afro-Americans were enrolled in academic and vocational high schools. Even when nonwhites had completed their schooling, "statistics indicated that the high-school-educated nonwhite was still at a disadvantage in the labor market." It seemed that discrimination based on color was the basis for hiring, rather than the lack of experience, or specific qualifications. Investigation showed that employers "frequently hired white candidates" because of their potential and these white persons developed into the personnel that continued to be employed. Thus "most secretaries, bookkeepers, etc., were developed through internal promotion, and employer sponsored training." [15]

Craft unions are still discriminating against nonwhites according to State Commissioner of Human Rights, Robert J. Mangum. He stressed one way in which discrimination was practiced that was through the use of aptitude tests. These tests act "as barriers to the employment of minority groups." [16] Many of the forms used to discriminate against nonwhites have been articulated in earlier chapters. They are still in vogue.

The impact of employment discrimination on the continuation of "the circle of discrimination," is described in the 1967 *Manpower Report* . . . and differs little, if at all from our earlier discription.[17] We have gone the full circle from 1625 to 1968.

Notes

CHAPTER 1

1. *William and Mary Quarterly,* ser. 3, VII (April, 1950), 199–222.

2. W. D. Jordan, "Modern Tensions and the Origins of American Slavery," *The Journal of Southern History,* XXVIII (February, 1962), 18–20.

3. O. Handlin, *Race and Nationality in American Life,* Boston 1957.

4. *Ibid.,* p. 9.

5. O. Handlin, *William and Mary Quarterly, op. cit.,* p. 203.

6. Mary and Oscar Handlin, "Letters to the Editor," *Comparative Studies in Society and History,* II (July, 1960), 490.

7. C. N. Degler, "Slavery and the Genesis of American Race Prejudice," *Comparative Studies in Society and History,* II (October, 1959), 52; *Out of Our Past: The Forces that Shaped Modern America* (New York, 1959), pp. 29–30.

8. C. N. Degler, "Slavery and the Genesis of American Race Prejudice," p. 52.

9. D. B. Davis, *The Problem of Slavery in Western Culture* (New York 1966), pp. 100–102.

10. C. N. Degler, *Out of Our Past,* pp. 29–30.

11. C. N. Degler, "Letters to the Editor, "*Comparative Studies in Society and History,* II (July, 1960), 492.

12. *The Journal of Southern History,* XXVIII (February, 1962), 29–30.

13. *Ibid.*

14. A. A. Sio, "Interpretations of Slavery: The Slave Status in the Americas," *Comparative Studies in Society and History,* VII (April, 1965), 289–300.

15. J. Viner, *Studies in the Theory of International Trade* (New York 1937), pp. 3–74; O. P. Chitwood, *History of Colonial America* (New York 1931), p. 202.

16. Davis, *op. cit.,* p. 114

17. A. J. Northrup, *Slavery in New York* (Albany, N.Y., 1900), p. 244.

18. *Ibid.,* p. 246.

19. *Ibid.;* T. R. R. Cobb, *An Inquiry into the Law of Slavery in the United States* (Philadelphia 1858), pp. 141–142.

20. W. G. Sumner, *Folkways* (Boston 1907), *introd.,* iv.

21. *Ibid.,* p. 67.

22. *Ibid.,* pp. 56–57.

23. *Ibid.,* pp. 94–95.

24. G. W. Williams, *History of the Negro Race in America from 1619–1880* (New York 1883), I, 139.

25. S. G. Nissenson, *The Patroon Domain* (New York 1937), pp. 5, 9.

26. *Ibid.,* p. 3.

27. P. J. Blok, *History of the People of the Netherlands* (New York 1898–1912), IV, 272.

28. E. B. O'Callaghan, *New York Colonial Documents*, I, 215.

29. E. B. O'Callaghan, *History of New Netherland* (New York, 1846), I, 385.

30. "Journal of the Slaver S. Jan.," Begun on the 4th of March of the year 1659. Cited in Elizabeth Donnan, ed., *Documents Illustrative to the History of the Slave Trade in America* (New York 1965), I, 141–142.

31. C. Wittke, *We Who Built America* (Cleveland 1939), p. 15.

32. Elizabeth Donnan, ed., *Documents Illustrative to the History of the Slave Trade in America*, III, 8.

33. Northrup, *op. cit.*, p. 248.

34. Davis, *op. cit.*, p. 108.

35. Northrup, *op. cit.*, p. 248; O'Callaghan, *Documents Relative to the Colonial History of New York*, I, 499; II, 474.

36. E. B. O'Callaghan, *Voyages of the Slaver St. John and the Arms of Amsterdam* (Albany, N.Y., 1867), introd., xiii.

37. D. H. Wabeke, *Dutch Emigration to North America, 1624–1860* (New York 1944), p. 20.

38. Wabeke, *op. cit.*

39. C. M. Andrews, *The Colonial Period of American History* (New Haven, Conn., 1937), III, 82.

40. Wabeke, *op. cit.*, p. 16; Northrup, *op. cit.*, p. 247.

41. E. B. O'Callaghan, *Documents Relative to the Colonial History of New York*, I, 40.

42. E. B. O'Callaghan, *History of New Netherland*, I, 384–385.

43. E. B. O'Callaghan, *Documents Relative to the Colonial History of New York*, I, 40.

44. *Ibid.*, p. 162.

45. E. B. O'Callaghan, *History of New Netherland*, I, 385.

46. W. G. Sumner, *Folkways*, p. 67.

47. Davis, *op. cit.*, p. 108.

48. E. B. O'Callaghan, *Documents Relative to the Colonial History of New York*, I, 343.

49. E. B. O'Callaghan, *Laws and Ordinances . . . , 1638–1674* (Albany, N.Y., 1868), pp. 36–37.

50. G. Myers, *History of Great American Fortunes* (New York), pp. 32–33; Northrup, *op. cit.*, p. 246 (italics added).

51. E. B. O'Callaghan, *Documents Relative to the Colonial History of New York*, I, 343.

52. Wabeke, *op. cit.*, p. 45.

53. *Ibid.*

54. E. L. Raesly, *Portrait of New Netherland* (New York 1945), p. 162.

55. G. E. Haynes, *The Negro at Work in New York City* (New York 1912), p. 66.

56. O'Callaghan, *Documents Relative to the Colonial History of New York*, I, 499 (Holland Documents: VI, *signed:* Gysbert Rudolphi, 7th of August July 1645; II, 474, "Declaration of the Farmers, Manhattan, 14 August, 1666, *signed:* Focke Jans and Hier Wolters).

57. A. B. Caldwell, *A Lecture: The History of Harlem* (New York 1882), p. 23.

58. Raesly, *op. cit.*, pp. 161–162.

59. Raesly, *op. cit.*, p. 162.

60. S. McKee, Jr., *Labor in Colonial New York, 1664–1776* (New York 1935), p. 113.

61. Northrup, *op. cit.*, pp. 260–261.

62. *Ibid.*

63. S. M. Ostrander, *A History of the City of Brooklyn and Kings County* (Brooklyn, N.Y., 1894), I, 171–172 (italics added).

64. E. B. O'Callaghan, *Documents Relative to the Colonial History of New York*, V, 39 (Lord Cornbury to the Board of Trade, February 10, 1708).

65. *Ibid.*, IV, 341–342.

66. M. Booth, *History of New York* (New York 1890), p. 270.

67. Northrup, *op. cit.*, p. 269.

68. McKee, Jr., *op. cit.*, p. 133.

69. *Colonial Laws of New York*, I, 764–765, Dec. 10, 1712.

70. *Ibid.*

71. *Ibid.*, p. 192, Nov. 2, 1717.

72. E. B. O'Callaghan, *Documentary History of New York*, I, 689.

73. McKee, Jr., *op. cit.*, p. 115.

74. U. B. Phillips, *American Negro Slavery: A Survey of the Supply, Employment and Control of Negro Labor as Determined by the Plantation Regime* (New York 1918), pp. 108–110; C. Bridenbaugh, *Cities in Revolt: Urban Life in America, 1746–1776* (New York 1955), p. 88.

75. Davis, *op. cit.*, p. 135.

76. H. A. Johnson, *The Negro in the New World* (London 1910), p. 231.

77. McKee, Jr., *op. cit.*, p. 133.

78. *Ibid.*, p. 142.

79. *Ibid.*

80. *Ibid.*, p. 143.

81. *Ibid.*

82. Northrup, *op. cit.*, pp. 260–261.

83. A. Caldecott, *English Colonization and Empire* (New York 1891), p. 193.

84. McKee, Jr., *op. cit.*, p. 124.

85. E. B. O'Callaghan, *Documents Relative to the Colonial History of New York*, IV, 510–511 (Signed: Earl of Bellmont, April 27, 1699).

86. Davis, *op. cit.*, p. 100.

87. Caldecott, *op. cit.*, p. 245.

88. L. A. Harper, "The Effect of the Navigation Acts on the Thirteen Colonies," in R. B. Morris, ed., *The Era of the American Revolution* (New York 1939), pp. 3–39.

89. C. M. Andrews, *The Colonial Period in American History* (New Haven 1937), III, 75–76.

90. 5 Geo. II., c. 22 (1732).

91. R. B. Morris, *Government and Labor in Early America* (New York 1946), p. 182.

92. McKee, Jr., *op. cit.*, pp. 52–53.

93. *Ibid.*, p. 183.

94. *Ibid.*, p. 11.

95. Morris, *op. cit.*, p. 183.

96. 5 Geo. II., c. 22 (1732).

97. Morris, *op. cit.*, p. 183.

98. *Ibid.*, pp. 148–149.

99. E. B. O'Callaghan, *Documents Relative to the Colonial History of New York*, IV, 307 (italics added), (signed: John Lewin, Gent. Agent . . . to your Royal Highness, May 24, 1688.)

100. E. B. O'Callaghan, *Documents Relative to . . .* III, 3.

101. McKee, *op. cit.*, p. 51.

102. H. Aptheker, *The American Negro Slave Revolts* (New York 1943), pp. 70–71.

103. A. H. Payne, "The Negro in New York Prior to 1860," *Howard Review* (June, 1923–1925), p. 21; Northrup, *op. cit.*, p. 243; L. Litwack, *North of Slavery: The Negro in the Free States, 1790–1860* (Chicago 1961), pp. 30–33.

CHAPTER 2

1. L. T. Greene, *The Negro in Colonial New England, 1620–1776* (New York 1942), pp. 100–123.

2. C. F. Adams, ed., *The Works of John Adams* (Boston 1850–1856), X, 380.

3. L. F. Litwack, *North of Slavery: The Negro in the Free States, 1790–1860* (Chicago 1961), p. 5.

4. W. H. and J. Pease, *Black Utopia* (Madison, Wis., 1963), p. 9; B. Drew, ed., *A Northside View of Slavery* (Boston 1856), pp. 88–89, 98, 186.

5. Litwack, *op. cit.*, p. 15.

6. H. D. Bloch, "The New York Negro's Battle for Political Rights, 1777–1865," *International Review of Social History*, IX (1964), 65–80.

7. R. B. Morris, *Government and Labor in Early America* (New York 1946), p. 183.

8. L. H. Butterfield, W. D. Garrett, and M. R. Sprague, eds., *The Adams Papers* (Cambridge, Mass.),

cited in *Life* Magazine, July 25, 1963, p. 4.

9. E. H. Roberts, *New York* (New York 1933), II, 455, 720.

10. *Ibid.*, p. 456.

11. *Census of the State of New York for 1855* (Albany, N.Y.), viii, ix.

12. *Negro Population in the U.S., 1790–1915* (Washington, D.C., 1917), pp. 51, 55.

13. "A New Image for an Old Industry," *Industrial Bulletin* (New York, June, 1963), pp. 7–8.

14. *Census of the State of New York for 1855, loc. cit.*

15. *Ibid.*

16. *Minutes of the Proceedings of the 4th American Convention of Delegates From Abolition Societies in 1797,* p. 37.

17. G. S. Johnson, "Black Workers in the City," *Survey*, March 1, 1925, p. 641.

18. *Life*, July 25, 1963, p. 4.

19. *Life, op. cit.*

20. . . . *American Convention of Abolition Societies* (New York 1803), p. 7.

21. . . . *American Convention of Abolition Societies* (New York 1805), p. 38.

22. W. J. Bromwell, *History of Immigration to the U.S.* (New York 1856), p. 15 ff.

23. *Negro Population . . . , 1790–1915*, pp. 51, 55.

24. *Census of the State of New York for 1855, loc. cit.*

25. O. Handlin, *The Newcomers* (New York 1962), pp. 6–7.

26. A. G. Lindsay, "The Economic Conditions of Negroes in New York Prior to 1860," *Journal of Negro History* (1921), p. 191.

27. *Ibid.*, p. 192.

28. G. E. Haynes, *The Negro at Work in New York City* (New York 1912), pp. 48, 144.

29. J. H. Griscom, ed., *The Sanitary Condition of the Laboring Population of New York* (New York 1845), p. 4.

30. C. C. Andrews, *The History of the African Free School* (New York 1830), p. 118.

31. E. S. Adby, *Journal of Residence and Tour of the U.S.* (London 1835), I, 358.

32. J. W. C. Pennington, *The Fugitive Blacksmith* (New York 1849), p. 55.

33. The New York *Mercury*, May 1830; *The American Daily Advertizer*, May 23, 1829.

34. Andrews, *op cit.*

35. . . . *American Convention of Abolition Societies* (New York 1821), pp. 52, 53.

36. . . . *American Convention of Abolition Societies* (New York 1828), pp. 20, 29, 62.

37. L. F. Litwack, "The Emancipation of the Negro Abolitionist," in M. Duberman, ed., *The Antislavery Vanguard* (Princeton, N.J., 1965), pp. 141–143.

38. *Colored American*, July 28, 1838.

39. Litwack, *op. cit.*, p. 142.

40. Andrews, *op. cit.*, p. 122.

41. *Colored American*, August 12, 1838; Dec. 22, 1838, *passim.*

42. W. Hugins, *Jacksonian Democracy and the Working Class* (Stanford, Calif., 1960), pp. 161–162.

43. *American Anti-Slavery Almanac*, I, no. 5, 1840, 21 (Caption reads: "Sanctified Hate, Legalized Hate").

44. *Ibid.*; W. E. B. DuBois, ed., *The Negro Artisan* (Atlanta, Ga., 1902), p. 134; the New York *Times*, Nov. 17, 1901.

45. Litwack, *op. cit.*, p. 159; *Colored American*, Sept. 16, 1837.

46. Pease, *op. cit.*, p. 186.

47. R. Ernst, *Immigrant Life in New York City, 1825–1863* (Port Washington, N.Y., 1949), p. 162.

48. *African Repository*, XXII, no. 8 (1846), 278.

49. Lindsay, *op. cit.*, p. 196.

50. D. R. Fox, *Decline of Aristocracy in the Politics of New York* (New York 1919), pp. 22–25.

51. H. C. Brown, *In the Golden Nineties* (New York 1928), p. 84.

52. A. Dyson, "Gerrit Smith's Efforts in Behalf of the Negroes in New York," *Journal of Negro History*, III, 355.

53. J. M. McPherson, *Struggle for Equality* (Princeton 1965), p. 233.

54. *The New Moral World*, June 29, 1844.

55. S. Spero and A. Harris, *The Black Worker* (New York 1931), p. 13; E. Abbott, *Women in Industry* (New York 1926), *passim*; Ernst, *op. cit.*, p. 67.

56. Ernst, *op. cit.*, pp. 104–105; Abbott, *op. cit.*, p. 137.

57. E. Abbott, *Historical Aspects of Immigration Problem* (Chicago, 1926), pp. 325–326.

58. A. P. Man, Jr., "Labor Competition and the New York Draft Riots, 1863," *The Journal of Negro History*, XXXVI (1951), 376.

59. J. H. Harmon, A. L. Lindsay, and C. G. Woodson, *The Negro as a Businessman* (Washington, D.C., 1929), p. 4.

60. *Maryland Colonization Journal*, III (1850), 103.

61. Ernst, *op. cit.*, p. 40.

62. J. G. Speed, "The Negro in New York," *Harper's Weekly*, Dec. 22, 1900, p. 1249.

63. M. W. Ovington, *Half a Man: The Status of the Negro in New York* (New York 1911), p. 29.

64. The New York *Tribune*, March 20, 1851.

65. McPherson, *op. cit.*, p. 231.

66. Ernst, *op. cit.*, pp. 73–79.

67. *The Citizen* (New York), March 4, 1854.

68. *Compendium of the Census of 1850* (Washington, D.C.), pp. 80–81.

69. Ernst, *op. cit.*, p. 67.

70. C. H. Wesley, *Negro Labor in the U.S., 1850–1925* (New York 1927), pp. 30–32.

71. *Preliminary Report of the 8th Census*, 1860 (Washington, D.C., 1862), pp. 80–81.

72. Ernst, *op. cit.*, p. 59; H. Jerome, *Migration and Business Cycles* (New York 1936), p. 40.

73. Ernst, *op. cit.*, p. 104.

74. Quoted in E. L. Franklin, *The Negro Labor Unionist in New York* (New York 1936), p. 21.

75. The New York *Tribune*, Nov. 27, 1853; *The African Repository*, XXVII, 110 (Quote taken from the Philadelphia *North American*).

76. The New York *World*, Aug. 2, 1862.

77. The New York *Tribune*, Nov. 25, 1862, and Jan. 24, 1863.

78. I. A. Hourwitch, *Immigration and Labor* (New York 1912), p. 231.

79. The New York *Tribune*, Dec. 1, 1862.

80. Committee of Merchants for the Relief of Colored People Suffering from the Late Riots in the City of New York, *Report of the Merchants for the Relief of Colored People Suffering from the Late Riots in the City of New York* (New York 1863), p. 10.

81. J. D. Burn, *Three Years Among the Working Classes in the U.S. During the War* (London 1865), pp. 22–23.

82. Committee of Merchants for the Relief . . . , *op. cit.*, pp. 3, 7, 9, 11.

83. McPherson, *op. cit.*, p. 232.

84. *Negro Population . . . , 1790–1915*, pp. 45, 51, 55.

85. Committee of Merchants for the Relief . . . , *op. cit.*, p. 10.

86. The New York *World*, March 16, 1867.

87. The New York *Age*, Feb. 9, 1889, and Sept. 16, 1889.

88. T. Boese, *Public Education in the City of New York* (New York 1869), p. 131.

89. W. E. B. DuBois, The New York *Times*, Nov. 17, 1901.

90. R. T. Berthoff, *The Immigrant in Industrial America* (Cambridge, Eng., 1953), p. 190; Ernst, *op. cit.*, p. 67.

91. *Ibid.*, p. 67.

92. *Ibid.*, pp. 81–83.

93. Department of Commerce, Bureau of Census, *Immigrants and Their Children, 1920* (Washington, D.C., 1927), Census Monograph no. 7, p. 26.

94. *American Academy of Political and Social Science*, "The Negro's Progress in Fifty Years," (Philadelphia 1913), pp. 34–35.

95. Census of 1870, *Statistics of Population* (Washington, D.C., 1872), I, 793.

96. M. R. Davie, *World Population* (New York 1936), p. 242.

97. *Ibid.*

98. Census of 1870, *op. cit.*, p. 793.

99. Hourwitch, *op. cit.*, p. 25; Davie, *op. cit.*, p. 243.

100. Spero and Harris, *op. cit.*, p. 177.

101. G. B. Barnes, *The Longshoremen* (New York 1915), p. 8.

102. R. F. Foerster, *Italian Emigration in our Times* (Cambridge, Mass., 1938), p. 334; R. S. Baker, "The Negro Struggle for Survival," *North American Magazine* (1907–1908), pp. 65, 479.

103. E. F. Frazier, "A Negro Industrial Group," *Howard Review* (June, 1924), p. 198; Barnes, *op. cit.*, p. 9.

104. Speed, *op. cit.*, p. 1249.

105. New York *Globe*, March 29, 1884.

106. Cleveland *Gazette*, Dec. 29, 1888.

107. W. E. B. DuBois, *Some Notes on Negroes in New York City*, *op. cit.*

108. G. Osofsky, *Harlem* (New York 1965), pp. 4–5.

109. Jerome, *op. cit.*, p. 41.

110. *Immigrants and their Children*, *op. cit.*, p. 27.

111. R. F. Foerster, "A Statistical Survey of Italian Emigration," *Quarterly Journal of Economics* (1908–1909), III, 79–81.

112. H. P. Fairchild, *Greek Immigration to the U.S.* (New Haven 1921), p. 117.

113. The New York *Age*, July 12, 1906.

114. P. Roberts, *The New Immigration* (New York 1920), p. 58.

115. Speed, *op. cit.*, p. 1250.

116. Roberts, *op. cit.*, p. 60.

117. The National Urban League, *Negro Membership in American Labor Unions* (New York 1930).

118. Spero and Harris, *op. cit.*, p. 337.

119. M. W. Ovington, "The Negro in Trade Unions in New York," *Annals of the American Academy of Political and Social Science* (May, 1906), p. 91.

120. Spero and Harris, *op. cit.*, p. 337.

121. "Negro Craftsmen in New York," *Southern Workmen* (1908), pp. 35, 48.

122. *Ibid.*, (1907), pp. 35, 54.

123. M. W. Ovington, *Half-A-Man: The Status of the Negro in N.Y.* (New York 1911), p. 93.

124. C. P. Larrowe, *Shape-up and Hiring Hall* (Berkeley, Calif., 1955), p. 49, *et seq.*

125. *The Colored Magazine*, XIII (October, 1907), 106.

126. Osofsky, *op. cit.*, p. 6.

127. "The Negro's Progress in Fifty Years," *op. cit.*, p. 34.

128. M. W. Ovington, *op. cit.*, p. 93.

129. *Negro Population in the U.S., 1790–1915*, *op. cit.*, p. 55.

130. M. W. Ovington, "The Negro Home in New York," *Charities*, Oct. 7, 1905.

131. C. L. Franklin, *op. cit.*, p. 41.

132. *Annual Reports of the Commissioner of Immigration.*

133. L. V. Kennedy, *The Negro Peasant Turns Cityward* (New York 1930), pp. 43–53.

134. 1910 Census, IV, *Occupations*, p. 180, *et seq.*; 1920 Census, IV., *Occupations*, p. 186, *et seq.*

135. C. S. Johnson, "Black Workers and the City," *Survey*, LIII (1925), 641–643; D. Dutcher, *The Negro in Modern Industrial Society* (Lancaster, Pa., 1930), p. 91.

136. Dutcher, *op. cit.*, p. 84.

137. Kennedy, *op. cit.*, pp. 88–89.

138. G. E. Haynes, "Effect of War Conditions on Negro Labor," *Proceedings of the Academy of Political Science*, VIII, 299–312; Women's Bureau, Bulletin no. 20, *Negro Women in Industry* (Washington, D.C., 1922), p. 7.

139. Kennedy, *op. cit.*, p. 91.

140. *Negro Membership in American Labor Unions* (New York 1930), p. 8 (italics added).

CHAPTER 3

1. T. J. Woofter, *Races and Ethnic Groups in American Life* (New York 1933), p. 133.

2. *Ibid.*

3. Report of the New York State Temporary Commission *Legislative Document No. 69* (Albany, N.Y., 1939), p. 14.

4. Roi-Ottley, *New World A-Coming* (Boston 1943), p. 115.

5. FEPC *Files*, May, 1944.

6. *Ibid.*, April 23, 1945.

7. *Ibid.*, May 27, 1944.

8. *Ibid.*, 1943.

9. Personal interview with Ramon Rivera, July 21, 1955; New York *Times*, July 26, 1955.

10. The New York State Commission Against Discrimination, *Railroad Employment in New York and New Jersey* (New York 1958), p. 1.

11. *Ibid.*, p. 5.

12. *Ibid.*, p. 6, *et seq.*

13. *Ibid.*, p. 21.

14. *Ibid.*, p. 25.

15. *Ibid.*

16. *Ibid.*, p. 26.

17. *Ibid.*, p. 28.

18. *Ibid.*, preface, ii, iii.

19. *Hotel*, June 17, 1963; *Hotel*, Sept. 16, 1963; *Electrical Union World*, Local 3, I.B.E.W., July 1, 1963; personal conversations with Peter Byrnes, secretary-treasurer, Local 144, B.S.E.I.U., AFL-CIO; Charles Chuisana, personnel director, Waldorf-Astoria Hotel, Oct. 1, 1963.

20. P. Byrnes, Nov. 5, 1963.

21. General Motors Department, UAW *Newsletter*, June 28, 1961, p. 5.

22. *Ibid.*, July 13, 1961.

23. Statistics obtained by author while research director of the Negro American Labor Council, 1960–1961.

24. Confidential Report dated Nov. 30, 1963.

25. *Ibid.*

26. *Ibid.*

27. *Holiday Magazine*, March, 1961, p. 161.

28. Greater Urban League of New York, *Advertising Agencies and the Negro* (New York, undated), p. 3.

29. *Ibid.*, p. 2.

30. *Ibid.*, pp. 10–11.

31. *Administrative Code of the City of New York*, B. 32-240.0 (1942).

32. The New York State War Council, *Committee on Discrimination in Employment*, First Report, March, 1941–July, 1944, p. 20.

33. *Ibid.*, First Quarterly Report, January-March, 1944, p. 32.

34. FEPC *Files*, Nov. 11, 1943.

35. The New York *Times*, May 8, 1959; personal interview with Elmer Carter, chairman of SCAD, January, 1961.

36. The New York *Times*, Jan. 23, 1964.

37. U.S. Commission on Civil Rights Report, *Employment* (1961), pp. 116–20, 153.

38. The New York *Times*, Sept. 11, 1962.

39. *Ibid.*, Aug. 1, 1963.

40. *Ibid.*, Jan. 27, 1964.

41. Ohio Civil Rights Commission, *Survey of Ohio College and University Placement Offices with Regard to Job Placement of Minority Students* (Columbus 1962), pp. 9–10.

42. *Hotel*, Jan. 20, 1964; interview with David Livingston, president of District 65, RWDSU, AFL-CIO, 1960.

43. *FEPC Files*, March 18, 1943.

44. *Ibid.*

45. *FEPC Files*, Jan. 27, 1945.

47. National Manpower Council, *A Policy for Skilled Manpower* (New York 1954), p. 219.

48. *Union Voice*, February, 1950, pp. 4–5.

49. *Ibid.*, pp. 3–4.

50. *Distributive Workers Union*, Feb. 4–5, 1950, p. 23.

51. National Association for the Advancement of Colored People, *Press Release*, June 4, 1946.

52. *FEPC Files*, April, 1944.

53. State Commission Against Discrimination, *Employment in the Hotel Industry* (March, 1958), p. 13.

54. *Ibid.*, p. 16.

55. *Ibid.*, p. 1; New York *Herald Tribune*, Dec. 3, 1957.

56. *Ibid.*, p. 11.

57. M. Hall, ed., *Made in New York* (Cambridge, Mass., 1960), pp. 94–95.

58. *Union Voice*, March 25, 1951, p. 6.

59. R. M. Lichtenberg, *One Tenth of a Nation* (Cambridge, Mass., 1960), pp. 220–221.

60. *Hotel*, Sept. 16, 1963.

61. *Hotel*, October, 1963, Jan. 20, 1964.

62. Interview with Peter Byrnes, Feb. 18, 1964.

63. C. E. Silberman, "The Businessman and the Negro," *Fortune* Magazine, September, 1963 (reprint), pp. 5–6.

64. Interview with author, August, 1963.

65. H. P. Miller, *Statement of Herman P. Miller, Special Assistant, Office of the Director, Bureau of the Census, before the Subcommittee on Employment and Manpower*, U.S. Senate Committee on Labor and Public Welfare, July 31, 1963, p. 4.

66. *Ibid.*, p. 3.

67. International Brotherhood of Teamsters, Chauffeurs, Warehousemen, and Helpers of America, Joint Council No. 16, *Press Release*, Aug. 26, 1963, p. 2.

68. *Ibid.*, p. 4.

69. Interviews with Moe Foner and Richard Logan, research director and education director, respectively, of Local 1199, RWDSU, AFL-CIO, January, 1964.

70. The New York State Temporary Commission Against Discrimination in Employment, Oct. 27, 1943.

71. *Ibid.*

72. Fiske University, *A Monthly Summary of Events and Trends in Race Relations* (October, 1944), p. 62.

73. U.S. Department of Labor, *Monthly Labor Review*, LX, No. 1, (1945), 5.

74. S. Tannenbaum, *Why Men Hate* (New York 1947), p. 117.

75. W. S. Woytinsky and Assoc., *Employment and Wages in the United States* (New York 1953), pp. 406–407.

76. "Labor's Race Problem," *Fortune* Magazine, March, 1959, p. 191.

77. *Ibid.*

78. *Ibid.*

79. J. L. Russell, "Changing Patterns in Employment of Nonwhite Workers," *Monthly Labor Review* (Reprinted, 1966), p. 503.

80. *Ibid.*, p. 504.

81. *Ibid.*, p. 508.

82. *Ibid.*, p. 509.

CHAPTER 4

1. P. Lazarsfeld and A. Zawarski, "The Psychological Consequences of Unemployment," *Journal of Social Psy-*

chology, 1936; K. B. Clark, *Prejudice and Your Child* (Boston 1955), pp. 63–65.

2. N. P. McGill and E. N. Mathews, *The Youth of New York City* (New York 1940), pp. 190–195.

3. J. Schiffman, "Employment of High School Graduates and Dropouts in 1962," *Monthly Labor Review*, July, 1963 (reprinted as Special Labor Force, #32), p. 6.

4. *Ibid.*, pp. 7–8.

5. *Ibid.*, p. 8.

6. *Manpower Report of the President and a Report on Manpower Requirements, Resources, Utilization and Training by the U.S. Department of Labor* (transmitted to the Congress, March, 1964), p. 105 (italics added).

7. *Ibid.*

8. *Ibid.*, p. 117.

9. U.S. Commission on Civil Rights Report (1961), *Employment* (Washington, D.C., 1961), p. 153.

10. Mayor's Council on Poverty, *Dimensions of Poverty in New York City* (New York, March 23, 1964), p. 153.

11. *Ibid.*

12. U.S. Department of Labor, Bureau of Labor Statistics, *Income, Education, and Unemployment in Neighborhoods, New York City, Brooklyn*, January, 1963, pp. 21, 2, 3, 4, 37, 53, 69.

13. The New York State Committee on Discrimination in Employment, *Annual Report for the Year Ending December 31, 1944*, p. 4.

14. Mayor's Council on Poverty, *op. cit.*, p. 4.

15. *Ibid.*

16. *Ibid.*, p. 5.

17. City Commission on Human Rights of New York, *Ethnic Survey of Municipal Employees* (March 19, 1964), p. 6 (italics added).

18. *Ibid.*, p. 7.

19. The New York State Commission on Discrimination in Employment, *op. cit.*, p. 4.

20. Manpower Report of the President . . . , *op. cit.*, p. 105 (italics added).

21. W. S. Woytinsky and Associates, *Wages and Employment in the U.S.* (preliminary draft, April, 1950), pp. 934–935. Ten years later, Herman Miller arrived at the same conclusion.

22. H. P. Miller, *Statement of Herman P. Miller, Special Assistant, Office of the Director, Bureau of the Census, before the Subcommittee on Employment and Manpower, U.S.* Senate Committee on Labor and Public Welfare, July 31, 1963, pp. 2–3 (italics added).

23. U.S. Department of Labor, *Family Income and Expenditure in New York City, 1935–1936*, I, 19.

24. The New York State Temporary Commission, *Legislative Document No. 69* (Albany, N.Y., 1939), p. 15.

25. Miller, *op. cit.*, p. 6.

26. *Manpower Report of the President* . . . , *op. cit.*, p. 275 (Table H-10); Miller, *op. cit.*, p. 7.

27. *Manpower Report of the President* . . . , *op. cit.*, p. 106.

28. *Ibid.*

29. *Dimensions of Poverty in New York City, op. cit.*, pp. 2, 3, 5, 6.

30. *Ibid.*, p. 6.

31. *Ibid.*, p. 3.

CHAPTER 5

1. Twenty-first Annual Eastern Seaboard Apprenticeship Conference, June 14–18, 1965, *Apprenticeship in a Changing World* (Atlantic City, N.J.).

2. P. H. Douglas, *American Apprenticeship and Industrial Education* (New York 1921), pp. 60–62; J. H. Ashworth, *The Helper and American Trade Unions*, The Johns Hopkins University Studies (Baltimore 1915), *passim*.

3. O. Klineberg, *Social Psychology* (New York 1940), pp. 39 ff.

4. S. Spero and A. Harris, *The Black Worker* (New York 1931), p. 56.

5. W. E. B. DuBois, ed., *The Negro Artisan* (Atlanta, Ga., 1902), p. 154.

6. *Ibid.*

7. W. E. B. DuBois, *Some Notes on Negroes in New York City* (Atlanta 1903).

8. J. R. Commons and Associates, *History of Labor in the United States* (New York 1936), I, 621.

9. *Ibid.*, p. 622.

10. Cigar Makers' International Union *Proceedings, 1865* (Johns Hopkins Library), p. 60; also, *Proceedings, 1867*, p. 136.

11. F. E. Wolfe, *Admission to American Trade Unions* (Baltimore 1912), p. 114.

12. National Typographical Union's *1852 Constitution*, Art. 10, sec. 1.

13. National Typographical Union's *1857 Constitution*, Art. 10, sec. 1.

14. *Ibid.*, By-Laws, art. V.

15. *Ibid.*, 1852 and 1857 constitutions, Art. 10, sec. 1.

16. International Typographical Union's *Convention Proceedings, 1879*, p. 9.

17. G. E. Barnett, "The Printers: A Study in American Trade Unionism," *American Economic Association Quarterly*, October, 1909, p. 33.

18. Wolfe, *op. cit.*, p. 68.

19. Carpenters and Joiners Union of the United States of America, *Proceedings of the First Annual Convention in New York, 1865.* (The current United Brotherhood of Carpenters and Joiners . . . , was formed in 1881.)

20. Wolfe, *op. cit.*

21. N. J. Ware, *The Labor Movement in the United States, 1860–1895* (New York 1929), p. 18.

22. G. E. Neill, ed., *The Labor Movement: The Problem Today* (New York 1887), pp. 134–171.

23. Wolfe, *op. cit.*, p. 114.

24. *The Workingman's Advocate* lists Cameron as both editor and publisher.

25. "The Address of the National Labor Congress to the Workingman of the United States," published in July, 1867 (reprinted in Commons and Associates, *Documentary History of American Society*, IX, 141–168).

26. Cameron, *loc. cit.*

27. *Ibid.*

28. *The Workingman's Advocate*, Aug. 24, 1867.

29. *Ibid.*, Aug. 31, 1867.

30. *Ibid.*

31. *Ibid.*

32. *Ibid.*

33. *Ibid.*

34. *The Workingman's Advocate*, Sept. 4, 1869.

35. The New York *Times*, Aug. 22, 1869.

36. *The Workingman's Advocate*, Sept. 4, 11, 1869; The New York *Times*, Aug. 18, 19, 22, 23, 1869.

37. *The Workingman's Advocate*, Dec. 11, 1869.

38. Wolfe, *op. cit.*, p. 114.

39. *Douglass' Monthly*, September, 1863.

40. Cigar Makers' *International Proceedings, 1865*, p. 60. (Johns Hopkins Library, Baltimore.)

41. *The Workingman's Advocate*, Sept. 26, 1868.

42. *Ibid.*, Oct. 21, 1869; the New York *Tribune*, Sept. 17, 1869 (italics added).

43. Executive Council, *A Study of the History of the International Typographical Union, 1852–1963* (Colorado Springs, Colo., 1964), p. 297.

44. The Washington *Daily Chronicle*, May 21, June 8, 1869.

45. *The Workingman's Advocate*, Oct. 8, 1870.

46. *Ibid.*

47. *The Workingman's Advocate*, Nov. 12, 1870.

48. *American Workman*, Sept. 30, 1871.

49. *The Workingman's Advocate*, Nov. 25, 1871.

50. *Bricklayers and Masons Proceedings, 1879*, p. 37.

51. *The Workingman's Advocate,* Jan. 28, 1871.

52. *Ibid.,* Jan. 21, 1871.

53. *Ibid.,* Jan. 17, 1874.

54. *Bricklayers and Masons Proceedings,* 1875, p. 39.

55. *Ibid.,* 1877, pp. 6, 17, 18.

56. Wolfe, *op. cit.,* p. 114.

57. The New York *Times,* March 2, 1869.

58. The New York *Tribune,* Aug. 23, 1871.

59. International Typographical *Proceedings,* 1879, p. 9 (italics added).

60. United Brotherhood of Carpenters and Joiners, *Constitution,* 1886, Art. III, sec. 3.

61. Commons, *et al.,* III, 167.

62. T. V. Powderly, *Thirty Years of Labor, 1859–1889* (Philadelphia 1890), p. 350.

63. Powderly, *op. cit.,* p. 347.

64. *Ibid.,* p. 348.

65. *Ibid.*

66. *John Swinton's Paper,* Oct. 17, 1886.

67. The New York *Freeman,* April 17, Dec. 18, 1886, Jan. 15, Sept. 10, 1887.

68. S. Kessler, "The Negro in the Knights of Labor" (Master's Thesis, Columbia University, 1950), pp. 48–50; Knights of Labor, *Proceedings of the General Assembly,* 1885: A geographic breakdown revealed that the City of Richmond, Va., had 12 all-Negro locals and one district assembly in 1885; Atlanta, Ga., in the same year, had at least two all-Negro assemblies, p. 31.

69. *John Swinton's Paper,* July 25, 1886.

70. *The Report of the First Annual Convention of the Federation of Organized Trades and Labor Unions of the United States and Canada 1881* (italics added).

71. *Gompers Letter Book,* Gompers to Jones, March 8, 1893.

72. *Report of the Proceedings of the 10th Annual Convention of the American Federation of Labor, 1890,* p. 29.

73. Gompers to R. T. Coles, April 28, 1891.

74. Duncan to Dadis, April 1, 1895 (italics added).

75. Duncan to O'Connell, March 27, 1895.

76. Wolfe, *op. cit.,* p. 117; Prentice Thomas, *Discrimination Against Negroes* (National Urban League), October, 1943.

77. *Proceedings of the AFL Convention,* 1900, p. 263.

78. P. S. Foner, *History of the Labor Movement in the United States* (New York 1964) III, p. 235.

79. *Ibid.*

80. Gompers, "Why Affiliate with the Federation" *American Federationist,* July, 1896, p. 103.

81. *Proceedings of the American Federation of Labor,* 1897, pp. 82–83.

82. *Official Report of the Second Annual Convention of the AFL,* 1887, pp. 4, 10.

83. L. L. Lorwin, *The American Federation of Labor* (Washington, D.C., 1933), p. 72.

84. Wolfe, *op. cit.,* pp. 117–118.

85. *American Federationist,* April, 1901, pp. 118–120; D. Brody, *The Butcher Workman: A Study of Unionization* (Cambridge, Mass., 1964), p. 41.

86. Wire Weavers *Constitution, 1894,* Art. III, sec. 1.

87. Switchmen, Subordinate Lodge *Constitution,* 1909, Sec. 141.

88. Maintenance of Way Employees, *Constitution,* 1909, Art. XI, sec. 1.

89. Railroad Telegraphers, *Constitution,* 1909, Art. XIV, sec. 1.

90. Railway Clerks *Constitution, 1906,* Art. II, sec. 1.

91. Commercial Telegraphers *Constitution,* 1908, Art. III, sec. 1.

92. Boilermakers and Iron Ship Builders, *Proceedings,* 1908, p. 494.

93. *Report of the Industrial Commission* (Washington, D.C., 1901), Vol. 17, p. 36.

94. April, 1903, p. 102.

95. Gompers to L. F. Klinger, July 18, 1891.

96. Bricklayers and Masons *Proceedings, 1881,* p. 7.

97. *Ibid.,* p. 26.

98. Bricklayers and Masons *Proceedings, 1883,* pp. 14, 21, 62, 63.

99. United Brotherhood of Carpenters and Joiners, *Constitution, 1886,* Art. III, sec. 3.

100. Cigar Makers' International Union *Proceedings, 1893,* pp. 5, 34.

101. Personal interview with Mr. Chall, retired member of Local 1, Plumbers Union, Brooklyn, N.Y., January, 1950.

102. C. L. Mangum, *The Operating Engineers* (Cambridge, Mass., 1964), pp. 2, 232, 233 (italics added).

CHAPTER 6

1. H. Feldman, *Racial Factors in American Industry* (New York 1934), p. 16; C. W. Johnson, *Black Manhattan* (New York 1930), p. 151.

2. I. De A. Reid, *Negro Membership in American Unions* (National Urban League, 1930), p. 26.

3. L. Wolman, *Ebb and Flow in Trade Unionism* (New York 1924), p. 26; AFL *Proceedings* for various years.

4. Wolman, *op. cit.,* pp. 22–23.

5. Reid, *op. cit.,* p. 26.

6. Letter addressed to Gompers from E. K. Jones and F. R. Moore, dated June 6, 1918 (files of the National Urban League, N.Y.).

7. *Report of Proceedings,* 38th Annual Convention of the AFL, June 10–20, 1918, pp. 198, 199, 205.

8. Reid, *op. cit.,* p. 29.

9. *Ibid.,* p. 30.

10. *Ibid.*

11. "Economic Conditions and Union Policy," in J. B. S. Hardman and Associates, *American Labor Dynamics* (New York 1928), p. 40.

12. *Gompers Letter Book,* Gompers to Jones, March 8, 1893.

13. Reid, *op. cit.,* p. 32.

14. *American Federationist,* XXXII, October, 1925, 878–879.

15. U.S. Department of Labor, Bureau of Labor Statistics, *Handbook of American Trade Unions,* (Washington, D.C., 1929).

16. R. R. Brazeal, *The Brotherhood of Sleeping Car Porters* (New York 1946), p. 128.

17. *Messenger,* August, 1925, pp. 304–305.

18. American Federation of Labor, *Convention Proceedings,* 1923, p. 122.

19. *Ibid.,* 1929, p. 137.

20. *Constitution* of the American Federation of Labor, art. xi, sec. 6.

21. *AFL Convention Proceedings,* 1929, p. 139.

22. Hotel Alliance *Constitution,* sec. 20; Reid, p. 37.

23. American Federation of Labor, *Report of Proceedings,* 1929, pp. 385–386.

24. Reid, *op. cit.,* pp. 96–98; C. L. Franklin, *The Negro Labor Unionist in New York* (New York 1936), p. 103.

25. Personal Interview with Edward L. Doty, 623 Bowen Avenue, Chicago, Ill., Feb. 12, 1961.

26. C. S. Johnson, *The Negro and Labor Unions,* Preliminary Report of a Study (National Urban League library, 1925); *ibid.,* The Negro in American Civilization (New York 1930), pp. 108–109.

27. Although the Railway Carmen's Union limited membership to "any white person between the ages of 16 and 65," it also had a special ruling covering some Negro American workers in the South. These black workers were organized into separate auxiliary bodies completely dominated by white locals, and accepted under special conditions. Their organization was effected only to

enable the union to maintain a monopoly control of the trade.

28. The Carmen's constitution differed from that of most others, since it stipulated that members must be "born of white parents."

29. The union's constitution permitted the organization of auxiliary locals only where the white local gave its consent.

30. *Handbook of American Trade Unions* (1929), p. 55.

31. Brazeal, *op. cit.*, p. 134.

32. *Ibid.*, p. 135.

33. Julius A. Thomas, former head of the Industrial Relations Department of the National Urban League, supplied this information in 1950.

34. The term "nominal" was used circumspectly, since many international union constitutions had no ban on Negro Americans, but individual local unions could discriminate against them. Frequently cited was the Operative Plasterers and Cement Finishers International Association, whose constitution read:

Any member or members that refuse to work with any other member in good standing in this association on account of race, creed, or nationality, thereby causing him to lose his job when such charges can be proven to the satisfaction of the Executive Board, he or they shall be fined the sum of One Hundred Dollars (*Constitution*, sec. 54, 15).

Field investigation revealed that this clause was simply window dressing. Each local had autonomy, which permitted it to admit or deny to membership on the basis of local conditions. There was nothing in the constitution that required a local to admit Negro Americans and many refused to do so. Too, exclusion from membership ruled out the rest of the section in the plasterers' constitution. A white worker's refusal to work with colored Americans cannot be questioned if they are not members of the local. Again, to prove loss of a job because of a union brother's refusal to work with a Negro American is not only difficult but somewhat

foolish when other means of evasion are at hand. The usual practice is to make life on the job so difficult that the Negro American will leave of his own accord. Also, according to most people who have been active in the craft unions, it is rather naive to think that one can prove discrimination to the satisfaction of the executive board. Finally, what the clause fails to mention is that the most important person in the triangle—Negro Americans, fraternal brothers, and management—is the business agent to whom the grievance is first presented. In 1964 an examination of Local 30's (Plasterers Union) membership rolls revealed no Negro American membership.

35. Similarly, the Painters and Decorators Union's constitution read:

Our general constitution does not prohibit the acceptance of Negro members, *it is a matter for local action.*

Hence, a cursory examination of the constitutions of many international unions may be misleading, since there is a difference between the written word and everyday practice. This was evidenced in the case of the bricklayers, where two out of the seven New York locals barred Negro Americans. The picture is complete when we examine the meaning of autonomy further. The AFL's executive board has no jurisdiction over local union practices, and in many craft unions the final say lies with the locals, not the internationals.

36. H. A. Millis and R. E. Montgomery, *Organized Labor* (New York, 1944), III, 279; P. Taft, *The AFL in the Time of Gompers* (New York, 1957), I, 202–210.

37. Reid, *op. cit.*, p. 102.

38. C. L. Mangum, *The Operating Engineers* (Cambridge, Mass., 1964), pp. 232–233.

39. H. Harris, *American Labor* (New Haven, 1939), pp. 159–162, 356.

40. Local 1888 was formed after World War I and for all practical purposes was a segregated local.

41. M. H. Vorse, *Labor's New Millions* (New York 1938), pp. 17–18.

42. Harris, *op. cit.*, p. 391.

43. Franklin, *The Negro Labor Unionist in New York City* (New York 1936), pp. 114–115.

44. *Ibid.*, pp. 125, 126.

45. E. Kine, "The Garment Union Comes to the Negro Worker," *Opportunity*, April, 1934, p. 107.

46. *Ibid.*

47. Franklin, *op. cit.*, p. 263.

48. *Ibid.*, p. 164.

49. *Ibid.*, p. 167.

50. *Ibid.*, p. 170.

51. *Electrical World*, April 1903, p. 102.

52. The New York *Times*, Oct. 18, 19, 1936.

53. Franklin, pp. 162–173. Unfortunately there were many omissions in Franklin's list. It was supplemented by material supplied by Lester Granger, formerly head of the National Urban League, and by material gathered by the writer while he was active in the labor movement during the 1930's.

54. H. Mulzac, *A Star to Steer By* (New York 1963), *passim*.

55. G. Hunton, *All of What I Saw—Part of Which I Was* (New York 1967), p. 83.

56. Federal Fair Employment Practices Committee (FEPC), Regional Office Files located in New York City (1945). Thanks is due to Edward Lawson, then regional director of the agency.

57. New York State Commission Against Discrimination, *The Airlines Industry*, July 1, 1945–Dec. 31, 1959.

58. Franklin, *op. cit.*, pp. 271–277.

59. Information supplied by members of Local 28 of the International Association of Sheet Metal Workers Union in 1946.

60. S. D. Spero and A. L. Harris, *The Black Workers* (New York 1931), pp. 62–63.

61. So listed in the New York *Telephone Directory* for 1944.

62. *Official Report of Proceedings Before the President's Committee on Fair Employment Practices in the Matter of: President's Committee ... v. Seafarers' International Union* (Oct. 10, 1944), held in New York City.

63. Based on letters on file with the Regional Fair Employment Practices Committee in New York City.

64. New York State *Legislative Document No. 69* (Albany, 1939), p. 47.

65. Personal interview with Mr. De Mar, Industrial Relations Secretary of the Urban League of Greater New York, April 17, 1944.

66. *Ibid.*

67. A similar situation existed in Baltimore, Md., during World War II among a group originally organized by E. Lewis, then head of the Baltimore chapter of the Urban League. Currently L. Pressridge is business manager of Local 542 of the Carpenters' Union, an all-colored local, and no district council has been formed in accord with the international union's constitution.

68. H. Northrup, *Organized Labor and the Negro* (New York 1944), p. 29; the situation remained unaltered in 1961 when Fred Andrews of Local 1888, then secretary treasurer of the local, was interviewed.

69. Carpenters' *Constitution*, April 1, 1959, p. 21.

70. G. Peterson, *American Labor Unions* (New York 1945), p. 89.

71. E. F. Frazier, "A Negro Industrial Group," *Howard Review*, June, 1924, p. 198; the late Professor Frazier maintained that the situation was the same in 1960, (the author was a colleague of his at that time).

72. *Ibid.*

73. *Ibid.*

74. Based on personal interviews with some members of Local 1, during May, 1945.

75. P. Thomas, *Discrimination Against Negroes* (National Urban League, N.Y., 1943), p. 2.

76. New York State Commission Against Discrimination, *The Airlines Industry*, July 1, 1945–Dec. 31, 1959.

77. R. A. Johnson, *Recent Trends of Membership in International Unions as They Affect Negro Workers* (National Urban League, N.Y., 1944), p. 1.

78. New York State Files on Discrimination, *Committee on Discrimination* (as recorded by Prof. Nicholas S. Falcone, then investigator for the committee), Oct. 23, 1943.

79. H. Kerns, *A Study of the Employment Opportunities for Negroes in Breweries of the United States* (New York Urban League, N.Y., 1951), pp. 15–16.

80. L. B. Granger, *Membership Policies of International Unions as They Affect Negro Workers* (National Urban League, N.Y., 1941), p. 2.

81. Based on a confidential study prepared by the ILGWU's research department entitled "The Negro and the ILGWU" (October, 1942).

82. P. H. Norgren, *et al.*, *Employing the Negro in American Industry* (New York 1959), 159.

83. J. Hope, Jr., *Equality of Opportunity* (Washington, D.C., 1956), pp. 85–89; also a personal interview with President Ralph Helstein in 1960.

84. The New York *Times* cited many instances where O. H. Knight, president of the Oil, Chemical and Atomic Workers Union, pressed charges against some of his own affiliates in the courts.

85. P. H. Norgren and S. E. Hill, *Toward Fair Employment* (New York 1964), p. 111; New York State Commission Against Discrimination. *The Airlines Industry*, July 1, 1945–Dec. 31, 1959, 1; E. P. Hohman, *History of American Merchant Seamen* (Hamden, Conn., 1956), p. 110. In 1951 the Seafarers' International Union "reached an agreement with the New York State Commission Against Discrimination to discontinue the SIU's practice of segregating white and Negro Americans by vessel in signing on stewards' department personnel." However, 10 years later (1961), the author was receiving affidavits alleging that the SIU still discriminated in job placement.

86. Information furnished by three Negro American members of Local 1814 of the International Longshoremen's Association in February, 1961.

87. Information based on a personal interview with a Negro American member of Local 2 of the Plumbers Union in January, 1961. This individual had his card and it was marked in *good standing*.

88. Interview with an "A" journeyman, a colored American, in April, 1967.

89. Interview with Mario Cinisomo, secretary-treasurer of Local 1814, ILA, AFL-CIO, 1961, further verified by three well-informed members of Local 1814.

90. *Union Electrical World*, official organ of Local 3, IBEW, Nov. 15, 1961.

91. Union survey conducted under the auspices of the Negro American Labor Council, December, 1960.

92. Information supplied by an oldtime foreman based on his personal experience on many public works projects in 1964.

93. Personal interviews held at the Negro American Labor Council's headquarters on Jan. 20 and 27, 1961, with Fred Randolph, Local 791, Le Roy Johnson, Local 1814, and Ebenezer George, Local 791.

94. State of New York: Executive Department, State Commission Against Discrimination on complaint of Fred Randolph, Complainant, against New York Shipping Association, International Longshoremen's Association Seniority Board, Local 791, ILA and Mr. Miskol, business agent, Respondent, dated: 16 of December, 1960.

95. The New York *Times*, June 8, 1963.

96. Civil Rights Bureau of Attorney General's Office of New York State, statement made by Assistant Attorney General Shirley A. Siegal at Workshop and Institute on Race Bias in Trade Unions, Industry and Government, sponsored by the Negro American Labor Council, Washington, D.C., Feb. 18, 1961.

97. Personal interview with W. O. Webb, January, 1961, at Negro American Labor Council's headquarters, 217 West 125th St., N.Y.

98. State of New York: Executive Department, State Commission Against Discrimination on the complaint of Waven O. Webb, Complainant, against John B. Kelly, Inc., and Bricklayers Local 41, AFL-CIO, Respondent, Complaint number C-6791-60.

99. Personal interview with Andrew Lawler, April, 1962.

100. Personal interview with Fred Andrews, secretary, Carpenters Local 1888, Oct. 17, 1961.

101. Roddie Brooks, Local 257, and Milton Abrams, Local 1888, interviewed on July 31, 1961 and Jan. 31, 1962, respectively. In addition to these two interviews, a spot survey was made by Negro American members in other carpenter locals, and they agreed with the statements presented in the text.

102. Taken from interview with Roddie Brooks.

103. *Ibid.*

104. Written communication from E. A. Bjork, vice-president, District Council of New York, United Brotherhood of Carpenters and Joiners of America, dated: July 19, 1961.

105. Rear Admiral R. K. James, Chief of the Bureau of Ships, Naval Shipyards Provide Essential Support to Vessels of the U.S. Navy, *Congressional Record*, Aug. 31, 1961, A6911-6914.

106. *Ibid.*, A6913. The same contention was expressed by both Mr. Andrews and Mr. Tumins of Local 1888.

107. R. B. Helfgott. W. E. Gustafson, and J. M. Hund, *Made in New York* (Cambridge, Mass., 1960), 94-95.

108. The New York *Times*, Jan. 5, 1961.

109. *Ibid.*

110. The New York *Times*, Jan. 12, 1962.

111. *Electrical Union World*, Jan. 15, 1962.

112. *Ibid.*

113. *Ibid.*

114. Remarks by Stanley H. Lowell, chairman, *New York City Commission on Intergroup Relations* upon Mayor Robert F. Wagner's announcement on the city's Contract Compliance Program.

115. Office of the Mayor of the City of New York, Executive Order No. 4, dated: Feb. 7, 1962.

116. The *Daily News*, Feb. 13, 1962.

117. The New York *Times*, Nov. 4, 1962.

118. *Ibid.*, Nov. 16, 1962; *Electrical Union World*, Dec. 1, 1962.

119. *Electrical Union World*, Dec. 1, 1962.

120. Letter from Oscar A. Durant, "Committee on Separate Charters," National Association of Letter Carriers, dated: October 13, 1962, and *Report of Committee on Separate Charters* (Denver, Colo., Sept. 2–8, 1962).

121. Personal conversations with Bertram Powers, president of ITU Local 6, and with Messers Boris and Schlesinger, chairman of the apprenticeship training committee and educational director of the local, respectively.

122. Bureau of National Affairs, *Union Labor Report*, March 8, 1963.

123. The New York *Times*, May 10, 1964.

124. AFL-CIO *News*, June 15, 1963.

125. New York City Central Labor Council, AFL-CIO, *Labor Chronicle*, June, 1963.

126. The New York *Times*, July 26, 1963.

127. H. Seidman, *Labor Czars* (New York 1938), pp. 68–93; District 65, RWSDU Local 1199, *Retail Wholesale, Department Store Workers Union* (RWSDU), Local 3, IBEW Local 342, Amalgamated Meat Cutters. All of the above mentioned demonstrated this proposition as late as 1965. There has been at least one successful

attempt to curb a large local union's power: this is the classic case of the Carpenters' Union under the tutelage of William L. Hutcheson. A good account of the power shift from local to international is given in R. A. Christie, *Empire in Wood* (Ithaca, N.Y., 1956), pp. 186–216.

128. *Preliminary Report of the Mayor's Action Panel,* July 11, 1963 *(signed by:* Samuel R. Pierce, Jr., Chairman, Brother Cornelius Justin, F.S.C., and the late [Dean] Harry C. Carman of Columbia University).

129. *Ibid.,* p. 1.

130. The writer, a former journeyman in the woodworking trades, was able to interview members of the District Council of New York, United Brotherhood of Carpenters and Joiners of America.

131. Marble, Slate, Stone Polishers, Rubbers and Sawyers, Tile and Marble Setters' Helpers and Terrazzo Workers' Helpers, International Association of, AFL-CIO Local 35, and Terrazzo and Mosaic Contractors Association of Greater New York, Agreement effective between 7/1/63 and 6/30/66; Bricklayers, New York Executive Committee, Locals 1, 9, 21, 30, 34, 37, and 41 and Building Contractors Employers Association, Inc., New York City and Long Island agreement, effective between 6/1/64 and 5/31/67; United Brotherhood of Carpenters and Joiners of America, New York City and vicinity District Council and the Cement League and Hollow Metal Door and Buck Association, Agreement effective between 7/1/63 and 6/30/66, etc.

132. City of New York, Office of the Mayor, July 18, 1963, p. 3.

133. *Ibid.,* p. 4.

134. The New York *Times,* June 22, 1963.

135. The New York *Times,* May 10, 1964.

136. *A Report of the New York Advisory Committee to the U.S. Commission on Civil Rights,* dated August, 1963.

137. Building Trades Employers Association, *News and Opinion,* December, 1963.

138. *Ibid.,* p. 5.

139. *Draft Report of the City Commission on Human Rights of Hearings on Employment Practices in the Building Trades, 1963.* The report issued for public consumption, the City Commission on Human Rights, *Bias in the Building Industry: An Interim Report to the Mayor, December 13, 1963,* was less inclusive in data contained in the draft, specifically in terms of naming specific unions.

140. *Draft Report of the City Commission . . . ,* C-1, C-2, C-3, C-4, C-5.

141. Information furnished by Sebastian S. Pugliese, formerly business agent for Local 6A.

142. Information obtained from union bricklayers in the greater New York vicinity.

143. Material for this table based on a composite of field work, oral presentation before the City Commission on Human Rights, and interviews with friends in official positions in the labor movement.

144. Based on personal knowledge of the operations of both locals.

145. *1199 Drug News* (official union publication), July-August, 1963; personal interview with Moe Foner, executive secretary of the local; The New York *Post,* June 27, 1963.

146. *Hotel,* Oct. 21, 1963.

147. Based on personal interviews with members of Locals 1 and 2 of the Dining Room Waiters Union. There was a second Negro American employed in Johnson's Steak House in Greenwich Village, but he was "forced out" by white waiters. The Negro American employed at Gallagher's obtained his post when the management changed hands and the restaurant's manager, a personal friend of the colored American "forced" his employment on a full-time basis with the "house."

148. The New York *Times,* July 26, and Aug. 6, 1963.

149. Based on confidential information furnished to the author by friendly local union officials.

150. Donald F. Rodgers, chairman, *Report:* Building Industry of New York City's Referral Committee, Dec. 18, 1963, p. 1.

151. Rodgers, *op. cit.*

152. *Draft Report of the City Commission for Human Rights of Hearing on Employment Practices in the Building Construction Trades* (1963), C-7 (italics added).

153. *Ibid.*

154. Earl B. Fullilove, chairman of the Board of Governors of the Building Trades Employers Association; hearing *Proceedings,* Aug. 14, 1963, p. 52.

155. Thomas A. McGuire, president, International Union of Operating Engineers, Union Locals 15, A, B, C, and D, Aug. 14, 1963, Transcript, p. 137.

156. *Draft Report of City . . . ,* C-8.

157. Ralph Dalton, International Union of Operating Engineers, Local 14, *Hearing Transcript,* Aug. 14, 1963, p. 127.

158. *Draft Report of City . . . ,* C-8, 9.

159. *Ibid.,* C-9.

160. Thomas Clarkson's testimony, *Hearing Transcript,* Aug. 14, 1963, p. 184.

161. City Commission on Human Rights *Transcript,* Sept. 9, 1963, 485–486.

162. Mr. Salzarallo, secretary-treasurer, Plumbers Local 2, *Hearing Transcript,* Aug. 20, 1963, p. 400.

163. Bureau of National Affairs, *Newsletter,* Aug. 30, 1963, p. 3.

164. The New York *Times,* Oct. 7, 1963.

165. D. F. Rodgers, . . . *Building Industry of N.Y.C. Referral Committee,* p. 1 (italics added).

166. *Hotel,* Jan. 20, 1964, p. 3.

167. *Ibid.*

168. *Ibid.,* April 20, 1964, p. 3.

169. Interview with Cecil Smith, program director of the project, 1965.

170. Interview with Ted Brown, official of CCHR, 1964.

171. The New York *Times,* Aug. 13, 1964.

172. *Ibid.,* June 6, 1965.

173. *Ibid.,* Nov. 25, 1964.

174. State of New York: Executive Department, State Commission for Human Rights, Opinion: Complaint Case No. C-9287-63; Notice of Order, Case No. C-9287.

175. Notice of Order, Case No. C-9287, 3–4.

176. *Ibid.,* 10–13.

177. New York *Times,* Aug. 24, 1964.

178. Information furnished by persons connected with the Bureau of Apprenticeship Training, U.S. Department of Labor.

179. Personal interviews with Nicholas Abandollo, vice president, and Moe Fliess, secretary-treasurer, of Local 432, Amalgamated Meat Cutters and Butchers Union, AFL-CIO, 1964.

180. The New York *Times,* Sept. 3, 1964.

181. The materials used in this section were based on:

(1) International Association of Heat and Frost Insulators and Asbestos Workers, AFL-CIO, Local 12, and the Asbestos Contractors Association of New York (Five Boroughs, plus Nassau and Suffolk counties). Agreement effective 7/1/63; expires, 6/30/66.

(2) International Brotherhood of Boilermakers, Iron Ship Builders, Blacksmiths, Forgers and Helpers, AFL-CIO, Lodge 5 and Boiler and Plate Work Erecting Contractors' Association. Agreement effective 7/1/63; expires 6/30/66.

(3) Bricklayers, New York Executive Committee, Locals 1, 9, 21, 30, 34, 37 and 41, and Building Contractors Employers Association, Inc. New York City and Long Island. Agreement effective 6/1/64; expires 5/31/67.

(4) United Brotherhood of Carpenters and Joiners of America, AFL-CIO, New York City and vicinity District Council and the Cement League and Hollow Metal Door and Buck Association. Agreement effective 7/1/63; expires 6/30/66.

(5) International Brotherhood of Electrical Workers, AFL-CIO, Local 3, and New York Electrical Contractors' Association, Inc.; Master Electrical Contractors' Association, Inc.; and Association of Electrical Contractors, Inc., New York City. Agreement effective 6/1/64; expires 5/31/66.

(6) Engineers, Operating, Local 14, and Building Contractors' and Mason Builders Association, the Cement League, Stone Setting Contractors' Association, Allied Building Metal Industries, Rigging Contractors' Association, Contracting Plasterers' Association. Agreement effective 7/1/63; expires 6/30/66. (Agreement applies to five boroughs of N.Y.C.); Engineers, Operating, Local 15-D, and the Cement League. Agreement effective 10/11/61; expires 6/30/66. (Agreement applies to five boroughs of N.Y.C.).

(7) Iron Workers, International Association of Bridge, Structural and Ornamental, AFL-CIO, Local 170 and Rigging Contractors Association of the City of New York. Agreement effective 7/1/63; expires 6/30/66. Iron Workers, Local 580, and the Allied Building Metal Industries. Agreement effective 7/1/63, expires 6/30/66.

(8) International Hod Carriers, Building and Common Laborers' Union of America, AFL-CIO, Locals 6-A, 18-A, and 20, the Cement League of Greater New York. Agreement effective 7/1/63, expires 6/30/66; Laborers, Mason Tenders' District Council of New York and Vicinity and Building Contractors and Mason Builders Association of New York City. Agreement effective 7/1/63, expires 6/30/66; Laborers, Local 66, and the Associated Brick Mason Contractors of Greater New York. Agreement effective 7/1/63; expires 6/30/66.

(9) Lathers International Union, the Wood, Wire and Metal, AFL-CIO, Local 46, and the Cement League (Greater New York). Agreement effective 7/1/63, expires 6/30/66; Lathers, Local 308, Master Contract (Bronx, Manhattan, and Staten Island). Agreement effective 1/1/65; expires 6/30/66.

(10) International Longshoremen's Association, AFL-CIO, Local 1474-1, Pipe Master Contract of Port of Greater N.Y. (Pipe covering companies). Agreement effective 10/25/64; expires 10/25/67.

(11) Marble, Slate, Stone Polishers, Rubbers and Sawyers, Tile and Marble Setters' Helpers and Terrazzo Workers' Helpers, International Association of, AFL-CIO, Local 35, and Terrazzo and Mosaic Contractors Association of Greater New York. Agreement effective 7/1/63; expires 6/30/66.

(12) Brotherhood of Painters, Decorators and Paperhangers of America, District Council 9 of New York City, and Association of Master Painters and Decorators of the City of New York. Agreement effective 8/1/65; expires 7/1/68.

(13) Operative Plasterers' and Cement Masons' International Association, Local 60 AFL-CIO, and Contracting Plasterers' Association of Greater New York. Agreement effective 6/28/62, expires 6/30/65; Plasterers, Local 780 and the Cement League (New York, Bronx, and Richmond counties). Agreement effective 7/1/64; expires 6/30/66.

(14) United Association of Journeymen and Apprentices of the Plumbing and Pipe Fitting Industry of the U.S. and Canada, AFL-CIO, Local 2, and Association of Contracting Plumbers of the City of N.Y., Inc. and Metropolitan Master Plumbers, Inc. Agreement effective 7/14/63, expires 6/29/66; Plumbers, Local 638, and Mechanical Contractors Association of N.Y. Agreement effective 7/1/63; expires 6/30/66.

(15) United Slate, Tile and Composition Roofers, Damp and Waterproof Workers' Association, AFL-CIO, Local 25, and Long Island and Brooklyn Roofing and Sheet Metal Contractors Association, Inc. Agreement effective 7/1/65, expires 6/30/68; Roofers, Local 8, and Composition

Roofers, Waterproofers and Damp-proofers Association of New York (5 boroughs). Agreement effective 7/1/63; expires 6/30/66.

(16) Sheet Metal Workers, International Association of Greater New York, AFL-CIO, Local 28, and Sheet Metal Contractors Association of New York City, Inc., and Mechanical Contractors Association of N.Y., Inc. Agreement effective 7/1/63; expires 6/30/66.

(17) Journeymen Stone Cutters Association of North America, AFL-CIO, N.Y. Local, Metropolitan District and Greater New York Cut Stone Contractors Association. Agreement effective 7/1/63; expires 6/30/67.

(18) International Brotherhood of Teamsters, Chauffeurs, Warehousemen and Helpers of America, Local 282, Master Contract (Excavating), New York City. Agreement effective 7/1/63, expires 6/30/66.

182. Senate Report No. 1827, 81st Cong. 2d. Sess., p. 13.

183. An expression of authorities favoring the closed shop: see Millis and Brown, *From the Wagner Act to Taft-Hartley* (Chicago 1950), pp. 439–440; J. P. Goldberg, *The Maritime Story* (Cambridge, Mass., 1958), pp. 277–282; Senate Report No. 1827, 81st Cong., 2d Sess. pp. 4–8.

184. *The Workingman's Advocate*, Aug. 31, 1867.

CHAPTER 7

1. W. Chambers, *American Slavery and Color* (London 1857), p. 37; also, *Things as They Are in America* (London 1854), p. 354.

2. L. Litwack, *North of Slavery: The Negro in the Free States, 1790–1860* (Chicago 1961), p. 31.

3. R. Logan, "The Negro in the Quasi-War, 1798–1800," *Negro History Bulletin* (1951), pp. 128–131; Litwack, *op. cit.*, p. 32.

4. C. Wesley, "Negro Suffrage in the Period of the Constitution's Making, 1787–1865," *Journal of Negro History*, April, 1947, pp. 148–149.

5. T. R. R. Cobb, *An Inquiry Into the Law of Negro Slavery in the United States of America* (Philadelphia 1858), pp. 287–290.

6. The New York *Times*, June 19, 1960.

7. J. S. Murphy, *Interesting Documents* (containing the Constitution of New York State with its amendments), New York, 1819.

8. C. Z. Lincoln, *The Constitutional History of the State of New York* (Rochester, N.Y., 1906) I, 170–171.

9. *Ibid.*, p. 172; M. W. Ovington, *Half a Man* (New York 1911), p. 11.

10. E. Olbrich, *The Development of Sentiment on Negro Suffrage to 1860* (Madison, Wis., 1912), pp. 16–17, 29.

11. C. Z. Lincoln, ed., *Messages from Governors* (Albany, N.Y., 1909), II, 237–239.

12. D. R. Fox, "The Negro in Old New York," *Political Science Quarterly*, June, 1917, p. 256.

13. Litwack, *op. cit.*, p. 14.

14. D. S. Alexander, *A Political History of the State of New York* (New York 1906), I, 11.

15. *Ibid.*

16. The New York *Spectator*, April 29, 1809.

17. *Ibid.*; J. D. Hammond, *Political History of the State of New York* (Albany, N.Y., 1811), pp. 143, 164, 351, 360.

18. *Journal of the Senate of the State of New York* (Albany, 1811), p. 143.

19. *Ibid.*, p. 360.

20. Olbrich, *op. cit.*, pp. 29–30.

21. *Reports and Proceedings of the Convention of 1821*, p. 212.

22. *Laws of New York State*, 37th Session, pp. 94, 95.

23. *Report of the Proceedings and Debates of the Convention of 1821*, pp. 197–199.

24. *Negro Population, 1790–1915*, pp. 45, 51, 55.

25. *Census of the State of New York for 1855*, pp. viii, xi.

26. *Negro Population, op. cit.*

27. *Census of the State of New York for 1855, loc. cit.*

28. *Journal of the Assembly of the State of New York* (Albany 1815), p. 475.

29. The New York *Spectator*, April 19, 1815.

30. A *Report of the Debates and Proceedings of the Convention of the State of New York* (Albany 1821), p. 185.

31. Fox, *op. cit.*, p. 256.

32. A *Report of the Debates . . .* , p. 185.

33. *Journal of the New York State Assembly* (Albany 1826), reproduced in the *Colored American*, March 25, 1837.

34. C. W. Johnson, *Black Manhattan* (New York 1930), p. 27; C. H. Wesley, "The Negroes in the Emancipation Movement," *Journal of Negro History*, January, 1939, p. 91.

35. J. Ashmun, *History of the American Colony in Liberia*, December, 1821–1823, (Washington City 1826), pp. 4–7.

36. *Resolutions of the People of Color at a Meeting Held on the 25th of January, 1831*, With an Address to the Citizens of New York in Answer to Those of the New York Colonization Society (New York 1831), pp. 1–8.

37. T. O. House, "Anti-Slavery Activities of Negroes in New York, 1830–1860," (Master's thesis, Howard University, 1936), p. 4.

38. *Address and Constitution of the Phoenix Society of New York* (New York 1833), p. 37.

39. *Minutes of the Fourth Annual Convention of the Free People of Color* (New York 1834) p. 13.

40. *American Anti-Slavery Almanac* (New York 1843), *Chronology*, May.

41. The *Colored American*, March 11, 1837.

42. *Journal of the Assembly of New York State* (Albany 1837), pp. 414–417.

43. The *Emancipator*, Oct. 5, 1837.

44. The *Colored American*, Oct. 20, 1838.

45. *Ibid.*, Nov. 17, 1838.

46. *Ibid.*, Dec. 15, 1838.

47. *Ibid.*

48. The *Colored American*, Nov. 3, 1838.

49. *Ibid.*, Nov. 17, 1838.

50. W. J. Simons, *Men of Mark, Eminent, Progressive and Rising* (Cleveland 1887), p. 1110.

51. S. R. Ward, *Autobiography of a Fugitive Negro* (London 1855), p. 25.

52. H. A. Garner, *A Memorial Discourse, February 12, 1865* (Philadelphia 1865), p. 33.

53. The *Emancipator*, May 6, 1841.

54. J. W. Edmonds, *The Statutes at Large of the State of New York* (Albany 1869), I, 127–128.

55. G. E. Baker, ed., *The Works of William H. Seward* (New York 1865), III, 237–238.

56. *Ibid.*

57. Garner, *op. cit.*, p. 44.

58. *Minutes of the National Convention of Colored Citizens* (Buffalo, Aug. 15–19, 1843), p. 6.

59. *Ibid.*, p. 7.

60. Garner, *op. cit.*, p. 43.

61. *The New York State Convention, 1846* (Albany 1846), p. 790.

62. The *Liberator*, May 23, 1845.

63. *Ibid.*

64. The *Liberator*, July 4, 1845.

65. *Report and the Debates and Proceedings in the New York State Convention for Revision of the Constitution, 1846* (Albany, 1846), p. 790.

66. *Ibid.*, p. 775.

67. *Ibid.*, p. 776.

68. *Ibid.*, p. 777.

69. *Ibid.*, p. 788.

70. *Ibid.,* p. 790.

71. *Ibid.,* p. 828.

72. *Ibid.,* p. 836.

73. *Tribune Almanac for 1870,* p. 53.

74. Garnett, *op. cit.,* p. 53.

75. Ward, *op. cit.,* p. 77.

76. *Proceedings of the National Convention of Colored People Held at Troy, N.Y.* October 6–9, 1847 (Troy 1847), p. 17.

77. *Ibid.*

78. The New York *Herald,* Sept. 6, 1847, p. 17.

79. *Ibid.*

80. The New York *Herald,* Oct. 3, 1851.

81. *Ibid.*

82. *Ibid.*

83. *Ibid.*

84. *Proceedings of the Colored National Convention,* July 6–8, 1853, (Rochester, N.Y., 1853), p. 9.

85. *Journal of the Senate, 1857* (Albany 1857), p. 67.

86. *Ibid.,* p. 354.

87. *Documents of the Assembly of the State of New York, 1857* (Albany, N.Y., 1857), pp. 11–12.

88. *An Appeal for Freedom,* made in the Assembly of the State of New York, March 7, 1859, by the Honorable Charles S. Spencer, p. 9.

89. *Journal of the Assembly of New York State, 1859* (Albany, N.Y., 1859), pp. 730–732.

90. *Ibid.,* pp. 64, 203, 532, 606, and 730.

91. W. C. Nell, *Property Qualifications or No Property Qualifications* (New York 1860), p. 3.

92. *Ibid.*

93. *Journal of the Assembly of the State of New York, 1860* (Albany, N.Y., 1860), p. 1129.

94. *Ibid.*

95. C. Z. Lincoln, *Constitutional History of New York* (Rochester, N.Y., 1906), III, 232–233.

96. *Journal of the Assembly, 1864* (Albany, N.Y., 1864), p. 32.

CHAPTER 8

1. New York *Spectator,* April 29, 1809.

2. S. W. McCall, *Thaddeus Stevens* (New York 1899), preface.

3. H. Minor, *The Story of the Democratic Party* (New York 1928), p. 295.

4. D. S. Alexander, *Political History of the State of New York* (New York 1909), III, 136.

5. *Elkins* v. *Wilkins,* 112 U.S. 94, 102 (1884).

6. *Ibid.*

7. Minor, *op. cit.,* p. 294.

8. *Ibid.,* pp. 294–295.

9. *Tribune Almanac and Political Register for 1866* (New York 1858–1889), p. 44.

10. McCall, *op. cit.,* p. 246.

11. *Ibid.,* pp. 247–249.

12. Mississippi, *Act of November 24, 1865,* as cited by McCall.

13. McPherson, *The Political History of the U.S. of America during the Reconstruction* (2nd ed.; Washington, D.C., 1875), p. 21.

14. The New York *Times,* June 18, 1968. One hundred and two years after its enactment, the U.S. Supreme Court cited the 1866 Civil Rights Act as being constitutional. This act goes beyond the 1968 Civil Rights Act, since it bans bias in "purchase, lease, sell, hold and convey [of] real and personal property."

15. *Congressional Globe,* 39 Cong., 1 sess., appendix, chap. XXXI, pp. 315, 316.

16. *American Cyclopedia and Register of Important Events* (New York 1865), pp. 614–615.

17. The New York *Tribune,* July 8, 1865.

18. *House Miscellaneous Documents,* No. 109, 39 Cong. 1 sess.; James G. Blaine, *Twenty Years of*

Congress (Norwich, Conn., 1884–1886).

19. *McPherson* v. *Blacker*, 146 U.S. 1 (1892).

20. *Saunders* v. *Wilkins*, 152 F (2d) 235 (1945).

21. *Ibid.*, pp. 235, 237–238, citing Willoughby, *Constitution*, 2d ed., pp. 626–627.

22. *14th Amendment, Sec. 1* (italics added).

23. *Slaughter-House Cases*, 16 Wall, pp. 36, 74 (1873).

24. *Scott* v. *Sandford*, 19 How. 393 (1857).

25. *Ibid.*, pp. 404–406, 417–420.

26. *McPherson* v. *Blacker, op. cit.*, p. 1.

27. *Horace Greeley to James R. Lawrence*, Dec. 16, 1866, (Greeley Papers, New York Public Library).

28. *Anti-Slavery Standard*, Jan. 7, 1865.

29. The New York *Independent*, Nov. 2, 16, 1865.

30. The New York *Tribune*, Dec. 14, 1865.

31. L. Fishel, Jr., "The Negro in Northern Politics, 1870–1900," *The Mississippi Valley Historical Review*, XLII, No. 1, June, 1955, 468.

32. The New York *Herald*, May 18, 1865.

33. The New York *Times*, June 7, 1865; The New York *Herald*, June 12, 1865.

34. *Annual Meeting of the Massachusetts Anti-Slavery Society*, "What the Black Man Wants" (Boston, April 17, 1865), p. 37.

35. *Ibid.*, p. 29.

36. The New York *Times*, June 2, 1865; April 24, 1865. Apparently, various New York Afro-American societies, including black chapters of the Freemasons, had sought in vain for permission from the Committee of Common Council to march in the Lincoln funeral procession.

37. The New York *Times*, June 2, 1865.

38. *Ibid.*, June 25, 1865.

39. *American Annual Cyclopaedia and Register of Important Events* (New York 1865), p. 615.

40. E. A. McPherson, *Handbook of Politics for 1868* (Phillips and Solomon, N.Y., 1868), p. 52.

41. *Ibid.*

42. *Ibid.*, p. 53.

43. McCall, *op. cit.*, pp. 257–264. The rupture between the majority of the Republicans and the President with regard to Reconstruction was partially revealed when Stevens' resolution to form a joint committee on Reconstruction to inquire into the condition of the Southern states was carried by 133 to 36.

44. McPherson, *op. cit.*, p. 53.

45. *Ibid.*, pp. 55–56.

46. *Ibid.*

47. *American Cyclopaedia and Register of Important Events* (New York 1866), p. 544.

48. The New York *Times*, June 6, 1866.

49. The New York *Times*, Sept. 8, 1866.

50. W. A. Dunning, "The Second Birth of the Republican Party," *American Historical Review*, XVI, 56.

51. A. C. Flick, ed., *History of the State of New York* (New York 1935) Vol. VII, 111.

52. Dunning, *op. cit.*, p. 57.

53. *Ibid.*, p. 61.

54. The New York *Times*, Oct. 23, 1866.

55. *Ibid.*, Nov. 20, 1866.

56. *Ibid.*

57. The New York *Times*, Nov. 23, 1866.

58. *Ibid.*, Nov. 22, 1866.

59. *Laws of the State of New York*, 1866, Ch. 812, Sec. 7.

60. The New York *Times*, Nov. 23, 1866.

61. *Ibid.*

62. *Ibid.*

63. *Ibid.*

64. The New York *Times,* Nov. 28, 1866.

65. Flick, *op. cit.,* p. 105.

66. W. H. Johnson, *Autobiography* (Albany, N.Y., 1900), p. 70.

67. *Documents of the Convention of the State of New York, 1867–1868* (Albany, N.Y., 1868), I, 2, 282.

68. *Proceedings and Debates of the Constitutional Convention of the State of New York* (Albany, N.Y., 1868), I, 200–263, V, 3560–3586.

69. *Ibid.,* I, 289.

70. The New York *Independent,* Aug. 1, 1867; D. C. Alexander, *Political History of the State of New York* (New York 1909), Vol. III, 185–186.

71. *Documents of the Convention of the State of New York, 1867–1868,* pp. 1181–1182.

72. *Ibid.*

73. *American Annual Cyclopaedia* (New York 1870), pp. 486–390.

74. The New York *Times,* March 18, April 15, Sept. 23, Dec. 8, 1869.

75. *Ibid.,* April 22, 1870.

76. E. A. McPherson, *The Political History of the U.S. of America during the Reconstruction* (2d ed., Washington, D.C., 1875), pp. 551–562.

77. "The Constitutional Commission, 1872," *Political Science Quarterly,* IV, June, 1889, 240–241, 258.

78. Alexander, *op. cit.,* p. 320.

79. *U.S.* v. *Reese.* 92 U.S. 214, 217–218 (1876); *U.S.* v. *Cruikshank.* 92 U.S. 542, 556 (1876).

80. *Laws of New York* (1870), p. 922.

81. F. A. Bailey, ed. *The Life and Times of Frederick Douglass* (New York 1941), appendix I, pp. 649–650.

82. E. L. Tatum, *The Changed Political Thought of the Negro, 1915–1940* (New York 1951), p. 76.

83. W. H. Johnson, *op. cit.,* pp. 94–95.

84. *Ibid.,* p. 214.

85. *Ibid.,* p. 68.

86. Unless otherwise stated, this section is based on articles and editorials in the New York *Times* for the period July 8, 1871 through February, 1872.

87. *Harper's Weekly,* July 22, 1871.

88. *Laws of New York* (1873), chap. 335.

89. The New York *Tribune,* Oct. 23, 1873.

90. C. McKay, *Harlem: Negro Metropolis* (New York 1940), pp. 124–131.

91. *American Annual Cyclopaedia* . . . (Albany, N.Y., 1872), pp. 585–586.

92. W. J. Simmons, *Men of Mark, Eminent, Progressive and Rising* (Cleveland 1887), p. 73.

93. *Ibid.,* p. 79.

94. The New York *Times,* Sept. 9, 1875.

95. The *New National Era,* Dec. 18, 1873; *Bee,* March 14, 1885.

96. Simmons, *op. cit.*

97. W. W. Brown, *The Rising Son: or the antecedents and advancement of the Colored Race* (Boston 1874), p. 253.

98. *Laws of New York* (1874), p. 925.

99. To gerrymander is to alter the political map of a state or county so that the voting districts are unfairly or abnormally arranged, for the purpose of advancing the interests of a particular party or candidate. To wit: "Mr. McKinley . . . was warmly supported by the popular vote, gaining considerably in his district, and he was defeated only by a gerrymander." C. W. Curtis, *Harper's Weekly,* March 28, 1891.

100. *Laws of New York, loc. cit.*

101. Bailey, *op. cit.,* pp. 477–491.

102. The New York *Times,* Sept. 17, 1876.

103. *Ibid.,* Nov. 3, 1876.

104. *American Annual Cyclopaedia* . . . , 1878, p. 623; *Tribune Almanac,* 1883, p. 42.

105. F. Douglass, "The Color Line," *North American Review*, June, 1881, p. 573.

106. New York *Freeman*, Nov. 28, 1885 (italics added).

107. The New York *Tribune*, Dec. 14, 1886.

108. *Tribune Almanac*, Dec. 14, 1886.

109. W. H. Johnson, *Autobiography* . . . , *op. cit.*, pp. 19, 35, 157.

110. The New York *Globe*, May 12, 1883.

111. T. T. Fortune, *The Negro in Politics* (New York 1886), pp. 58–59.

112. The New York *Age*, Aug. 25, 1888.

113. The New York *Tribune*, Dec. 14, 1886.

114. H. Minor, *The Story of the Democratic Party* (New York 1928), p. 361.

115. *The New York State Cleveland League, Colored Citizens State Democratic and Independent Organization* (New York, May 26, 1892), p. 11.

116. *The Afro-American in Politics*, an address by T. McCants Stewart, Esq., Oct. 27, 1891, p. 6.

117. *Ibid.*, p. 9.

118. *The Address of C. H. Lansing, Jr., President of the Colored Citizens Chapin Club* (New York 1889), p. 5.

119. The New York *Tribune*, Oct. 11, 1889.

120. *Ibid.*, Dec. 19, 1889.

121. *Ibid.*, Dec. 10, 1889.

122. *Ibid.*, Oct. 28, 1894.

123. *Ibid.*, July 4, 1895; Oct. 20, 1898.

124. The New York *Times*, July 10, Aug. 17, 1895.

125. E. E. Morison, ed., *The Letters of Theodore Roosevelt* (Cambridge, Mass., 1951–1954), I, 357.

126. The New York *Post*, Aug. 21, 1900.

127. G. Osofsky, *Harlem: The Making of a Ghetto* (New York 1966), p. 159.

CHAPTER 9

1. C. Bridenbaugh, *The Colonial Craftsman* (Chicago 1960), pp. 4–7.

2. A. Caldecott, *English Colonization and Empire*, p. 245.

3. R. F. Weld, *Brooklyn is America* (New York 1950), p. 154.

4. C. Bridenbaugh, *Cities in the Wilderness* . . . (New York 1955), p. 7.

5. *Laws of New Netherland*, p. 36; Stokes, *Iconography*, I, 24.

6. C. N. Glaab and A. T. Brown, *A History of Urban America* (New York 1967), pp. 1–2.

7. P. d'A. Jones, *The Consumer Society* (New York 1965), pp. 16–23.

8. Bridenbaugh, *Cities in the Wilderness*, *op. cit.*, p. 6.

9. G. Myers, *History of Great American Fortunes* (New York), *passim*.

10. C. Bridenbaugh, *The Colonial Craftsman*, *op. cit.*, p. 160.

11. S. M. Lipset and R. Bendix, *Social Mobility in Industrial Society*, (Berkeley, Calif., 1960), Introd., pp. 2–3.

12. C. Bridenbaugh, *The Colonial Craftsman*, p. 160.

13. F. L. Olmstead, *Slaves States* (New York 1959), p. 274.

14. C. S. Johnson, *Shadow of the Plantation* (Chicago 1934), p. 1; E. F. Frazier, *The Negro in the United States* (New York 1949), p. 274.

15. S. M. Elkins, *Slavery* (Chicago 1959), p. 54.

16. L. Litwack, *North of Slavery: The Negro in the Free States, 1790–1860* (Chicago 1961), pp. 22–23.

17. Committee of Merchants for the Relief of the Colored People Suffering from the Late Riots in the City of New York, *Report of the Merchants for the Relief of Colored People Suffering from the Late Riots in the City of New York*, p. 14.

18. J. T. Headley, *The Great Riots of New York, 1712–1873* (New York 1873), p. 169.

19. J. McPherson, *Struggle for Equality* (Princeton, N.J., 1964), p. 232.

20. S. L. Spero and A. L. Harris, *The Black Worker* (New York 1931), p. 56.

21. Although the American Federation of Labor's constitution makes no specific mention of the Afro-American worker, the parent body did require a pledge from all of its potential affiliates, from 1886 to 1896, that they would not discriminate on account of color, creed, or other condition. For example, the International Association of Machinists was refused a charter in 1887 because its constitution contained a Caucasian clause. Report of the Industrial Commission, *The Relations and Conditions of Capital and Labor* (Washington, D.C., 1900–1911), XVII, 36. The IAM was admitted to the AFL when it substituted a ritual clause for its Caucasian clause. After 1896 such craft unions as the Boilermakers and Iron Shipbuilders were granted AFL charters even though their constitutions banned Afro-Americans (P. Thomas, *Discrimination Against Negroes*, National Urban League, N.Y., 1943, p. 4).

22. G. E. McNeill, *The Labor Movement—The Problem Today* (Hazen, N.Y., 1887), pp. 124–171.

23. *The Electrical World* (April, 1903), p. 102.

24. The New York *Times*, Oct. 18, 19, 1936.

25. *FEPC Files*, dated Feb. 11, 1943; also *Official Report of Procedures Before the President's Committee on Fair Employment Practices in the Matter of: President's Committee on Fair Employment Practices v. Seafarers' International Union of North America* (New York, October 10, 1944).

26. *FEPC Files*, April 23, 1945.

27. Horace Sheffield, International Representative for the UAW, January, 1961; UAW General Motors Department *Newsletter*, July 12, 1961.

28. Community Council of Greater New York, *Poverty in New York City*, (New York, November, 1964), p. 18.

29. *Ibid.*, p. 19.

30. The New York *Times*, Sept. 19, 1965.

31. C. Shaw, *et al.*, *Delinquency Areas* (Chicago 1929), p. 214.

32. *Progress Report of Findings of New York Citizens' Council of the National Council on Crime and Delinquency* (Sept. 21, 1962), p. 2.

33. Community Council of Greater New York, *op. cit.*, p. 12.

34. *Ibid.*, p. 11.

35. *Ibid.*, p. 10.

36. S. and E. Glueck, *Unraveling Juvenile Delinquency* (Cambridge, Mass., 1955), and *Family Environment and Delinquency* (Boston 1962), *passim*.

37. R. A. Cloward and E. Ohlin, *Delinquency and Opportunity: A Theory of Delinquent Gangs* (Chicago 1960), *passim*.

38. Shaw, *op. cit.*, p. 203.

39. The New York *Times*, July 27, 1968.

40. Justice J. W. Polier, *Everyone's Children, Nobody's Child* (New York 1941), pp. 238–239; E. Peterson, "Working Women," *Daedalus*, Spring, 1964, pp. 668–687; "Report of the President's Commission on the Status of Women," *American Women* (Washington, D.C., 1963), pp. 4, 5, 22, 27.

41. *Ibid.*

42. The Community Council of Greater New York, *op. cit.*, p. 13.

43. H. Gerth and C. Wright Mills, *Max Weber: Essays in Sociology* (New York 1946), p. 181.

44. Fisk University, A *Monthly Summary of Events and Trends in Race Relations*, May, 1947, p. 10.

45. S. Tannenbaum, *Why Men Hate* (New York 1947), p. 232.

46. Joint Council No. 16, International Brotherhood of Teamsters, Chauffeurs, Warehousemen and Helpers, *News Release*, Aug. 26, 1963; Dr. H. P. Miller, Special Assistant, Office of the Director, Bureau of the Census,

before Subcommittee on Employment and Manpower; Census of Population, II, pt. B, *Occupation by Earnings in Education;* The Community Council of Greater New York, *op. cit.*, pp. 30–31.

47. The New York *Times,* Sept. 19, 1965.

48. *Ibid.*, May 26, 1965.

49. Community Council of Greater New York, *op. cit.*, vii, and pp. 30–32.

50. The New York *Times,* Sept. 19, 1965.

51. U.S. Department of Labor, *Monthly Labor Review,* 60 (1945), 5.

52. *Business Week,* "The Negro Drive for Jobs," Aug. 17, 1963, p. 74.

53. *Ibid.*, p. 52.

54. U.S. Department of Labor, *Family Income and Expenditures in New York City, 1935–1936,* I, 19.

55. U.S. Department of Labor, *The Economic Situation of Negroes* (October, 1960), p. 15.

56. New York State Temporary Commission . . . (1939), *op. cit.*, p. 15.

57. The New York *Times,* Aug. 4, 1963.

58. U.S. Department of Labor, Bureau of Labor Statistics, *Income, Education and Unemployment in Neighborhoods, New York City, Brooklyn, Queens, Bronx, and Richmond,* January, 1963, pp. 21–2, 3, 5, 21, 37, 53, 69.

59. The Community Council of Greater New York, *op. cit.*, p. 29.

60. The New York *Times,* July 31, 1963 and Nov. 11, 1963; H. P. Miller, *op. cit.*; The Community Council of Greater New York, *op. cit.*, pp. 30–32.

61. B. M. Fleisher, "The Effect of Income on Delinquency," *American Economic Review,* March, 1966, pp. 133–137.

62. P. H. Douglas and A. Director, *The Problem of Unemployment* (New York 1937), pp. 26–27.

63. J. L. Toner, *The Closed Shop* (Washington, D.C., 1944), p. 165.

64. *Conference between Judge Sulzberger and Mr. De Mar,* Director of Industrial Relations for the Urban League of Greater New York, appeared as an interoffice communication to Edward Lewis, head of the Urban League, dated May 8, 1945.

65. C. Golden and S. Ruttenberg, *The Dynamics of Industrial Democracy* (New York 1942), pp. 120–150.

66. U.S. Bureau of Census, *Characteristics of the Population,* II, Table 58, (1950); *Ibid.*, Table 106 (1960).

67. The Community Council of Greater New York, *op. cit.*, p. 27.

68. B. M. Fleisher, "The Effect of Income on Delinquency," University of Chicago, Center for Social Organization Studies, 1965, *Working Paper No. 40,* pp. 28–29.

69. B. M. Fleisher, "The Effect of Unemployment on Juvenile Delinquency," *Journal of Political Economy,* December, 1963, pp. 553–544, 548.

70. L. D. Singell, "An Examination of the Empirical Relationship Between Unemployment and Juvenile Delinquency," *American Journal of Economics and Sociology,* October 1967, pp. 376–386.

71. D. Glazer and K. Rice, "Crime, Age and Employment," *American Sociological,* October, 1959, pp. 679–686.

72. The New York Citizens Council of the National Council on Crime and Delinquency, *Progress Report of Findings of the New York Citizens Council* (September, 1962), p. 2.

73. Office of Manpower, Automation and Training, U.S. Department of Labor, *Training Needs in Correctional Institutions* (Washington, D.C., 1965), p. 4.

74. Polier, *op. cit.*, "Report of the President's Commission on the Status of Women," *American Women, op. cit.*

75. Shaw, *op. cit.*, p. 203.

76. C. N. Glaab and A. T. Brown, *History of Urban America* (New York 1967), pp. 94–95.

77. *Ibid.*, p. 95.

78. *Ibid.*, p. 96.

79. *Ibid.*, pp. 246–247.

CHAPTER 10

1. C. W. Andrews, *The History of the African Free School.*

2. The *Colored American*, July 28, 1838; Litwack, *op. cit.*, p. 142.

3. H. Aptheker, *A Documentary History of the Negro People of the United States* (New York 1962), p. 144.

4. The New York *Tribune*, March 20, 1851.

5. *Ibid.*, Feb. 27, 1857.

6. *Proceedings of the Colored National Convention Held in Rochester, N.Y., July 6–8, 1853.*

7. The New York *Tribune*, March 20, 1851.

8. The New York *World*, March 16, 1867.

9. The New York *Age*, Feb. 9, Sept. 16, 1889.

10. T. Boese, *Public Education in the City of New York: Its History, Conditions and Statistics, An Official Report to the Board of Education* (New York 1869), p. 131.

11. M. Delaney, *Conditions, Elevation, Emigration and Destiny of the Colored People* (Philadelphia 1852), pp. 92–109.

12. Aptheker, *op. cit.*, pp. 420–422.

13. G. Osofsky, *Harlem: The Making of a Ghetto*, p. 34.

14. *Ibid.*, pp. 93–97.

15. The *New Era*, Feb. 17, 1870.

16. C. H. Wesley, *Negro Labor in the United States*, *op. cit.*, p. 55.

17. The New York Colored Mission, *Annual Report for 1871* (New York 1872), p. 7.

18. *Ibid.*, *Annual Report for 1872*, p. 5.

19. *Ibid.*, *Annual Report for 1893*, pp. 13–15.

20. A. Meier, *Negro Thought in America, 1880–1915* (Ann Arbor, Mich., 1963), pp. 128–129.

21. Osofsky, *op. cit.*, p. 56; Meier, *op. cit.*, p. 134.

22. A. N. Adams, *The Neglected Period of Anti-Slavery in America* (Gloucester, Mass., 1964), p. 73; Aptheker, *op. cit.*, p. 623.

23. *Address and Constitution of the Phoenix Society of New York* (New York 1833), p. 35.

24. Woofter, *Survey*, p. 133.

25. Roi-Ottley, *New World A-Coming* (Boston 1943), pp. 114–116.

26. Urban League of Greater New York, *Annual Report of 1940*, *passim.*

27. Roi-Ottley, *op. cit.*, pp. 114–116.

28. Franklin Delano Roosevelt Document 41–45, filed June 25, 1941 (No. 8802), amended by No. 9346, May 27, 1943.

29. *The Story of the City-Wide Citizens' Committee on Harlem*, May, 1943.

30. The New York *Times*, Sept. 26, 1948.

31. Urban Management Association, *Demonstration in Harlem* (New York 1945), *passim.*

32. *Report of the Mayor's Commission* (reprinted in the *Amsterdam News*, May 29, 1935).

33. *New York Legislative Document No. 63* (Albany, N.Y., 1938), p. 13.

34. The New York *Times*, July 26, 1955.

35. *Ibid.*, Dec. 29, 1957.

36. *Ibid.*, Feb. 10, 1958.

37. *Ibid.*, Sept. 12, 1962.

38. Confidential source, original materials in the author's files.

39. *Electrical Union World*, Local 3, IBEW, AFL-CIO, July 1, 1963; *Hotel*, Jan. 20, 1964.

40. *Wall Street Journal*, July 3, 1963.

41. *Ibid.*

42. The New York *Times*, Aug. 8, 1963.

43. *Ibid.*, Aug. 8, 1963.

44. *Ibid.*

45. The New York *Times*, Sept. 26, 1963; author consulted with Mrs. Maria Marcus of the NAACP's Legal Defense and Educational Fund on this case.

46. The New York *Times*, April 29, 1964.

47. The New York *Tribune*, Jan. 18 and Feb. 15, 1855.

48. E. F. Frazier, "A Negro Industrial Group," *Howard Review*, June 1924, p. 198.

49. *Ibid.*

50. *The Workingman's Advocate*, Aug. 31, 1867.

51. M. K. Staupers, R.N., *No Time for Prejudice* (New York 1961), p. 1.

52. B. Minton and J. Stuart, *Men Who Lead Labor* (New York 1937), p. 148.

53. *Ibid.*, p. 150.

54. *Ibid.*, p. 152.

55. R. R. Brazeal, *The Brotherhood of Sleeping Car Porters*, p. 151.

56. U.S. Department of Labor, *Handbook of American Trade Unions* (1936 ed.), p. 256.

57. I. De. A. Reid, *Negro Membership in American Unions*, p. 96.

58. *Messenger*, VII (1925), 296.

59. Reid, *op. cit.*, p. 131.

60. *Official Proceedings of the National Negro Congress* (Washington, D.C., 1936).

61. City Commission on Human Rights, *Hearings on Employment Practices in the Building Construction Trades* (Hearings, August, 1963), pp. 421–439.

62. Local 144, BSEIU, AFL-CIO, *25th Anniversary Celebration*, 1967 (no pagination); also personal conversations with Peter Ottley and Peter Byrnes, president and secretary-treasurer, respectively, of Local 144.

63. Quoted by L. E. Lomax, *The Negro Revolt* (New York 1963), pp. 264–265.

64. Personal interview with Cleveland Robinson at District 65, in 1955.

65. Agreement dated February, 1965.

66. Interview with Cleveland Robinson, March, 1967.

EPILOG

1. U.S. Department of Labor, "The Employment Situation for Negroes," *Employment and Earnings and the Monthly Report on the Labor Force*, Sept., 1967, p. 15.

2. *Ibid.*

3. *Ibid.*

4. *Ibid.*, p. 17.

5. U.S. Department of Labor, "Jobless Trends in 20 Large Metropolitan Areas," *Monthly Labor Review*, May, 1968, p. 17.

6. *Ibid.*, p. 26.

7. "The Employment Situation for Negroes," 19; *Manpower Report of the President and a Report on Manpower Requirements, Resources, Utilization, and Training*, April, 1967, p. 75.

8. *Ibid.*, p. 75. Subemployment refers to a person already a worker, or should and could become one with suitable help, was either jobless or not earning enough for living above the poverty level.

9. Lowell E. Gallaway, "Interindustry Labor Mobility Among Men, 1957–1960," *Social Security Bulletin*, September, 1966, pp. 10–22; A. P. Garbin and John A. Ballweg, "Intra-Plant Mobility of Negro and White Workers," *The American Journal of Sociology*, Nov. 1965, pp. 315–319.

10. U.S. Department of Labor, "Occupational Mobility of Employed Workers," *Monthly Labor Review* June 1967, pp. 35–38.

11. *Equal Employment Opportunity Commission* derived its information from *Employer Information Reports*, the EEO-1, are received from employers of 100 or more employees covered by Title VII of the Civil Rights Act of 1964 and all holders of Federal contracts of $50,000 or more with 50 or more employees. Hearings were held in New York between January 15 and January 18, 1968.

12. OEEC, *Hearings*, p. 7.

13. OEEC's *Employment Opportunities for Minorities in New York City: Introduction*, January, 1968, p. 5.

14. OEEC's *White Collar Employment in 100 Major New York City Corporations*, (Summary Report, Jan. 1968), p. 3.

15. *Employment Opportunities*, pp. 6–8.

16. *Newsday*, Dec. 3, 1968.

17. *Manpower Report of the President*, pp. 83–84.

Index

Abolition party, 181
Abolition Societies, 22, 23–24, 25, 155.
  See also New York Abolition Societies
Abolitionists, 35, 180
Abrams, Charles, 227–28
"Act for Regulating Slaves, An," 9
"Act for the Gradual Abolition of
  Slavery Within this State, An," 155
Adams, Abigail, 21, 23
Adams, John, 20, 21, 23
Administrative Code of the City of
  New York, 125
African Free School, 25, 26, 27, 178,
  221
Afro-American League, 224
Afro-American Realty Company, 223
Aid to Dependent Children (ADC),
  205
American Academy of Political and
  Social Science, "Annals" of, 42 f.
American and Foreign Anti-Slavery
  Society, 222
American Colonization Society, 158, 165
American Equal Rights Association, 181
American Missionary Association, 35
American party, 181
Anastasia, President, 115
Andrews, C. W., 28, 221
Anglo-French War, 20, 26
Anthony, Susan B., 181
Anti-Slavery Society, 27
Arma Corporation, 56–57

Back to Africa Movement, 233
Beecher, Henry Ward, 35
Bell, Ruby, 49, 209
Berg, Richard, 208–209
Black Muslims, 234
Black Worker, The, 48

Black Workers and the New Unions,
  48
BMT subway lines, 107
Boykin, Herman, 59, 72
Brennan Committee, 135–36
"Brennan Plan," 134–35
Brown, John, 178
Building Industry of New York City
  Referral Committee, 137
Building Trades Council, 135, 136
Building Trades Employers Association,
  132

Cameron, A. C., 82–83, 89, 90
Cathers, W., 83, 230
Chapin Democratic Club, 192
Charter of Freedoms and Exemptions,
  6
"City-Wide Citizens' Committee on
  Harlem," 226
Civil War, 20, 33, 34, 37, 38, 43, 154,
  169, 172, 177, 178, 180, 183, 218
Clarion, 161
Clark, Kenneth, 233
Cleveland, Grover, 191–92
Colonization report, 1846, 29
Colored American, 27, 28, 159, 160
Colored Freeholders of the City and
  County of New York, 160–61
Committee of Merchants for the Relief
  of Colored People Suffering from the
  late Riots in the City of New York,
  35
Committee of 70, 186–87
Committee on Elective Franchise, 163
Committee on the Right of Suffrage,
  183
Congress of Racial Equality (CORE),
  128, 134, 228, 229, 233

Conscription Act, 1863, 35, 85, 202
Consolidated Edison Company, 231
Consumer Arbitration Board, 226
Crabb, Alice, 9, 12

Darnall, James, 182–83
Davis, William, 162, 165
Day, Horace, 84
Declaration of Independence, 166
Degler, Carl N., 1. *See also* Degler-
  Handlin dispute
Degler-Handlin dispute, 2–3
Democratic party, 180–81, 183–84, 186,
  187, 188–89, 191–94
Democratic-Republicans, 156, 169
Depression: 1930's, 63–64, 69, 207;
  post-War of 1812, 26
*Discriminatory Employment Retrench-
  ment*, 209–10
Douglass, Frederick, 103, 166, 178, 179,
  181, 185–86, 187, 188, 190, 191,
  222, 233
Douglass' Weekly, 178
Downing, George T., 31, 179, 187, 191
Dred Scott Case, 175, 183
DuBois, William E. B., 37
Dutch Reformed Church, 8–9
Dutch West India Company, 3, 4–8,
  199

Electrical World, 93, 109, 202
Elk v. Wilkins case, 171
Employment, 55
Equal Employment Opportunity Com-
  mission (EEOC), 237

Fair Employment Practice Act, 226
Fair Employment Practices Committee
  (FEPC), 49, 50, 54–55, 56–57, 64,
  112, 114, 232
Farmer, James, 228, 233
Federal Emergency Relief Administra-
  tor's report, 63
Federalists, 155, 156, 157
Fenton, Governor, 176–77
Flore, President, 102
Folkways, 3–4
Foner, Moe, 232
Foner, P. S., 91
Fortune, 62
Franklin, C. L., 107–109
Franklin, Dorothy, 228
Fraunces Tavern, 22, 223
Free Suffrage Convention, 166
Freedmen's State Central Committee,
  162

G. I. Bill of Rights, 59
Garnett, Rev. H., 161, 162, 164, 167,
  178

Garveyism, 233
General Motors, 53, 203, 229
George, President, 85
George III, King, 16
Gimbel's, 58, 61
Gompers, Samuel, 89–93, 97–100, 102,
  232
Grand Army of the Republic, 192
Grand party, 186
Grant, Ulysses S., 178, 187
Greater New York Coordinating Com-
  mittee for Equal Opportunities, 232
Greeley, Horace, 176, 183
Green, William, 100–101, 102, 103,
  112
Grenville Act, 199

Hamilton, Alexander, 155
Handlin, Mary, 1. *See also* Degler-
  Handlin dispute
Handlin, Oscar, 1. *See also* Degler-
  Handlin dispute
Harlem Hospital, 128, 144
Harpers Ferry, 178
Harper's Weekly, 31 f., 186
Hawk, John, 113–14, 203
Hayes, Rutherford B., 189
Haymarket bombing, 89
Holland, Susan, 235
Hotel and Motel Worker, 61
Hotel Association, 59–60
Hotel Trades Council, 134
Hunter, Governor, 10

Institute of Defense Analysis, 205
Insurrection of 1712, 10
IRT subway lines, 107
Ives-Quinn Act, 117

Jay, John, 155
Jefferson, Thomas, 181
Johns Manville Company, 225
Johnson, Andrew, 170, 171–72, 179
Johnson, Lyndon B., 205
Johnson, Dr. W. H., 183, 186, 187, 191
Jones, Elizabeth, 181
Jordan, W. D., 2

Kennedy, John F., 128, 129, 229
King, Martin Luther, Jr., 233

Labor Management Relation Act, 139–
  40
Lamb, Anthony, 200
Lamb, John, 200
Lansing, C. H., Jr., 192
"Learn Trades or Slave!" 103
Legal Defense and Educational Fund,
  229–30

Lennon, John B., 90
Let's Find Out, 136–37
Liberal party, 188
Liberator, 159
Liberty party, 162
Lorillard tobacco factory, 34, 85
Lowell, Stanley, 125, 136

McBride, John, 90
McCune, Dr. James, *see* Smith, Dr.
James McCune
McFadden, James J., 137
McKee, S., Jr., 13
McPherson v. Blacker case, 176
Manpower Report, 1964, 75; 1967, 238
"Manpower Report of the President
and a Report on Manpower Require-
ments, Resources, Utilization and
Training," 71. *See also Manpower
Report*
Manumission Society, 155
Markowitz, Justice, 139
"March on Washington," 226, 233
Maryland Colonization Journal, 31
Mason-Dixon Line, 175
Massachusetts Anti-Slavery Society, 178
Matthews, James C., 187–88, 191–92
"Matthews' Great Bonanza," 191 f.
Meany, George, 118–19, 123, 128–29
Messenger, 231
*Minutes of the Proceedings of the 4th
American Convention of Delegates
from the Abolition Societies*, 22
"Modern Tensions and the Origins of
American Slavery," 2
Molasses Act, 199
Monroe, James, 158
Montserado, 158
Moreland Commission on Welfare, 206
Mountain Pacific Case, 140, 142, 143

Napoleon, 20
Napoleonic era, 25
Napoleonic Wars, 24
National Alliance for Business, 235
National Association for the Advance-
ment of Colored People (NAACP),
58–59, 128, 226, 228, 229, 233
National Convention of Colored Citi-
zens of Buffalo, 162
National Convention of Colored Men,
167
National Industrial Recovery Act
(NIRA), 106, 108
National Labor Relations Act, 143
National Labor Relations Board, 128,
137–38, 140
National Negro Congress, 232
National Recovery Administration, 48
National Relief Association, 192–93

National Urban League, 62, 98, 224,
225, 226, 228, 233. *See also* Urban
League of Greater New York
Negro American Labor Committee, 119,
213, 233, 234
Negro Labor Congress (World Negro
Congress), 100
Negro Leadership Conference, 233
New Deal, 48, 232
New Jersey Division Against Discrimina-
tion, 50–51
New Moral World, 31
New York Abolition Societies, 27
New York *Age*, 225
New York African Society for Mutual
Relief, 224
New York Anti-Slavery Society, 159,
163, 177
New York Building and Construction
Trades Council, 134
New York Central Railroad, 40
New York City Board of Education, 42,
139
(New York) City Charter, 188
New York City Colored Mission, 224
(New York) City Commission on Hu-
man Rights, 74, 118, 127, 130, 132,
134–35, 136, 228, 232, 234
New York City Common Council, 28
New York City Department of Health,
25
New York City Department of Wel-
fare, 205
New York *Echo*, 193
New York Fair Employment Practices
Committee, 59
New York *Globe*, 39
New York Hotel and Motel Trades
Council, 137
New York Mission Society, 25
New York Navy Yard, 59
New York *Observer*, 159
New York Shipping Association, 120
New York Society for the Encourage-
ment of Faithful Domestics, 26
New York State Board of Registrars, 182
(New York) State Central Committee
of Colored Citizens, 183
New York State (Civil Rights) Com-
mission, 73, 74 f.
New York State Commission Against
Discrimination (SCAD), 50–52, 54,
55, 57, 58–59, 60, 120–21
(New York) State Committee on Fed-
eral Relations, 184
New York State Constitution: 1777,
154, 164, 167, 169, 183, 184–85;
1846, 184; Convention, 1894, 193
New York State Employment Service
(NYES), 55, 59–60, 65, 139
New York State Human Rights Com-
mission, 118, 127, 138, 139, 147

(New York) State Industrial Commissioner's office, 54
New York State Legislature, 117, 185, 218, *passim*
New York State Supreme Court, 139, 156, 182
New York *Sun*, 88 f.
New York *Times*, 84, 87, 110, 124, 186, 189, 191, 226
New York Trades Council, 59–60
New York *Tribune*, 87, 177, 193
New York *World*, 35 f., 222
Northern Star, 178
Northrup, Herbert, 115

O'Donnell, Senator, 179
O'Dwyer, William, 226
Oil Transfer Company, 112
"On the Condition of the Urban Colored Population," 227
"Origins of the Southern Labor System," 1
Ottley, Peter, 232–33
Ovington, M. W., 32, 40–41, 42, 43

Payton, Philip A., Jr., 223
Peckham, Attorney General, 186
Pennington, Rev. J. W. C., 26
Pennsylvania Railroad, 49–50, 58–59, 203, 207
Phelps, A. W., 83, 85–86
Phillips, Wendell, 163, 177
Phoenix Society of New York, 158
Plans for Progress, 62, 126, 235
Political Improvement Association of New York City, 159–60, 161
Powderly, Terence V., 87–89, 90, 232
President's Committee on Equal Employment, 125
President's Committee on Equal Opportunity, 62, 128
President's Committee on Government Contracts, 227
Provost, Anthony, 28

Quill, Michael, 107

Race and Nationality in American Life, 1
"Race First, and then Party," 191
Radical Republicans, 170–71, 173, 184
Randolph, A. Philip, 100, 101, 102, 128, 226, 231, 232, 233
Reason, Charles L., 160, 161, 223
Reconstruction Committee, 170
Recruitment and Manning Operations of the War Shipping Administration (RMO), 113
Redistribution Act of Virginia, 174

Republican party, 177, 180, 183–84, 186, 187, 188–94. *See also* Radical Republicans
"Restoration of the Rebel States and the Claims of the Black Man, The," 178
Revolution, American, 11, 17, 20, 21, 23, 153, 154, 199, 200, 202, 221, 223
Robinson, Cleveland, 233, 234
Rockefeller, Nelson, 229
Roosevelt, Franklin D., 48, 112, 203, 226, 232
Roosevelt, Theodore, 194
"Rough Riders," 194

Scrottron, Samuel, 42, 43
Seward, William, 162
Shaughnessy Report, 132
Slaughter-House Cases, 175
Smith, Gerrit, 164
Smith, Dr. James McCune, 32, 222, 224
Southern Negro Leadership Council (SNLC), 233
Spanish-American War, 194
Speed, J. G., 31 f., 38 f.
"Spirit of Liberty Call to the Franchise, The," 161
Stanton, Elizabeth Cady, 181
Stephens, Uriah, 87, 89
Stevens, Thaddeus, 170
Stewart, McCants, 192
Stewart, Michael, 139
Stuyvesant, Peter, 8
Sumner, Charles, 170

Taft-Hartley Act, 142
Tailor Trade Association (N.Y.), 32
Tammany Hall, 194
Taney, Chief Justice, 175, 176
Totten, Ashley, 231
Townshend Act, 199
Trade Union Committee for Organizing Negro Workers, 232
Trans-World Airlines, 227
Truman administration, 229
Tweed, Boss, 186

U.S. Army, 154
U.S. Bureau of Labor Statistics, 70, 236
U.S. Civil Rights Act: 1866, 171, 173, 186, 187; 1964, 118, 119, 126, 208, 233
U.S. Civil Rights Commission, 55, 72, 131
U.S. Civil Service Commission, 49, 194
U.S. Constitution, 154, 167, 168, 170, 172, 173, 174, 175, 177, 180, 181, 183, 184, 185–86, 187, 189, 193
U.S. Department of Commerce, 49

U.S. Department of Health, Education and Welfare, 205–206
U.S. Department of Justice, 128, 208
U.S. Department of Labor, 70–71, 75, 76, 134, 210, 211, 228
U.S. Employment Service (USES), 49–50, 54–55, 56–57, 203
U.S. House of Representatives, 170
U.S. Marines, 154
U.S. Navy, 154
U.S. Supreme Court, 59, 174, 175, 185
U.S. Weather Bureau, 49
Union party of 1862, 180–81
Unions: American Federation of Labor (AFL), 58–59, 80, 89–96, 97–107, 109, 110–12, 116–17, 118–19, 123, 126, 128–29, 139, 231, 233; Colored National Labor Union, 84, 230, 231; Committee of Industrial Organizations (CIO), 64, 106–107, 112, 117, 118–19, 123, 126, 128–29, 139; Federal Labor Union, 91–92; Federal Workers Union of the CIO, 64; National Labor Union (NLU), 80, 82–84, 85, 86, 87, 96, 230; National Trades Union, 81; *passim and*
Civil Service—
American Federation of State, County and Municipal Employees Union, 55; Federal License Officers Association, 54; National Association of Letter Carriers, 127
Communications—
Commercial Telegraphers Union of America, 104; Journeymen Printers, 81; National Typographical Union (International Typographical Union), 81, 85, 86, 127; New York Typographical Society, 80; Order of Railroad Telegraphers, 104; Railway Mail Association, 104; Telegraphers Union of North America, 110
Construction, building services—
Bricklayers and Masons' Union, 81; Bricklayers, Masons and Plasterers International Union of America, 121; Bricklayers Union, 86, 93–94, 117, 141, 145; Brotherhood of Painters, Decorators and Paperhangers of America, 105; Building Service Employees International Union, 133, 232; Carpenters and Joiners of New Haven, Conn., 83; Carpenters of New York, 80; Carpenters Union, 85, 122, 130; Caulkers of Boston, 80; Cement and Concrete Workers Union, 132; Colored Caulkers Trade Union, 84; Colored Painters Society, 84; International Association of Journeymen Plumbers, 104; International Union of Building Service Employees, 109; Lathers and Plasterers Union, 122; National Carpenters Union, 81; Operative Plasterers and Cement Fin-

ishers International Association, 104, 131; Ornamental and Structural Iron Workers Union, 109, 122; Painters Union, 115, 119; Plumbers International Union, 128, 136, 137; Plumbers Union, 122; United Association of Journeymen Plumbers and Steamfitters, 131; United Brotherhood of Carpenters and Joiners of America, 94, 105, 111, 115; United Hod Carriers Association, 84
Hotel, food, food service—
Amalgamated Meat Cutters and Butchers Workmen, AFL-CIO, 139; Brewers Board of Trade, 234; Cooks and Waiters Union, 104–105; Hotel and Restaurant Employees, 105; Hotel and Restaurant Employees International and Bartenders League of America (Hotel Alliance), 101–103, 111; Waiters and Dining Room Employees, 134
Manufacturing—
Amalgamated Clothing Workers of America, 107; American Wire Weavers Protective Association, 104; Asbestos Contractors Association, 139; Brotherhood of Shop Crafts of America of the AFL, 58–59; Cigar Makers International Union, 94; Cigar Makers' Union, 81, 85, 86; Flint Glass Workers of North America, 104; Furniture Workers of America, 108; Hat, Cap, and Millinery Workers Union (Headgear Workers), 107; International Association of Insulators and Asbestos Workers, 110; International Association of Machinists (IAM), 90–91, 95, 104, 110; International Association of Sheet Metal Workers, 104, 112–13; International Brotherhood of Boilermakers, 104; International Brotherhood of Electrical Workers, 93, 104, 109, 110, 117, 119, 126, 131, 202; International Ladies Garment Workers Union (ILGWU), 105, 107, 109, 111, 123, 212; Iron Molders and Machinists, 81; Iron Molders Union, 81, 82; Iron Shipbuilders and Helpers of America, 104; Journeymen Tailors' Union of America, 105; Oil, Chemical and Atomic Workers Union, 117; Sheet Metal Workers International Association of Greater New York, 138; Sheet Metal Workers Union, 109, 122, 146–47; Shipbuilders and Helpers of America, 104; Shipwrights of New York, 80; Steamfitters of the United States and Canada, 104; Steamfitters Union, 136; United Auto Workers (UAW), 107, 229; United Steel Workers, 107; United Steel Workers of America, 128; United Textile Workers, 104; Upholsterers, Carpet and Linoleum Mechanics International Union of Ameri-

ica, 108; Wire Weavers Protective Association, 110

Professional, misc. service—
American Federation of Teachers, 104; American Nurses Association, 231; Brotherhood of Blacksmiths, Dropforgers and Helpers Union, 112; Drug and Hospital Employees Union, 134; International Alliance of theatrical and Stage Employees and Moving Picture Machine Operators, 103; Garage Carwashers and Cleaners Union, 114; International Brotherhood of Blacksmiths, Drop Forgers and Helpers, 90, 104, 212; Journeymen Barbers International Union of America, 105; Laundry Workers International Union, 105; Motion Picture Projectionists Union, 105, 114, 213; National Association of Colored Graduate Nurses, 231; Retail, Wholesale, Department Store Workers Union, 133, 134, 233; United Association of Colored Motion Picture Operators, 103, 231

Transportation (*see also* Communication)—
Airline Pilots Association, AFL-CIO, 112; American Federation of Express Workers, 104; American Federation of Railroad Workers, 104; American Railway Association, 110; American Train Dispatchers Association, 104; Brotherhood of Dining Car Conductors, 104; Brotherhood of Dining Car Employees, 231; Brotherhood of Locomotive Firemen and Enginemen, 93, 110, 128; Brotherhood of Railroad Trainmen, 110; Brotherhood of Railway and Steamship Clerks, Freight Handlers, Express and Station Employees Union, 105–106, 110, 123; Brotherhood of Railway Carmen, 104; Brotherhood of Railway Clerks, 104; Brotherhood of Railroad Trainmen, 104; Brotherhood of Sleeping Car Porters, 100, 102; Brotherhood of Station Employees and Clerks, 104; Colored Engineers Association, 84; Flight Engineers International Association, AFL-CIO, 112; Grand International Brotherhood of Locomotive Engineers, 104; International Brotherhood of Teamsters, 105, 234; International Longshoremen's Association (ILA), 105, 111, 112, 114, 115, 118, 119, 120; Marine Firemen, Oilers and Water Tenders and Wipers Association of the Pacific, 110; Masters, Mates and Pilots, 110; National Brotherhood of Dining Car Employees, 231; National Organization of Masters, Mates and Pilots of North America, 104; National Union of Steam Engineers, 94; Order of Railway Conductors, 104, 110; Order of Railway Expressmen, 104; Order of Sleeping Car Conductors, 104; Order of Switchmen's Union of North America, 110; Order of Train Dispatchers' Association, 110; Railroad Yardmasters of America, 104; Railroad Yardmasters of North America, 104; Sailor's Union of the Pacific, 128; Seafarers' International Union (SIU), 113, 128, 203, 212, 213; Switchmen's Union of North America, 104; Transport Workers, 107

Other—
American League of Colored Laborers, 224; American Negro Labor Congress, 232; General Trades Union of New York City, 80–81; Hebrew Union Trades, 232; Knights of Labor (K. of L.), 87–89, 96; Knights of St. Crispin, 81; United Packing House Workers, 117

United African Republic Emigration Society, 165–66

Urban League of Greater New York, 50, 53–54, 65, 127–28, 202–203, 225, 227. See also National Urban League

Van Arsdale, Harry, 129
Veale, Mary, 58

Wagner, Robert F., 72, 74, 125, 129–32
War Labor Board, 76
War Manpower Commission (WMC), 50, 56, 112
War of 1812, 154; depression following, 26
War Shipping Administration, 113
Ward, Samuel, 161, 164
Washington, George, 22
"WASPS," 56
WCBS, 136
Webb, Waven O., 120–21
Weber, Max, 206
Whig party, 181
White, Walter, 226
Wilkerson, William, 167
Wilkins, Roy, 233
Williams, Thelma, 49–50, 203
Wirtz, Willard, 132
Wolfbein, Seymour, 64
Workingman's Advocate, 82
Workingman's Convention, 80
World War I, 21, 38, 45, 97, 108, 115
World War II, 48, 56, 58, 112, 203

Young, Whitney M., Jr., 228, 233

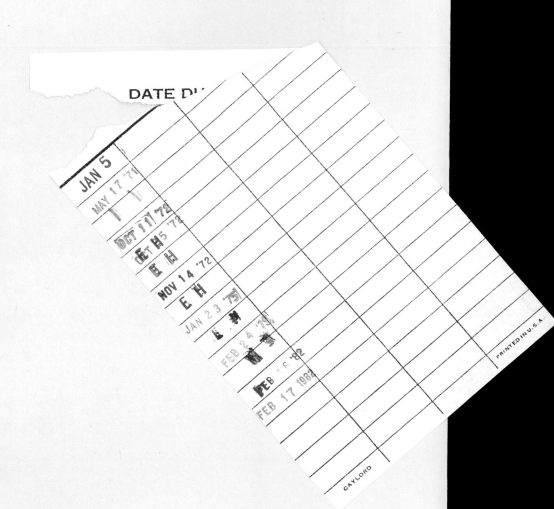

DATE D[U]

JAN 5

MAY 17 '7[?]

OCT 11 '72

OCT 15 '7[?]

NOV 14 '72

JAN 23 75

FEB 24 '75

FEB 16 '82

FEB 17 1982

PRINTED IN U.S.A.

GAYLORD